MONEY TALKS

Books by Walter Wagner

Money Talks

God's Prison Gang (*with Chaplain Ray*)

Beverly Hills: Inside the Golden Ghetto

Heavenly Humor

You Must Remember This: Oral Reminiscences of the Real
  Hollywood

Solomon in All His Glory (*Novel*)

The Trip Beyond (*with Brian Ruud*)

To Gamble, or Not to Gamble

The Trouble with Wall Street (*with Lewis A. Bracker*)

The Man from Miracle Valley (*with Don Stewart*)

Turned on to Jesus (*with Arthur Blessitt*)

Born to Lose, Bound to Win (*with A. A. Allen*)

The Chaplain of Bourbon Street (*with Bob Harrington*)

The Golden Fleecers

MONEY TALKS

How Americans
Get It, Spend It, Use It and Abuse It

WALTER WAGNER

The Bobbs-Merrill Company, Inc.
INDIANAPOLIS   NEW YORK

Library of Congress Cataloging in Publication Data

Wagner, Walter, 1927–
  Money talks.

    1. Wealth—United States.   2.   Money—United States.
I. Title.
HC110.W4W33   332.4'973   77-15431
ISBN 0-672-52144-X

For my wife, Maxine
With love, with gratitude

CONTENTS

DOWN PAYMENT

The getting and spending of money consumes more time, effort and attention than any other human activity, including sex. Hence this book, a journey into the money styles of representative Americans, speaking intimately of their economic struggles, triumphs and defeats.

The impact of money on our lives is more profound than most of us realize. Money, or the lack of it, determines where we live, what and how much we eat, where and how hard we work, how we spend our leisure time, and—often—whom we marry and how many children we have. Money, in short, is indispensable to survival, to the quality of life—and, yes, to happiness. For as a study cited in this book points out, the more money an individual has, the higher his quotient of happiness is likely to be. There are exceptions, of course. Maid-housekeeper Bertie Williams, who tells her story in these pages, appears to be more content than multimillionaire restaurateur Rocky Aoki. And ex-Hollywood producer Marvin Schwartz is a perfect example of a man who feels he attained happiness only after abandoning the pursuit of material wealth. On the other hand, money or the lack of it has dictated the direction and the quality of the lives of Watts resident Stuart Bayless, prostitute Lynn Robbins, and senior citizen Zola Primm. Their stories are three of several in this book that explore the connections between money and race, money and gender, money and age.

Money, despite revolutionary economic and political upheavals throughout history, has never been distributed evenly or rationally. Examples of the disparity—which is inextricably woven into the fabric of our society—between those who have and those who have not abound in this book. Among the former are Caroline Leonetti Ahmanson, one of the world's richest women; Andreus Vargo, mortgage banker; and entertainer-millionaire Art Linkletter. Among the latter are Roberto Suarez, an illegal immigrant who lives on $125 a month; and Weldon Greenlee, a truck driver forced to use food stamps because of frequent layoffs.

In fact, according to William Ryan, professor of psychology at Boston College, "At least seven out of ten families are economically vulnerable, with at least an even chance of spending some years of their lives in economic distress. It is not merely some vague minority called 'the poor' who stand in economic peril; it is the majority of Americans."

In my investigation of how money impinges on the lives of people, I discovered that, for many, the Horatio Alger myth is dead. The majority of those interviewed in this book, though they work hard and are thrifty, remain in an economically precarious position. But then the Horatio Alger dream has always come true for only the lucky few. Luck, it should be noted, apparently has much to do with who is poor and who is rich. It is often more important than education, well-connected parents, or working twelve hours a day.

Above and beyond everything else in their lives, Americans worry about money. It's been that way for decades; perhaps it was always that way. According to the George Gallup polling organization, economic concerns are the most frequent cause of worry for American families today, as they were ten and thirty years ago. Those questioned cited most frequently such worries as the high cost of living, inflation, taxes, the fear of unemployment, fear of illness, the cost of educating children, and the fear of not having enough money for retirement. All of these concerns are voiced by those who speak in these pages.

Emerson said, "A man's treatment of money is the most decisive test of his character—how he makes it and how he spends it." That observation sums up one of the goals of this book: to discover the quality of humanity vis-à-vis money in the men and women I've interviewed.

Before proceeding with this investigation of money in all its guises, I wish to express my gratitude to my agent, Jane Browne, whose unflagging determination to see the concept in print was a constant source of encouragement.

I am also deeply in debt to my editor, Diane Giddis, who shared my initial enthusiasm for this project. Her patience, editorial buoyancy and insight were a source of inspiration, and to say thanks is to say not enough.

Above and beyond the dedication of this book to my wife Maxine goes an additional round of thanks for her constant interest in the work and for her reassurance. The book would not have been possible without her.

Finally, I wish to express my debt to Iona Darland for transcribing the hundreds of miles of tape-recorded interviews. She brought a sense of excitement as well as enormous efficiency to a task that in other hands would perhaps have been tedious.

So much for this brief "down payment." Now let's listen to those willing to tell why and how *Money Talks*.

—WALTER WAGNER

MONEY TALKS

The View
from the Couch

Money is a way to reduce anxiety.

—Arthur F. LeBlanc

ARTHUR F. LEBLANC

Dr. LeBlanc is a fifty-two-year-old clinical psychologist with formidable credentials. He's been an associate therapist at Dr. William Glasser's Institute for Reality Therapy, and the chief psychologist at the children's division of California's Camarillo State Hospital; he has taught at USC, UCLA, the Fuller Graduate School of Psychology, Immaculate Heart College, and California Lutheran College. Since 1970, he has served as co-director of Los Angeles's Institute for Human Studies, where he sees private patients and conducts workshops for psychiatrists, school guidance directors, rehabilitation counselors and para-professional groups.

Money is a way to reduce anxiety. In the United States money is a prerequisite to mental health. If you don't have money, you should be anxious. You first must get your survival needs met— food, clothing and shelter—and the way you do it is with money. Money is a necessity, like oxygen.

Psychologically, money isn't good or bad; it's indifferent. What matters is what you do with money. There is more potential good than bad in money. But if a man's going to spend his whole life chasing money as the only way to reduce anxiety, then it's bad. It isn't money in itself but the chase for money that can be destructive. I see a lot of people because of the chase.

I'm seeing a man now who has ample money and a big retirement fund. Every day of his life he makes a parking attendant break a dollar bill for him as he leaves his office. He puts the change in a mayonnaise jar. At the end of each month he takes the mayonnaise jar to the bank, even though he's a multimillionaire.

Every day this man studies the interest rate at the bank. He moves his money maybe five times a week. When I play golf with

2

him, he hauls out the worst damn ball you've ever seen. So I always give him a new ball and say, "Here, cheap ass, hit my ball." I mean, this man is loaded. But he'll never have enough money, because his fantasy is that he's going to die in Chicago with the rats in a cellar, like his mother did.

He has severe symptoms, ulcers and migraine headaches. All we talk about during his therapy hour is money. He keeps asking me if he'll have enough money. And I tell you, this man will never have enough money, even though he's sixty years old and couldn't spend all he has if he wanted to.

Most of my clients are rich. You have to be fairly well off to come to see me. I charge forty dollars an hour, sometimes fifty, depending on my mood. If I don't like you, I charge more.

What I'm finding is that my rich clients are asking, "Is money what life's all about? I have a tennis court, I have a Jaguar, I have this and I have that." I tell them, "Yes, this is what life is all about. Life is breathing, laughing, fooling around, playing tennis." But they want more, and I don't know where to go to get it for them, except to dip into mysticism, which isn't my thing.

I think people want too much. If you've got your car, your wife, your kids; if you're in good health, have a beautiful home; if you've got your tennis and sailing, your parties, your relaxing, what the hell else do you want? This is all there is. This is all we've got. I don't really see that there is more in this world.

These wealthy people are in therapy with me because they want to create a new world with their money. But they are not gods. All that their money is going to do is make them comfortable in the world we've got. But they don't buy that; they aren't satisfied with that.

Freud described the world as a very crappy, miserable place where you spend your whole lifetime using defense mechanisms to ward off evil: the evil in you, called the id, and the evil out there, called external pressure. The humanists came along, and in the revolt against Freud they gave us a lollipop picture of the world. And they talked about self-fulfillment and being and growth, flowery and poetic stuff that the flower children of the sixties bought. But I think Hermann Hesse is closest to reality when he says that life is crazy and unpredictable. You've got wars, famine, misery in a hundred guises. Okay, so it's crazy out there, but my id is not crappy. The thing that I have is a sense of humor. And if I have a sense of humor and money, I can handle the crap. If I have no money, I can't handle it. But with money and a sense of humor, I've got it made. You can go to the bank and do the hoarding thing as long as you don't have symptoms as the result of it. If you can hoard and there are no symptoms, if you can laugh on your way to the bank, okay. You can go out and buy condominiums until they are swimming out of your ears if you laugh and have fun doing it.

I was skiing a few years ago with a doctor friend of mine, and I left my wallet in the lodge. I asked my friend if he had any money, and he said sure. He took a big roll out of his pocket — a lot of it was ones—and a little boy who was watching us came up and said, "Hey, is that real money?" And I told him, "There is no real money. It's all play money. It's all to be played with. You just play with this stuff called money. And if you ever think it's for real, you're finished."

When you go to school you're supposed to be average, not too bright, because if you're an egghead you're put down. I think it's the same with money. Don't make too much, because if you do, you are violating something sacred. On the other hand, don't be too poor; make a living wage. But a living wage is a crappy wage in the United States. If you come out and say you want to make a lot of money, you are violating one of the commandments. You are avaricious. You are not virtuous if you want to make a lot of dough. That doesn't make sense.

To talk about money the way I do scares some people. I gave a symposium in Canada where I said, "I think the goal of a man my age should be to make an awful lot of money while having fun." Now, when you say that, you are saying something sinful. There was a lot of growling and muttering in the room.

I don't think our parents wanted us to use language like that in regard to money. The parents always said, Make a living; get by. When I got back from a trip to Europe, the first thing my father said was, "How's business?" "Great," I said. And he said, "Oh, then you can pay for the trip." He didn't ask me anything about the trip, if I'd had a good time—only could I pay for the trip.

I want to make $55,000 a year and work three days a week. I think that's a decent, obtainable goal. A number of my colleagues are working three days a week and earning $75,000, and they're playing more often with their children, playing on their boats, playing tennis, jogging.

A three-day week that brought in $55,000 would be a pretty nice living. That would let me play the other four days. I'd golf, ski, travel, go to the beach. Hell, I enjoy just going to the hardware store or the supermarket for my wife.

I'm two years away from my goal. Right now, I'm working four days a week and feeling fine and joyful and happy. I don't see why three days a week wouldn't add to that.

When I worked seven days a week, I developed psychosomatic symptoms. I wasn't sleeping that well. I was anxious if I missed a day's work. I wouldn't take a vacation. I would go an entire year without a vacation because I was too guilt-ridden to take a day off. It would be too much for me to take a week off. That would be an unpardonable sin. In fact, I just came from a three-week vacation, and I could have stayed a fourth or fifth week. It was the first time in my life that I could have stayed another week or two. Ah, it's a marvelous sensation, not feeling guilty anymore.

The sorriest people in America—and there are a lot of them— are those who stockpile money as a way of avoiding the reality of death. In other words, if I get a pile big enough, the gods won't be able to strike me dead. The most horrendous reality is death, but through stockpiling I can avoid it. How can I die if I have so much? You know, what would happen to the company? and so on.

That's not for me. I'm perfectly well aware of my mortality. And while I can, I'm going to work as little as possible and play at the game of spending—and enjoying—my money.

STEPHEN SYKES

A psychiatrist since 1954, Dr. Sykes practices in a conservative, churchgoing community near a large industrial city. He was raised on a small farm and "struggled like Jesus to get through school."

Despite severe financial and professional setbacks, neurosis and *psychosis provide him the wherewithal to live in a $175,000 home and buy a new Lincoln every year. His fee for an hour of therapy is $70.*

I suppose one of the oldest questions in the world is: Can money buy happiness? From a psychological point of view, money definitely cannot buy happiness. You have it or you don't. No one can buy happiness, any more than anybody can give anybody else happiness.*

Money only buys material things. Those material things can be lost. Only when money is used as an expression of sharing does it result in a healthy relationship in human beings. That is the key and fundamental yardstick.

The rich man concerned with power can get carried away. As his desire for power grows, he strays from his own natural humanity. That gives rise to conflicts, which can lead to such psychological ailments as depression, anxiety, a sense of futility.

A man who makes his first $100,000 feels exhilarated; he's caught up in the power thing. But often he doesn't build up any sense of internal value or internal worth. Then he makes $500,000, but he still doesn't feel that he has internal worth. When he makes $1 million he has more friends who are friendly to his money but not friendly to him. So he goes on and makes $2 or $3 million, and he may get to the place where he becomes totally despondent, not just depressed. He can reach the point where he becomes absolutely devoid of any feeling as to what his relationship to the world really is. Then he jumps off the roof of his skyscraper.

People pay too high an emotional price to earn money. They get caught up in the whole game of feeling that if they just work hard they will make money, and that money or material things will bring security. But it's far more difficult doing the emotional homework of finding inner security, which is what matters. To

---

*Many therapists disagree. *Psychology Today* magazine, reporting on experiments conducted by Dr. Paul Cameron, said: "He studied handicapped persons, retarded individuals and normal individuals of various ages, and found no consistent differences in happiness among them. Physical wholeness, mental capacity and age didn't seem to matter; income did. 'We know money talks,' he concluded, 'and our research suggests it also makes us happy. Apparently affluence is one of the few things that generally improves life satisfaction.' "

develop a relationship with one's self where you know you have an intrinsic value, where you place a nonmonetary value on yourself, is certainly a much more challenging responsibility for every human being. But that's harder to do; it is easier to simply work eight, ten, twelve hours a day to get money. By doing that, we somehow get the idea, if I make more money, then I am successful; therefore, I must be secure. Usually I find some sort of confrontation with this particular problem somewhere along the middle years of life. A person has gotten into a profession, wrestled for money; then, all of a sudden, either through a dramatic experience and some kind of despair or despondency, or else in gradual little ways, he's faced with an emotional crisis in his life. He asks himself, Hey, wait a minute, what kind of a rat race am I in? What's the idea of accumulating? Generally it happens imperceptibly in the patients I see—they slowly get a feeling that the accumulation of money and material things is not the most important thing in their lives.

I'm aware that many therapists are also guilty of this syndrome, that they practice only for money, and that they're accused of charging too much. But such therapists will face their own emotional confrontations sooner or later. As to the cost of psychiatric care, I buy the classic Freudian idea that unless one sacrifices or unless one hurts financially, one doesn't achieve anything working with a therapist.* When Ronald Reagan was governor of California, he said much the same thing about

---

*In 1913 Freud wrote that ". . . the value of the treatment is not enhanced in the patient's eyes if a very low fee is asked . . . . the whole relationship is removed from the real world, and the patient is deprived of a strong motive for endeavoring to bring the treatment to an end."

Other psychiatrists concur, among them Karl Menninger, who said: "The analysis will not go well if the patient is paying less than he can reasonably afford to pay. It should be a definite sacrifice for him."

Interestingly, in a 1975 study three Yale psychologists selected 424 patients at random to determine whether the amount of the fee influenced recovery. Fifty-six percent of the patients paid nothing; 12 percent had their fees paid by welfare; 15 percent had insurance to cover the fees; 9 percent paid $1 to $14 per session; and 8 percent paid the standard $15 fee.

The researchers found that the fee had no effect on the success of treatment. Those who paid nothing recovered or failed to recover at the same percentage rate as those who paid the full fee. The researchers' report said that "psychotherapists who charge high fees for the patient's sake will have to find another rationalization for those extreme charges."

taxes—that they should hurt. Freud believed that the therapist's fee should hurt so that the patient becomes motivated
to help the analyst help him. Freud himself was éxpensive in his
day.

I'd say that no matter what therapy costs, it's a good investment—better than a home, better than a cabin in the
mountains, better than a new car. An investment in therapy
provides the techniques and the skills to grow and master one's
problems. It gives the analysand the ability to cope, to stretch his
emotional legs, to make an investment in his future. Whether he
invests $5,000, $10,000 or more in therapy, it's well worth it.

I'd like to add, contrary to what many believe, that the poor
and the middle class are not frozen out of therapy because they
can't afford it. In my own personal experience and that of
colleagues I know, it just doesn't happen. I never refuse any
individual aid if I see clearly that he sincerely wants help, even
though he can't afford my normal fee. If the emotional needy
who are ready for therapy don't have any money, I don't charge
them anything.

I have my own neurotic problems about money, though most
of them have been refined and resolved over the years. It goes
without saying that even psychiatrists have a need for security. I
grew up with the notion that material things were closely connected to security. I was a poor farm boy, and I was made aware
very early in life that in order to survive you had to work hard;
you had to joust with the land in order to get a crop, and when
the crop was sold, you had just enough money to pay the grocer
for all the bills you had run up during the year. So it was
inevitable that I began to equate some kind of personal security
with material things.

I have to be honest: when the chips are down, so far as money
is concerned, virtually everybody becomes his lesser self. When
someone wants to take what is rightfully yours, you regress to the
basic attitude you developed early in life, no matter how
sophisticated you are, no matter how polished the veneer you
present publicly.

I speak from personal experience, after having gone through
a divorce and bankruptcy.

While we were married, my ex-wife and I never had so much

as one disagreement about the sharing of material things, which as I think back and reflect was a dreadful mistake, because she was so naïvely trusting and satisfied with me as a husband and a father and a provider. Without any selfish desire, I was single-mindedly directed toward providing for the family.

I think that my experience was the same as that of countless thousands of other husbands regarding the sharing of love, romance and fun. I'd worked hard for years; then I got the idea that just working hard, all work and no play, makes Jack a dull boy. It occurred to me that there must be some other reason for working and existing and struggling. That's far from the Puritan idea that to work hard and be miserable in this life will earn a good life in some other world. I began to take a more open-minded view of God, love and happiness. I left my wife and five children.

That changed the whole financial picture. The lesser side of my ex-wife came into play. She wanted her share—more than her share—of our joint assets. The divorce was a bitter experience. The court awarded her half of all we had, but I had to pay both her attorney's fee and my own attorney's fee, which really became a terribly immoral kind of thing in terms of the total cost. The bill for the attorneys ran to over $50,000 in after-tax dollars. Then my wife was surprised and disillusioned to learn that her attorney was demanding an additional $13,000 from her. He'd sold a piece of property the court awarded her, and that was his fee, and she had to pay.

Instead of demonstrating Solomonic wisdom, which would have divided everything down the middle, the courtroom unfortunately became a strange arena where things were not done fairly, that is to say, as sensible people would arrive at a solution through negotiation. For example, her attorney claimed that my good name or what we call goodwill was worth something like $350,000. My clinic was making money at the time, but much of it was plowed back into overhead and the growth of the business. Ironically, I left my wife during the best year I've ever had—an income of $129,000 after taxes. So obviously it was difficult to plead in court, no matter what kind of explanation I gave, to go easy on me in the face of a ledger that showed $129,000. Our household expenses were running about $3,000 a month; we had a lovely home, and all the children were in private schools. I offered to pay $3,000 a month alimony and child support, which seemed to me fair and reasonable. But instead they asked for $5,500 a month, plus half the money I didn't have for my good name. I finally told the court that she could have any part of my good name she wanted; I would sell out to her.

We settled at last on $4,000 a month, which I paid for nearly two years. Then I was forced, totally forced, into bankruptcy. I was still suffering the blow of her lawyer's fee, and the monthly payment to my wife became an awesome burden. At the same time, business at my clinic declined dramatically.

I had been given the clinic and the accounts receivable, which amounted to about $150,000. But that $150,000 had not been collected, and of course no taxes had been paid on that sum of money. I also had a staff of fourteen, and I had to dismiss all of them because referrals dried up. This is a very church-conscious town, and all the gossip surrounding the divorce, the fact of the divorce itself, helped destroy me. There was an ungracious and uncharitable feeling in town that I was some kind of monster. How could I walk away and abandon my wife and children? No one looked at the situation from my point of view. In addition, when all the legal skirmishing was over, I still owed my ex a note for $60,000. That, too, was part of the settlement. Therefore, at the end of seven years I would have the pleasure of paying her $60,000 plus interest—and it just seemed completely impossible to meet that kind of demand. Bankruptcy became inevitable.

I left my wife in 1972. It seems like fifty years ago. Since that time I've gradually been able to rebuild the business. I have a staff of three now—a biofeedback technician, a clinical psychologist and an occupational therapist.

I've remarried and everything is going well. I've got a $100,000 mortgage on the house, but I'm not worried. Fortunately, I'm in a profession where I can earn a decent income, but I have to be very careful about my expenses.

Frankly speaking, it's one thing to tell patients they shouldn't be overly concerned with money. However, it's quite another pot of beans when it's your own money that's at stake.

LORIENE CHASE

Loriene Chase is a strikingly pretty psychologist who numbers many film luminaries among her patients. Her French-Norman home in the Hollywood Hills is modest in comparison to the $600,000 mansion she once occupied in tony Bel Air. The bridesmaids at her wedding to a wealthy California businessman were Rhonda Fleming; Jeanne Crain; Ann Miller; Mrs. David Rose, wife of the composer; and Princess Atti of Egypt, King Farouk's sister. The Los Angeles Times *headlined the nuptials:* CINDERELLA MARRIES INDUSTRIAL TYCOON. *They were divorced eight years later. She won't discuss the reasons for the breakup except to remark, "Let's just say that Cinderella's glass slipper didn't fit."*

My father was a grocery clerk. I was raised on a quiet, sort of middle-class tree-lined street in Sacramento. After I earned my doctorate at the University of Southern California, I was devoted to my practice.

When I met my future husband, it was a new world. I'd never been around people with wealth, security and social position. It was a completely different atmosphere from anything I'd known. I came up, so to speak, through the ranks, a card-carrying Cinderella who married the prince. My husband once said, "I don't know how Loriene does it. She can ferret out the wine, the château and the year like a beagle. Yet she's a peasant." And I was. Being a peasant, I was delighted to find that I met some of the nicest people I've ever known while I was living at the summit. Throughout this period, I maintained a full-time practice.

I've lived at three socioeconomic levels, and the differences are damned interesting. The lesser level—not the poverty-stricken, but around the $10,000-a-year bracket—will characteristically fight and argue in public whenever they feel like it. The men are butt pinchers; they flirt, and they go to bed with the wives of their friends and neighbors. Getting drunk or drinking heavily is not considered negative behavior among this group.

In the middle class, professional people and businessmen who haven't gone through that invisible wall to the top rung, there is also butt pinching, flirtations and infidelities, but not so much. But open arguments and drinking to excess also occur frequently.

The ground rules at the pinnacle are completely different. There is a whole set of unwritten laws. Open drunkenness is out: you must know how to handle your liquor. And you don't fight with your wife or your husband in public. You must know protocol at the dinner table. No butt pinching or flirtations—which is not to say, of course, that the wealthy don't have extramarital affairs. Another taboo is anti-Semitism. You just don't hear prejudicial remarks about any minority. That is as severely frowned upon as pinching the butt of your friend's wife, getting drunk, or losing money in the stock market. People obviously have their own private prejudices, but they are never manifested in the conversation of the rich, not even subtly.

The accumulation of money isn't a crime so long as you don't hurt yourself or others in the process of amassing it. And I don't know many people who have a lot of money who just hold onto it. Some of them do, but most find ways of helping others. For example, probably more money is raised for charity in Beverly Hills than in any other city in the world. As I look back at the other levels of society where I've lived, it was quite unusual to find anyone who'd gained some amount of disposable income who'd given any important money to charitable organizations.

The average person pictures the rich as having servants and doing nothing. People who haven't been wealthy or haven't been around wealthy people think of them as dilettantes. Or that they just live it up. It's quite the opposite. The equation is that the more people you have working for you, the busier you are, the more things you must attend to, the more responsibilities you have. No one has enough competent help to handle everything by himself.

When I had seven servants, it was the hardest work of my life, and I'm accustomed to working long, hard hours. You become like the general manager of an institution. Every morning it's going around and making sure that this and that are done. And you can't tell them one day and not the next. You have to tell them every day, and nicely. It was a fantastic experience to realize that the lady of the house had to work very hard.

To prepare for a black-tie sit-down dinner—to make it successful you never have more than twenty-four guests—the hostess must do all the planning herself, because if something isn't letter-perfect she will be blamed. It's also worth mentioning that a social dinner party is a place where the rich can escape, where they can enjoy privacy among their peers. They know they're safe. No one is there to bother them or to try to take advantage of them. No one has an ulterior motive. Talking business at dinner is as gauche as getting fat. It becomes a kind of mutual protection league.

I have found that having money—and I am talking about having a lot of money—can be a problem. There are so many enticements for the rich, so many diversions. Usually, I've found that people who are highly successful financially almost inevitably need some kind of emotional upheaval in their lives. That doesn't necessarily mean a financial disaster. It simply means something that shakes them to the point where they must look inward. That's why so many are in therapy.

The emotional symptoms I see among my rich, troubled clients are depression, stress, anxiety. Many have physical symptoms—palpitations of the heart, ulcers, or the beginnings of arthritis.

Some rich male patients are in therapy with me because, having attained financial success, they don't feel successful. They've come to realize that money is not the answer. They are no longer interested in acquiring more money, so they become restless. After all, how much can you buy; how much can you have? Many wealthy men over thirty-five begin to search themselves, if they do not have some kind of spiritual guide to their lives. Therapy is the only way they can overcome feelings of being lonely, dry, unfulfilled, unworthy.

Wealthy women who come to me say they feel useless, lonely, separated from life. Many are alcoholics or drug addicts. Sleeping pills, pep-up pills and travel are popular among them—all sorts of things that are escapes.

I call such feelings "high lonesome." "High lonesome" is my term for people who've achieved their financial goals and then find money isn't satisfying. They feel isolated from life.

I feel very strongly that money can do a tremendous amount of good when used correctly. And it can be the devil himself when not used correctly. It is a matter of how important money is to the person, what position they give it in valuing themselves.

Professionally, I'm notorious for my low fees. My only motive is to help people. I believe all of us should help one another. I have complete faith that there will always be an abundance for me, or at least as much money as I need. I charge $35 to $45 an hour. Some pay $25 because they just absolutely can't afford to pay any more and they need help. And then, of course, I take some for nothing.

I keep expenses down by having clients come to my home. I don't need the Beverly Hills office, the reception room, the secretary, all of that. I make my own bookings, I make my own hours, I take my own calls, I collect my own money.

Patients pay as they go. If they can't afford to pay me, I keep the therapy going, but I just wipe their bills off the books, just wipe it off. I never carry money on the books.

Let me give you an illustration about how I think of money. I have many clients write down a list of all their possessions, everything they own. Then I ask them to burn the paper and imagine that everything on that paper is gone. Because that literally can happen very quickly. The person who is mentally stable must be able to burn the paper and still feel that he has value. If the client burns the paper and expresses regret, then he is in trouble. That test shakes people up quite a bit.

I took that test myself, mentally, when I divorced my husband, and it shook me up temporarily. The big home, the servants, and all the other trimmings had vanished. That kind of wealth now seems like a dream. Yet it didn't destroy me; far from it. I was able to restructure myself, and now I feel that I am living an exciting, useful life, personally and professionally.

WILLIAM ZEHV

"An income of $10,000 a year is quite adequate for a family of four, despite inflation. Such a family must have the right psychological attitude about the spending of money. They must recognize that the latest car isn't the most important thing in the world, as long as they have

transportation. Having all the latest gadgets in the house is not that important, as long as they have the immediate necessities. If it is recognized that certain luxuries aren't really necessities, I would say that the $10,000 figure isn't out of line for a healthy, realistic, emotionally rounded family."*

Dr. Zehv practices in middle- and upper-middle-class Encino, California, where most incomes, including those of his patients, exceed the $10,000-per-annum mark. He's a $35-an-hour clinical psychologist and marriage counselor who earns $30,000 a year. Born in 1919, he's a child of the Depression, an experience which lingers.

When I was growing up, the psychological aspect of money, the social pressure concerning money, was thrift. You saved. Now the social pressure is to spend. Consumption. Even during the recent economic recession, I found that the tendency among my friends and my patients was to spend and consume, if they hadn't lost their jobs. We had a property tax rebate in California not long ago. What was the purpose of that? It reflected our national hang-up with spending. It was a political maneuver designed to encourage people to put money back into circulation. The politicians of our country condition us to spend.

Our society places a very high value on consumerism, but did you ever stop to think how fragile consumerism is? For example, we have about nine million alcoholics in this country, and God knows how many borderline alcoholics. Yet the liquor industry is important to our economy. What if 10 percent of all the people who drink suddenly stopped drinking? We would really have a depression then. At the height of the energy crisis, it became very fashionable for a while to buy a bicycle. Everybody had to have a ten-speed bicycle, which costs well over a hundred dollars. That contributed to the affluence of our industrial society and to employment. Then, all at once, it wasn't fashionable to have bicycles. What impact did that have on our society and our employment rate?

When I was in high school, the ethic was that in order to get

---

*According to the Department of Labor, the typical urban family of four requires $16,236 a year to maintain a moderate standard of living, and the same family can live at an austere level for $10,000 a year. Per capita income in America is $7,375.

something valuable out of life you had to suffer for it. I don't agree with that. Suffering does not encourage a significant or a happy life. I suffered enough. I know. The thing is that an individual, a child growing up, has to recognize the significance and the meaningfulness of working hard, of being ambitious. But at the same time he has to put it into perspective. After all, a job is only a means to an end, not an end in itself. It's like money, which is also not an end in itself but a means to an end.

Money is an excellent index of a person's behavior and personality. I had a client who was earning $18,000 a year. He and his wife came to came to see me because they were at their wits' end. They were on the verge of divorce. They were tearing each other's hair out because they were so deeply in debt. The wife couldn't go to the doctor because she wasn't paying him. The husband was a guy who was working to make money solely for status, which isn't a very desirable motivation. Moreover, he didn't know how to use money. They spent two years in therapy with me, and I helped them get almost out of debt. Then, suddenly, when they were on the verge of seeing financial light at the end of the tunnel, the husband went out and bought a new house and an expensive boat. And of course they were back in debt again, heavily.

After two years of learning how to manage his money, being disciplined about the spending of money, using money correctly, he just couldn't stand it any longer. Buying the house and the boat gave him self-satisfaction. He thought he owed those things to himself and to his family. He had a wife and four children, and he wanted the children to go to the proper Catholic schools, where there is expensive tuition. He never learned the meaning of thrift, of living with money realistically. He was a country mile away from the concept of delayed gratification. He left therapy, and I'm sure by now he's in a morass of more overspending and the consequent psychological problems that can create. I'm afraid his behavior is all too typical of too many Americans, whether they're rich or poor.

I worked for six years in an outpatient clinic. The majority of the people who came there could afford very little or nothing at all in the form of a fee. The thing that struck me most vividly was that these people felt they were entitled to certain luxuries, in spite of their poverty. The luxuries, small as they were, made life bearable for them. A number of them were on welfare. Being on welfare, in spite of all they say in the newspapers, is no picnic. The amount of money they get is very little. Nevertheless, a family, typically, would take some of the money from welfare and go out with their children to have a hamburger at McDonald's. But even a McDonald's hamburger for four or five people amounts to quite a bit of money. They could have had a much better cooked meal at home. But such behavior is a form of self-assertion. They have got to do something for themselves to make themselves feel good. It isn't that they feel society owes them money, but they feel, on the basis of what they've seen on TV and in the other media, that there is much affluence around. Other people eat out. So many other people can afford so many things. Therefore they conclude that they have to reach out for something to assert their individuality, their ego. It makes them feel like people again.

Unfortunately, in our society money is often equated with love. Take an executive on the financial make. He is busy trying to achieve; he's under a tremendous amount of pressure, both at the office and at home. The executive makes more and more money, and he uses that money to buy luxuries for his wife and children. He is buying their love, since he cannot give anything of himself because he doesn't have the time. The wife is caught too. She wants her husband to be successful and ambitious; she wants him to make money. But she also wants him to work a nine-to-five job so he will have time for her and the children. But he can't do both. I see that type of case very often.

I tell my clients that the use of money depends on them. As a psychologist I try to get across the notion that the individual has to determine what would satisfy him in his life and therefore to use whatever money he earns to get that kind of satisfaction. Suppose an executive in an advertising firm says he would rather be an artist or just live on a farm. Well, if that's what he wants to do, if that is meaningful to him, that's fine. But he also has to recognize and must accept the responsibility that he cannot earn the same amount of money.

Many people are caught in a financial-emotional bind. A husband, a wife and their seventeen-year-old son came to consult with me. The problem was that the son had run away for the summer and spent his time just knocking around. Now that he was back, he was attacking his father's conservative political beliefs. The son resented the fact that his father supposedly had no social conscience or social ethic. I turned to the son and said, "Look, you're almost eighteen years old, and on the verge of going to college. If that's the way you feel about your father, why don't you do as you did before, run away again, take off and be on your own?" The son thought for a moment, then replied, "Well, I like the idea of my father giving me a car and an allowance." I said: "Then you cannot have it both ways. You can't keep attacking your father while he provides so generously for you. You can't have your cake and eat it too."

So far no one has done any formal research that I know of about the sexual side-effects of unemployment, but in case after case I've found that the unemployed husband definitely experiences a deflation of libido. One such husband told me: "How can I make sexual overtures to my wife? Being unemployed, I feel less of a man. I don't feel I deserve the pleasures of sexual intimacy."

At a cocktail party, a woman of about thirty cornered me and whispered: "There's something wrong with my husband. Ever since our marriage, he's been an ardent lover. He'd follow me into the bathroom when I bathed, he'd chase me around the bedroom, he'd often plead and beg. But lately he hasn't been doing it. I'm worried. There's something wrong. Maybe he doesn't love me anymore. Maybe he's sick."

"Is your husband unemployed?" I asked.

"How did you know?" she said.

As the unemployed person is obliged to lower his standard of living, he suffers a decline in self-worth, and that plays havoc with his sex life. Because he's making less money, he's less interested in sex.

Then there was the high-priced hooker who came to me for counseling. She wondered if something was wrong with her. "Suddenly I find that the men in my life are no longer interested in me," she said. "Perhaps it isn't you at all," I said. "Maybe it's just that your customers can't afford you anymore.

These are hard times, and the first thing a man gives up is unnecessary luxuries."

"Since when," she asked, "has sex become unnecessary and a luxury?"

"Since the men in your life began wondering where their next meal was coming from."

I concluded by telling her that the plunge in her income now afforded her the opportunity to enter a more desirable profession.

You see, there's a silver lining in every problem, even one that occurs when an individual or the nation is facing a financial crisis.

"There's No Business Like Show Business"

A million dollars is no money anymore.

—ART LINKLETTER

HARRY REEMS

The star of Deep Throat *and* The Devil in Miss Jones *is in deep financial and judicial trouble.*

From a small Hollywood office donated by Rod McKuen and from another tiny beachhead on East 56th Street in New York, he tirelessly solicits money on the phone and in letters. His letterhead, in large, bold-faced type, reads: "Harry Reems Legal Defense Fund." Recipients are advised that "Tax deductible contributions should be made payable to The Bill of Rights Foundation, Inc." In a column at the left of the letterhead are the names of fifty-nine famous people who support his cause, the luminaries including: Bella Abzug, Edward Albee, Lauren Bacall, Warren Beatty, Dick Cavett, Ramsey Clark, Jules Feiffer, Ben Gazzara, Gene Hackman, Hugh Hefner, Dustin Hoffman, Garson Kanin, Norman Lear, Jack Lemmon, Shirley MacLaine, Mike Nichols, Jack Nicholson, Rex Reed, Barbra Streisand and Gay Talese.

Reems is slightly built and dark-eyed, not particularly impressive off screen as a sex object; in fact, it is startling to realize that this short, intense, average-looking unmarried thirty-year-old has been the world's most celebrated male star of cinematic erotica.

I was born in Manhattan and grew up in the Bronx. Then we moved to Westchester. I went to synagogue when I was young. The atmosphere at home emphasized middle-class morality and values, a job, a home, security, a family, that sort of thing.

As a kid I never wanted to be an actor. I never thought about it till I was in my late teens. I started by working in off-Broadway productions. Then I went to dramatic school. I would say my early career was an awful lot of studying and a lot of showcase, workshop, ensemble and repertory. I nearly starved to death.

It got to the point where I was on welfare. I was a full-time

21

student at dramatic school and I was doing shows in the evening, and I had no time to make the rounds. At that time there was a provision in the welfare law that said a full-time student who had no time to look for a job couldn't receive aid. So I lost my welfare eligibility.

I started sort of nickeling and diming my way, waiting on tables, working at market research firms, taking surveys, doing carpentry work, and whatever other odd jobs I could pick up to make some money.

I never had money to pay the rent, never had money to eat, never had money to go to the theater. I'd always sneak in at the second half of Broadway shows. When the shows broke at intermission, the audience would come out of the theater and meander around the streets until the curtain went up again for the second half. I used to slide into the crowd and filter my way back into the theater with the crowd. I saw an awful lot of second acts that way.

The first time I went on film was in 1968. I did three Wheaties commercials. I did a little extra work in *Klute* and on whatever other films were shooting in New York.

But I wasn't making it. I was a starving actor and I needed to supplement my income, and I was tired of waiting on tables. So in 1969 I made my first film in the sex genre. It wasn't only the fact of making money, but I did the film because there was also a little titillation involved, a little curiosity, a little experimentation.

When *Deep Throat* came along, I was initially a member of the crew. By now I'd done a number of films in that genre, and I had worked my way behind the cameras. My interest sort of evolved to that point because what was happening in front of the cameras was really no challenge; it offered no test of anything I had learned. So I began developing an interest in film technique, the whole film process, the lighting, the sound, the camerawork.

I originally went down on *Deep Throat* as a lighting man. They were having trouble casting that particular part opposite Linda Lovelace. The director had seen my work and asked if I would act. I said sure.

The film turned out to be a lot of fun; I enjoyed it. I did my comedy and sex scenes with Linda, and had no reluctance doing the film, because I was doing it as a straight acting job. At this point, remember, I was bored with what I was doing as an actor.

My only reasons for performing in the film were again curiosity, my own titillation, and my own sexual pleasure. Technically or artistically, there was very little to be gained from it.

I worked one day on *Deep Throat* and was paid $100. The film has probably grossed $40 million. I think Linda Lovelace made $1,200 for her acting role. Subsequently she did a lot of promotion and advertising for the film and was paid fairly well. Linda, I believe, has just had a baby, and I don't think she has any kind of career going for herself. She doesn't consider herself an actress. She is a *cause célèbre*. I hope that if money was a goal in her life, she took advantage of a situation that could have paid off extremely well for her. I don't know if she did or not. I have no relationship with her.

The popularity of *Deep Throat* was not a result of the movie, of any outstanding qualities in the movie or outstanding subject matter. It was the legal harassment that brought the film to the attention of the press and public. Suddenly it gained tremendous notoriety around the country as a film that declared itself not obscene and yet had explicit sexual material in it. And this created a lot of controversy. People started talking about the question of obscenity as something criminal or not criminal. All this generated curiosity about *Deep Throat*. Everybody went to see what it was all about.

After *Deep Throat* I continued to work in that market and continued to work in the theater. It wasn't *Deep Throat* that made me successful. It was the combination of that film and a similar role I took in *The Devil in Miss Jones*. Once I had participated in two blockbuster hits, my name was connected to that genre of film. I became a salable commodity. People wanted to see Harry Reems. Harry Reems sold tickets. When you reach that, when you are marketable, you can suddenly go above scale and demand a percentage on the number of tickets you are going to sell. I'm intelligent and I have a business sense, and I had good lawyers who said I should be asking for pieces of the pictures I was doing. They said I should be getting a good salary, so no longer did I work for $100 a day. I was getting all sorts of offers in that genre, and I was able to pick and choose very carefully. I had good taste—I mean the films that I was connected with were the ones that did the biggest business in that market.

Christ, my money escalated up to $10,000 or $15,000 for

three, four days' work. Financially, I was doing about $50,000 to $60,000 a year, making only two or three films a year.

Then I went to Europe for three years and developed a nice film career over there, not in sex films but in comedies and adventure films.

When I came back to the States for a visit, about two and a half years after I'd participated in *Deep Throat*, I was arrested by the FBI and charged with conspiracy to distribute. I was extradited to Memphis, Tennessee and was brought to trial there. I sat in that town for ten and a half weeks. If you know anything about the violation of the conspiracy laws, you realize that the accused is responsible for everything that happens in the course of that crime. So the fact that I had acted in *Deep Throat* meant I could be charged with the distribution of *Deep Throat* under the conspiracy laws. I was formally brought to trial on a conspiracy charge of interstate transport of obscene materials.

The trial took place in Memphis because the government had found itself a very sympathetic prosecutor there, and the government was fairly confident it could find a sympathetic jury in that geographical region. Memphis, Tennessee is antiquated; it's provincial; it is moralistically Victorian. It has no business judging what is acceptable for Los Angeles and New York City. And this being a federal case, a Memphis jury decided what was acceptable for the United States of America.

The trial cost me more than $30,000 of my own funds. The bills outstanding are probably equal to that. And the bills yet to come will probably amount to close to $100,000. I was convicted on federal obscenity charges, but in April 1977 I was granted a new trial because my work in *Deep Throat* had taken place prior to a U.S. Supreme Court ruling on obscenity in 1973.

I am doing very poorly trying to get money for my defense. I am not a professional fund-raiser. I don't know how to go out and solicit dollars. It's a very embarrassing situation, a very awkward situation for me and for those whom I address myself to. Nevertheless, it's a case that has caught the attention of every civil liberties group in the nation. It has caught the attention of everybody in the theatrical community, and they are extremely receptive and sympathetic to it. It has been compared to the Ellsberg trial; it has been called one of the hugest miscarriages of justice of our time, of this century.

Many people have made contributions in one way or another—by letting me use their names, for example. Some of them haven't yet made dollar contributions, but that's because they are waiting to see if their names can generate money. It's like, for instance, when Jimmy Carter was running for president, Warren Beatty attended a fund-raising dinner for him. The fact that Warren Beatty was there sold a hundred tickets at $100 a head, and that is $10,000. Warren Beatty didn't necessarily make a dollar contribution himself to Carter's campaign, but his name did. That basically is the way it works.

Los Angeles is a tough town to crack financially, because most celebrities are approached daily—five times a day—for all kinds of good causes. I sympathize with them, because it is difficult to say no to a cause that has bona fide serious implications. I'm basically a New Yorker, and to reach major celebrities I usually have to go through their agents or managers, whom I usually never hear from again. But I find that when I can talk to people directly, they usually are aware of the case and will make a contribution.

In more than a year, I've raised about $45,000 against the $150,000 I need. The case is going to drag on a long time. There will be an appeal, perhaps a retrial, and if I'm convicted again we'll probably go all the way to the Supreme Court, if I can support that effort. I'm also scheduled to be tried, in the same place and for the same so-called crime, for my participation in *The Devil in Miss Jones*. That trial will cost another $150,000 to $200,000, depending on its length.

If my conviction stands, I think that what has happened to me could happen to Charlton Heston or Steve McQueen. I don't think—I know! Any actor, potentially, can be indicted. I don't think I'm being an alarmist in saying that major stars could find themselves in courtrooms in small towns all over America under the current conspiracy laws.

Once my legal troubles are over, I hope to go back to work, and I hope to make a nice comfortable living, doing films that I want to do.

I can't put a dollar figure on a comfortable living, but I want certain things in life, a piece of land, a family, freedom to not work if I choose not to. If I want to take a week off and go up in the hills somewhere, I want to be able to do that.

For me, money isn't a goal in life. Money is a key to obtaining the goals in life that I want. I would use money to put a smile on my face. Money itself would not put a smile on my face. What I use the money for would put a smile on my face. Money is dangerous, it is exotic, it's a threat to happiness, it's a conduit to happiness. It's violent. It's peaceful. And unfortunately it's the key to false happiness.

I've paid a tremendously high price in financial terms, never mind the emotional scars, for earning $100 in *Deep Throat*. All I did was take an acting job. I'm the victim of an injustice. I'm not a criminal. I'm not guilty of anything. It's the goddamn government of the United States coming down on my neck and trying to throw me in the slammer.

Right now, I can't work. All my time has to be devoted to raising funds.

The court case cost me everything I had. I'm officially bankrupt. I now live from day to day on the generosity of others.

ALEXANDER TUCKER

The Hollywood business manager, the efficient, sleek éminence grise operating quietly in the background, has traditionally been a close-mouthed breed, rarely publicized, since an ethical obligation exists to keep clients' financial affairs private.

Occasionally a gigantic underground tussle between business manager and star surfaces. Example: Doris Day won a suit against her manager after charging him with fraud and malpractice. At stake was no less than $22 million.

"Sure, there are crooked business managers," says Tucker, one of the most respected financial minds in Hollywood. "That sort of thing is being done, and that's about as much as I can say on that subject, except that unfortunately a license isn't required to be a business manager."

Born in 1908 in Bangor, Pennsylvania, he received his law degree from Georgetown University. "When World War II was over, I had the opportunity of going back to Washington, where I had been special assistant to Homer Cummings, the attorney general of the United States. I decided to stay in southern California and pursue whatever happiness it would become my good fortune to possess."

Tucker's mere presence invites confidence. He is impeccable in a gray suit, striped tie and blue shirt; his brownish-gray eyes peer out from a solid, mustached visage. He exudes charm—but bluntness, too.

I became an employee of another business manager, with whom I stayed for a period of seven years, learning my trade. During that period, I handled Tyrone Power, Howard Hawks, Dinah Shore, George Montgomery, all the Marx Brothers— mainly people in the motion picture business, because television had not as yet become important enough to bother with.

After that lengthy apprenticeship, I was able to go out on my own. My present clients—there are eighty or ninety of them— include Anthony Quinn, Glenn Ford, George Peppard, Telly Savalas, Earl Holliman of *Police Woman,* and directors like Fred Zinnemann and Richard Fleischer.

The charge for our services is 5 percent per annum of the client's earned income. Our annual volume is between $5 million and $15 million; I wouldn't care to pinpoint it any more than that. We don't necessarily derive 5 percent of that, because a lot of that money may be earned by clients from investments; our income accrues from the flat 5 percent charge.

This is a one-man organization in the sense that I do not have any associates. I have twenty-seven employees, several of whom participate in profits, but they are not my partners. They all work for me.

Some people think that I won't handle anyone who earns less than $50,000 a year. That's not so. Valerie Perrine, Robert Redford and Peppard all came to me when they were earning $15,000 a picture, and I accepted them as clients. I no longer handle Redford. He moved to New York City, and he preferred to have somebody there, which is perfectly all right with me.

These people come to me because what I offer them mostly is my reputation and the confidence of the people who have seen fit to recommend them to me. We do everything for them in a financial way that it is possible to do. We try to stay out of anything personal. Frequently we can't do that, because, for example, a divorce suit requires tax handling and usually division of property.

In a roundabout way, we play father confessor and psychologist to our clients. It very rarely works. It doesn't happen often, but if an actor wants to give his girl friend a Rolls-Royce, he is going to do it. At the bottom line, there's nothing we can do to keep a client from making an imprudent investment. We try to make the best of it when that occurs, and we try to get the client into a position where he will buy something that has future value.

I have never refused to handle a famous client, but I have asked some well-known clients to leave the office because they repeatedly disregarded our advice or because they made themselves obnoxious. They couldn't get along with the personnel in the office, with the people who were assigned to them. We would reassign them to other people, and they couldn't get along with them, either. I don't handle any client personally. I handle all but I handle none. They are all assigned to a particular individual, but the client has the right to come to me at any time to discuss his problems.

All our clients have agents. The agent gets the check first, sees that it is for the correct amount, deducts his commission, and sends the remainder to us. We endorse it after the proper entries have been made and deposit the check in the client's bank account.

The client doesn't see his money as a rule. The only time a client is likely to see his money is when he gets a residual check, because the Screen Actors Guild has a rule of passing those on directly.

My ultimate objective is to manage the finances of clients and increase their wealth, so that hopefully they will accumulate enough money to give them financial security at a time when they can't get a job.

We do that in many ways. We have people who send us deals from all over the United States—real estate deals, oil and gas deals, licenses, patents, manufacturing, franchises, limited partnership deals involving businesses of different kinds. We also put clients into banking certificates of deposit; sometimes we invest in government bonds or municipal bonds. But we don't use municipals as much today. We haven't, for example, bought any New York City bonds in several years. We were able to anticipate that situation.

I don't make any investment decision by myself. If any of the deals are worthy, I bring them to the client. Maybe there are three which are possibilities. That gives the client a way of comparing and perhaps a way of more easily forming a judgment or preference. When necessary, I discuss the deal with the client's attorney and go through it with him. If the attorney approves, we then try to cement the deal in the manner and shape and form which we think is most desirable.

In some deals, a number of our clients come in. Ten of them recently participated in the purchase of a 622-unit apartment building in Marina del Rey. The purchase price was $16 million, and I think the property has a natural replacement value now of $23 million. So in that situation we have made on paper $7 million for our clients.

In real estate, we usually stick pretty close to southern California. We will go from Santa Barbara to San Diego. I don't know how many apartment deals we've made, but they are numerous. And the apartment buildings are always very, very large. They are easier to handle that way. We have one in Downey that consists of 460 units. We have three-hundred-odd apartments in Santa Barbara. And we have a lot of smaller ones in various locations of between 100 and 150 apartments.

We go into every deal with the knowledge that it is going to be tax-sheltered. But we won't take a deal just because it is a tax shelter. It has to be a good deal first and then a tax shelter second. If you would ask me the question, "Would you buy a deal that isn't tax-sheltered?" the answer is no. A good deal is one where we can see all the figures, the taxes, the expenses, the whole financial layout, one that looks like it should intrinsically be a good deal.

I think I've been successful over the years in making money for my clients. The question is, Do they make only a small amount or a large amount? Naturally, when clients earn a small amount of money, they have to start slowly. As they go up the income ladder, they will be able to get into larger deals, where the profits are greater.

For our clients we also handle mortgage payments, charge accounts and personal accounts. We handle everything, because it is all money, and money must be accounted for. Every check we write has two signatures, mine and the client's. The client sees every check we write. Clients can write checks on their own—they have small personal accounts. But we keep those personal accounts at a certain level, usually no more than $500. They don't need more than that. They have charge accounts, and they can always get checks, unless they are away a long time in Europe. It's also true that some of our clients who have taken liquidity positions can put their hands on, if they wish, up to $2 million in cash.

I think stars today are more knowledgeable about money than a lot of the old-timers who lost their money. That's because there are more business managers, people with expertise. I think stars have come to realize that they need financial advice. Now there are more people who can give it to them. When I first started out, there were just a very few in this business; there was virtually no one to go to.

There's another important factor that necessitates a business manager. The tax laws have continuously changed. Practically every year since 1939, Congress has meddled and interfered and screwed up our tax laws in such a way that only an expert can understand what they are talking about. And much of the time even an expert can't interpret the tax laws without going into a court of law.

Stars also get financial advice from their attorneys and bankers. And the stars talk to one another. Money is their favorite subject. Whenever they get together at a party, money becomes the thing they talk about most, how to get it or how to keep it. One looks at the other and says, "He's got money put away for his future, and that's what I want. If he can do it, I can do it." Some stars put money before everything else—marriages, children, personal aggrandizement, and sex.

Clients who come to us usually don't have complicated financial affairs, because we generally get them when they are very young, and their careers zoom very quickly. If they are going to make it, they make it fast. Valerie Perrine became a star within a year. That $15,000 per picture she was making when she first came to us is way, way up there. Offhand I don't remember her last figure, but I think it's close to $250,000 a picture now. If she continues to climb and takes her career seriously, she is going to be one of our great actresses.

I would say Cary Grant is the richest star in Hollywood, because he owns every picture he ever made. His picture deals
were made on the basis of a seven-year release. The studio had
them for seven years, but then he got them back. I don't know
how many pictures Cary made, but I would say that his poorest is
worth not less than $500,000 for one or two plays on a network;
perhaps it's worth $1 million. And he has at least thirty or forty
of these pictures, plus all the other money he never spent. Cary
was very careful; he is not a great spender.

Neither are a lot of other stars great spenders. There was a
time when they were much looser with their money. I find they
are getting tighter and tighter. I find them holding onto their
money. It's because they are getting better advice.

I think all the major stars today are very wealthy. There might
be some who are heavily loaded with deals that are not panning
out at the moment, but generally speaking all the top stars I
know are rich. I would define rich as having anything from $1
million up.

I also think that Hollywood, contrary to what you read, is in
excellent financial shape. Paramount has increased profits 60
percent. Universal has so much money it doesn't know what to
do with it. Even poor Columbia is paying off its debts because
they have four or five pictures that are bringing in a lot of
money.

My clients are making more money than ever. There's more
money available for motion picture and television projects for
people who can produce at the box office.

John Wayne certainly has the longest and best record of bringing people into the theaters. But in today's market there are
perhaps a dozen actors who make from three to ten times more
money than Wayne does, and their pictures gross and net maybe
three to ten times more than a John Wayne picture. Redford,
Paul Newman, and Steve McQueen are three stars in that category.

But if young hopefuls in Milwaukee and Omaha and Toledo
are licking their lips over the fabulous amounts of money stars
are making, they better forget about it. Stars aren't created the
way they once were. There's nobody going into Schwab's to
discover Lana Turner. Valerie Perrine was fortunate; she was a

showgirl at Las Vegas when Monique James, in charge of casting at Universal, found her. The new Valerie Perrines will come from Broadway or off-Broadway or from the talent pool that's already out here. The little farm girl who once came to Hollywood and made good here is, I think, almost nonexistent. Actors and actresses nowadays must have training.

Basically, the motion picture business is a very unfortunate one to be in. You are only as good as your last picture. It's an old statement, but it's true.

You have a situation now where some stars are making gigantic amounts of money, while at the same time there is very high unemployment in Hollywood. The reason? It's simple. There are too many people in the business who shouldn't be in it. They should never have come to Hollywood in the first place.

MARVIN SCHWARTZ

John Wayne's son Michael, an old friend, has loaned Schwartz his unoccupied suburban lakeside home during his short visit back to Hollywood. He is dressed in a white T shirt, jeans and a rope belt. His feet are bare. Forty-nine years old, he is blue-eyed and gray-haired, with perfect white teeth. A few feet away, coiled in a saffron robe, is an American-born Buddhist nun. The young woman and Schwartz, eating from paper plates, are finishing a lunch of noodles and hash. Schwartz, who moved to Los Angeles when he was four years old, conveys the impression of a man at rest, a man who doesn't have a care in the world.

In the late fifties I became a partner in one of the most successful publicity firms in Hollywood. Some of our clients were Cary Grant, Tony Curtis, Yul Brynner, Chrysler Corporation for television, and the cities of Reno, Nevada and Long Beach, California.

For a while I enjoyed publicity. I was making around $30,000 or $40,000 a year, something like that, which at that time was considerable money, I guess. Then I moved into production. My first picture was for Universal. It was called *Blindfold,* and it starred Rock Hudson and Claudia Cardinale. It wasn't a successful picture, but I made a lot of money on it by charging a hefty packaging fee. The book cost so much, the screenplay so much, the stars so much. I then added my up-front price for putting the whole project together—$150,000.

I then did three pictures in quick succession, mostly on location in Spain: *The War Wagon,* with John Wayne and Kirk Douglas; *101 Rifles,* with Raquel Welch; and *Hard Contract,* which starred James Coburn and Lee Remick. Of the three, I only made profits on *War Wagon.* So few pictures make money. What you try to do is get as much money as possible in front to protect yourself in case the picture doesn't go into profit. Even if a picture does make money, studios have so many ways of hiding profits. They have so many of their own costs that they take off, you never see your profits anyway. I mean, studios can make money on pictures that show a loss on paper. So I didn't really make that much on *War Wagon,* though it was pretty successful. Some checks have started coming in during the last year or two, a couple of thousand dollars. But overall I did well with the picture because it also brought me a packaging fee of $150,000.

I then made *Tribes* with Jan-Michael Vincent for television. It was a story about a kid with long hair who gets drafted into the Marine Corps and is confronted by the traditional tough sergeant. I co-authored the teleplay, and the show won an Emmy and a Writers Guild award.

I was a success, on the surface. Inside I wasn't feeling that good. I had a big house with a swimming pool in Benedict Canyon, and I drove a Ranchero. I'd been divorced twice but I had chicks. I had everything I wanted. I mean I could go anywhere, and I had every credit card ever issued, and anything I wanted to buy I could. I could eat in any restaurant in L.A.— they all knew me, and I got the best tables. I had writers working on deals, and all this stuff.

But that's not what makes you happy. Things don't make you happy. We are oriented in this society to think that things make us happy. Temporarily, you get money and you go out and buy stuff, and that's terrific. But you keep wanting. So you keep working harder to make more money to buy bigger houses, bigger cars, more clothes, more things. They are all temporary highs. But every time you get a high, remember that you are going to get a low. Those highs are terrific for a while, but those lows are what's eating up your fucking guts.

You know when you're not feeling good. You know when you're suffering inside because of your chick, because of your kids, because of your payments, because of the shit you take in your work, because of the revenge you want to get, because of ego. Ego—whoo, ego is a word.

I woke up one morning, looked in the mirror and didn't like what I saw. I told myself there has got to be a better way to live, some way to feel better more of your waking hours.

In two weeks I had sold my house and given away my furniture. I packed two suitcases and a suit bag and headed for the airport. I said, "I want to take a plane to where it's warm." On impulse, I took a flight to the Canary Islands.

I didn't know what I was going toward; all I knew was that I had to leave. I just wanted out. I had to get out of the environment I was in, which was a total downer, all money-oriented.

In the Canary Islands I was living on six dollars a day. The Benedict Canyon pad, with all the booze and stuff, had been costing me three grand a month.

I met a freak with long hair and I asked him, "Where can I score some dope?"

"I'll show you," he said. Then he said, "What are you doing here?"

"I don't know what the hell I'm doing here," I said.

"How would you like to go up in the mountains and live in a cave?" he asked.

"All right," I said.

He asked if I had a sleeping bag, and I said No, but I'll buy one.

I had enough clothes with me to outfit a small regiment. I had a big caribou shoulder bag, and I had a cowboy hat, cowboy boots, cowboy jeans with a big buckle, the whole Hollywood cowboy thing.

I sent my suitcases to a friend in London. I got rid of my cowboy outfit. I got rid of my Grecian Formula 16; I'd been dying my hair so chicks wouldn't think I was too old.

Then the freak and I bought some food. He said, "We're

going to hitchhike to the south end of the island." I hadn't hitched since I was a kid.

It took ten days of walking to reach the cave. I stayed up there, living in the cave, for about a month. We met this other guy, and then we moved into an empty shepherd's house with a couple of chicks and stayed there for a while, and I kinda got myself oriented.

You see, mostly what man spends his waking hours doing in the United States is working and paying bills. Now, all of a sudden, I was into a whole new number. How would you feel, how would you adjust if I took you and lifted you out of the atmosphere in which you function? You've been trying for the top, trying to grab a golden rung, but suppose suddenly you don't have to worry about anything; you just have to start learning how to feel good.

That's what happened to me. I started getting into myself. Not into meditation—I didn't know anything about meditation then. I was just starting to learn a lot of new things; about nature, for example. I saw a butterfly one day and watched it. I didn't even know butterflies did what they do.

After the Canaries, I took a boat to Marseilles and hitched through Europe. In Amsterdam I bought a used 1966 Volkswagen van and built a bed in the back and drove through some of the Iron Curtain countries. I went through East Germany, Czechoslovakia and Yugoslavia and then down to Greece, where I sold the van.

I spent some time on Crete, then hitched my way to Turkey. Then I decided to go to Africa. So I hitched my way to Syria and Lebanon and went by boat to Beirut. The border there was closed, and the only way I could get in was to fly. I don't like to fly, not because I'm afraid, but because you don't see anything. But I did fly to Cairo, and from there I went through twenty-two countries in Africa on foot.

I was seeing countries in a whole new way. Most of us fly to Paris or Rome and get a hotel room and do this and that and go to some restaurants. And then you are a city-watcher. When you are on the road and hitching, something happens to you every day. I met groovy people. I'd been in Paris eight times and never had a good time. I was lonely in Paris in a $100-a-day suite at the George V, with a car and a chauffeur. In Africa, I lived in villages with the Bantu, the Ebo, the Masai. I ate monkey and crocodile and termite stew. I lived in Africa for a year on what it used to cost me for a very quiet month in Los Angeles.

I still had no idea what I was going toward, only what I was going away from.

In Zambesi, in the Congo and in other places in Africa, I saw the greatest poverty that exists anywhere in the world. I mean, I saw people starving to death who didn't have the slop we feed our pigs. I saw people who didn't have a glass of water to drink.

We live behind a wall. When you go there and you see people actually dropping dead because they don't have a glass of water or a piece of bread to put into their mouths, it's totally indescribable. No American, no Westerner can understand it without seeing it.

In other places in Africa where they don't have much, what they have they will share with you. That's what's great about the bush. If the Africans have food, you are their guest. I've stayed in villages where I would come in and ask to meet the chief. I'd tell him I needed something to eat and a place to sleep. They would always feed me and give me a hut to sleep in. They would never ask for money. A lot of times the mammas would wash my clothes without my asking. I would come in from being out all day, and my clothes would all be clean and hanging over the bushes.

The interesting thing is that they have nothing, and they say, "Wow! America! America is terrific!" They want to be like Americans, because they think America has everything, that everybody in America is rich.

But what they've got in many ways is more than we've got. They've got togetherness. The whole family, the whole village works together to stay alive. It's the feeling that maybe we had in the early West when the pioneers were settling it. They still have that, and you really feel good with them. People there aren't out only for themselves. They've never heard of the profit motive.

From Africa, I hitched to India, and there I got interested in becoming a spiritual person. I took my first meditation course in Varnasi, the holy city on the Ganges where the people come and bathe in the morning, where they burn the dead and sprinkle the ashes in the river. My friends who meditated had a look of happiness in their eyes. I came down from Katmandu, where I'd been staying, and took the course because I envied their serenity and peace.

It just blew me out. It changed my whole life. I found new muscles. I broke old habits. I learned to get inside myself. I discovered a new relationship with the world. I realized there were people I didn't like because I saw something in them that I didn't like in myself. Now I like myself, and I like other people much better and get along with them well.

I've become a Buddhist. Buddhism isn't a religion as such; it's a way of feeling good inside. Buddhism says there is wisdom in knowing yourself. It's all right to make money—they don't have anything against making money, but money shouldn't obsess you. And you should make it in such a way that you are not hurting anybody, and you should spend it in a way that will do people good.

Buddhism says that the only reason you need material things is that you must eat; you must feed your body and you need a place to sleep. The monks and nuns usually have what they call a benefactor, somebody they know who will send them a few dollars a month. If they don't have a benefactor, they beg for their food. For them, there is nothing shameful about begging. It's very good karma for someone to help a monk.

I came back for a few months to see my kids and family. And I got a little tired physically of traveling. I wanted to sit for a while. Also, I decided that in order to help people, I'd take a job with one of the UN food programs. The UN accepted me; they're doing the security check right now. They want me to go back to India for them. But I've decided not to take the job. I haven't even told them that yet. I think I can help more people by taking more Buddhist teachings. And getting purer, trying to go for enlightenment, because I see the effect I have on people by just being with them. That's the way I'm going to spend my life, by learning more through meditation.

I still have a few bucks left. I don't know how I'm going to support myself in the future. But I don't care. I don't worry about it.

I'm going back to India in a few weeks. My biggest expense will be getting there. I have enough money for that. When I get there, it won't cost that much to live. Bombay is the most expensive city in India. There it costs me roughly maybe $3 a day. In Varnasi there's a really nice hotel that costs five to eight rupees—let's say sixty cents a night for a really nice room, with clean sheets and everything. It costs another buck to eat. You take trains. I have a student card, so I get 50 percent off for traveling second class. And if I have to, I'll beg.

Since I've been back, a friend of mine who is the head of a studio offered me a deal to produce pictures. He said, "I'll set you up. I need help, and I want you to come in with me." But I said I still didn't want it.

I may come back someday and make a lot of money in the picture business in order to put up some meditation centers in this country.

If someone offered me a million dollars I'd take it. I'd find something really nice to do with it. I would probably give it to people to help people. I don't really need it or want it myself.

What I'm interested in is helping people. I'd like to help you, because you are competing; you are in the marketplace. I know. I've been there. If I could help you feel better through meditation, it would make me feel better.

My friends here all dig me, but it ain't the same. They are, in their various ways, envious of me. But they don't want what I've got. They would all like to see me once in a while but not often. I guess they feel uncomfortable with me.

My friends are all in the movie business, and that's what they talk about all the time. That's what I used to talk about all the time. That's what I used to do all the time. Now that I'm not in it anymore, I'm not interested in it anymore.

When I came back, I said I'm going to see everything that clicks. I'm going to see every movie. I saw a few and then I got bored. Also, I don't drink anymore and I don't smoke dope and I don't drop acid. So I guess I'm a bore. What my friends don't know is that I get the biggest high in the world just sitting here meditating. I am sorry I can't see my friends as much, but I have to back off. I'm sorry if they feel guilty around me.

When I first got back, some of them said, Oh, you left because business is bad; you left because your ex-wives were hassling you, blah, blah, blah. Right away, they had the rationalizations. They all, in their own way, want to be happy, but they can't accept what I have to offer. They're still out for money.

Money makes you suffer. In America you are taught to be a success. You are not taught to make just enough money to live on, to be comfortable. You are taught to want more, always more, because that's what built this country. What you are taught is insanity, because you are never satisfied with what you have.

Jesus, I really have compassion for people who work only for money. It is so painful for them. I wish I could take them on my trip for a minute and just say, "Close your eyes for sixty seconds and let me show you what it is to be serene."

My good Jewish mother used to say, "Be a doctor, be a lawyer, be a professional man, make money. If you're a professional you'll always have money and security." The more money you had, the happier you would be. So we all wanted to be J. Paul Getty. We were always looking up to people who had money and position. Money, position, things, attachments. That's what we were taught to believe in.

It's shallow, it's wrong. It's not for me.

ART LINKLETTER

Art Linkletter is the envy of Hollywood, regarded as a financial genius. A tanned, healthy sixty-five, he's the most amiable of men, a lesson in how to be self-confident. He appears on TV these days only in an occasional special, preferring the life of a businessman. He's on the board of directors of MGM, Western Airlines and seven other corporations. He has interests in more than sixty businesses, ranging from Peruvian copper mines to a sheep ranch in Australia.

I get angry when people ask me how much I'm worth. The first question that almost all writers and reporters ask is, "How much money are you making and how much are you worth?"

That's such a private and personal thing. Also, these days it's a defensive thing, because anybody who is in the chips has to be careful that he isn't reminding a lot of potential kidnappers and rip-off artists and burglars that he's available. These guys peruse the newspapers. But above and beyond that, we are such a materialistic society that how much a person is worth seems to be more important than other qualities such as the things you write, the programs you do, the interesting people you know, your philosophy, the number of charitable and philanthropic activities you are in, all kinds of accomplishments. It all seems to come down to dollars and cents.

Not that I mind talking about money. Naturally, I've had a healthy concern for it all my life. Especially because I was the adopted son of a traveling Baptist preacher, and we were so poor that when the Depression hit, we didn't know it. All the Depression meant to me, in retrospect, was that practically everybody else was living the way we were.

We always lived in little houses in back of big houses. I never had an address that didn't have half a number on it until I was in my late teens. It was always something like 4326½ Van Dyke Street. And, you know, they left baskets of food for us on the doorstep on holidays so they wouldn't embarrass us.

I've never forgotten one incident concerning money that happened when I was just a little kid, working at anything I could find. One day a woman asked me if I would pick up the rocks in her front yard. She said it would look so much better if the rocks were taken away. So I got a big pail and did the job. At the end of a long hot afternoon, after I'd removed all the rocks, the woman asked what I would charge. I was kind of embarrassed at the thought of negotiating, which I had never done in my life. I didn't even know what the word meant, of course.

I said, "Oh, I couldn't charge you anything," feeling that she would protest and pay me something. But she said, "Well, in that case, thank you very much." And I walked away without a nickel.

Years later when I negotiated a contract and added an extra, unseemly amount of money, I just said to myself, "That's for the rocks."

A matter of $5 changed the direction of my life, shortly after I graduated from college. I had a job at KGB, the CBS radio outlet in San Diego, which paid me $125 a month. I was offered $120 a month to teach school. I really wanted to be a college professor, and I told them, "If you can give me the same amount I'm making at the station, I'll do it." They couldn't come up with the extra $5. Still, it was a very close decision; it could have gone either way, and I gave very serious consideration to not going on in radio.

At the time, I'd been a radio announcer for over a year. And the first so-called glamour of a young college guy getting a job as a radio announcer had worn thin. It was very hard work, sixty hours a week. I sold spots, I made personal appearances for sponsors, I did news, I did sound effects, I did everything. The worst thing about it was that I couldn't see how I could ever be a star. Because I couldn't see that I had any talent. I didn't sing or play a musical instrument. I didn't dance, act, or tell dialect stories. All the established stars in show business in 1934 had come from Broadway, Hollywood or vaudeville. Besides having no talent, I didn't have any of that background. Yet I didn't want to remain an announcer, because that obviously had a very limited horizon.

Fortunately, *People Are Funny* and *House Party* came along, and the success of those shows changed the picture for me. *People Are Funny* ran on radio and television for nineteen years, *House Party* for twenty-five years.

House Party began on radio about 1943. Budgets in those days were very low. The budget for the whole show—and this was a coast-to-coast show—was around $10,000 or $12,000 a week. I made $2,000 or $3,000 a week—I forget which. Then it got up to $35,000 and $40,000, and I made $8,000 or $10,000 a week, which seemed like a lot of money then.

I remember at one time I was making $12,000 a week, and I met Clark Gable at a party. Somehow the talk got around to salaries, and Gable said rather proudly, "I get $5,000 a week." And I thought, My gosh, here's this big star, and I make more than he does. But that was because he had a fifty-two-week noncancellable contract, which was the system at MGM and the other studios. A guy like Harry Cohn of Columbia was paying big stars $200 a week and loaning them out for $100,000 a picture.

I made it in show business, I suppose, because I was a good communicator. And I was a good salesman, a good persuader, a good talker. Then I became a good businessman because I was driven into it by the Internal Revenue Service, which takes an unholy chunk of the money earned by creative or productive people.

When I was making my biggest money in show business, federal and state taxes together were taking 96 percent of my earnings. So when you only have four cents left out of every dollar that you sweat and work for, you are forced to take advantage of tax shelters and loopholes. In other words, if the government is going to hit you over the head with a club, you have a constitutional right to defend yourself with a shield. You are a damn fool if you don't use the shield. The word loophole is actually a misnomer. That makes it sound like something sleazy and dirty, and it just burns me up. A loophole is a legal way of avoiding taxes, just as the government has a legal way of taking your money. You might just as well say you are looking for the loopholes in the government's right to take your money. It's a bad word; loophole implies evasion and something that somehow isn't right.

Money is just a scorecard for me. I don't live lavishly. I don't spend wildly. And I don't buy boats or airplanes or expensive cars. I don't gamble; I don't have a big wardrobe. I just don't feel any need for those things. So when I make a deal I make it because it's an interesting situation. And because I'm curious. People who make fortunes are all curious.

I do allow myself one luxury, the luxury of turning down anything I don't want to do. Money gives you the freedom to say no. Most people spend their lives scrambling and doing things they don't really want to do, because they have to. And when you don't have to, that's the greatest luxury you can have.

I keep at it because it's inside me to be a winner. But more than that, I'm intrigued by challenges. You are either that kind of person or you're not. You don't turn off when you have attained money; you are still the same person. It's like when I was playing champion handball. I played just as hard in a pickup game as I did in a tournament. I wanted to win. It didn't make any difference whether anybody was there while I was playing. Either you play to win or you don't.

One of my closest friends is D. K. Ludwig, who put the super-tanker on the high seas. He has interests in oil, minerals, cattle, farming and land development. I suppose D. K. is worth better than a billion dollars. Here's a man who is eighty years old who works harder today than he did twenty-five years ago. He lives in comparative frugality. He has a beautiful home, but he doesn't have a chauffeur or a private airplane. He doesn't gamble and he doesn't go to the theater, so what is he working for? The answer is, he feels he's creating something. It's the same feeling a person gets whether he's creating a painting, a book, a symphony, or a serum to prevent polio.

I think these days almost everybody is overpaid, particularly entertainers and sports figures. You see a bunch of kids, rock stars, standing on a stage wearing ragged clothes and knocking off $4 million or $5 million a year. That makes me feel the way I imagine Pancho Gonzales feels when he sees some nineteen-year-old kid making $200,000 a year hitting a tennis ball. And he made $12,000 a year as a world champion.

On the other hand, entertainers aren't overpaid if you keep in mind that it's a very cruel business. And whereas you are over-paid when you do well, you are cut off before you should be when you aren't doing well. That's the way the game is. So you have to make it when you get a good roll of the dice.

Stars my age are working for less now, with the possible excep-tion of Bob Hope. They are working for less or doing things they don't particularly want to do. Like Bob Cummings, who's out playing the theater-restaurants for $3,500 to $4,000 a week, working very hard, living in all kinds of cities he doesn't espe-cially want to live in.

Many stars are doing commercials and making good money, in some cases almost as good as when they were stars. They used to look down their noses at me in the forties when I was a star and doing commercials. Now you notice they are all doing it. John Wayne, Henry Fonda, Jimmy Stewart, Gregory Peck, Laurence Olivier, Helen Hayes. You name them and they are doing com-mercials.

I don't have a golden touch in every deal. Nobody has. The cattle business, in which I was a large investor, has gone to hell in the last five years and has cost me a lot of money. And I lost, oh, a half-million or so in a food item called Toasta Pizza. A bunch of us got together and backed that product. We got a big flour company to make a pizza which you could put into your toaster. And while it worked when made in small, limited quantities, we never could get it to work right when we got nationwide production. It was one of those things. The product gummed up the toaster, and a lot of other things happened beyond my control. I saw it all work in a laboratory, and I saw it all work on a limited-distribution basis; and I saw the whole thing take off and then fall flat because it wouldn't work on a mass-production basis. We couldn't lick the problems and couldn't guarantee the quality of the product.

My most successful venture has been the McMoRan Exploration Company. That's a company that drills for oil. I went into it with a few of my close friends. We got H. L. Hunt to give us the deals he was turning down because they were too small for him. He only went for elephants, as they call them in the oil business. And I was very, very happy to have camels. We did so well that the company went public about six years ago. When we started we had zero in reserves. We just had another oil company. But from zero, I would say that McMoRan today has oil reserves worth about $200 million. I own a substantial part of the company.

There isn't a secret to making money, but there is a flair for it and there is a feel for it. It comes from some kind of mysterious chemistry which combines daring and good judgment, knowing the time to strike and when to go.

Really cautious people—accountants, for example—ordinarily never make any money. There is a certain class of lawyer that never makes any money because they are noncreative. They tell you what you can't do, tell you the trouble you could get into. By the time this type of lawyer is through figuring out all the ways to keep you out of trouble, the good businessman has gone in, made his deal, and gotten out.

People who make money are generally people who have an element of the gambler in them, gambling tempered with a good analytical and mathematical idea of the odds. I would compare a successful businessman to a stunt man. You see the stunt man dive through a window into the flames. It looks as though he's going to kill himself, but he knows every inch of the way and has figured every possible safeguard, and that's what a guy who makes money does.

I think kids today have more opportunity than I did. There are better chances in everything today. Show business has a bigger payoff now, even though the chance of success is smaller because they don't give you as long to make it. But if you do make it, you make it bigger.

If I were starting out today and didn't have any show business talent and I wanted to be in some kind of money-making scheme or field, I would buy land, because the government can't print land. If I didn't have money to buy land, I'd get into the energy business. I would study solar and other forms of energy, since that's going to be our biggest need in the next fifty years.

I'd also advise a young man to be aware of taxes, and when he's in a position to do it, to hire a good tax man. Bob Cummings made a fortune as a star, but he got into the hands of a tax man who devised a scheme to avoid taxes legally. But the scheme was so flimsy that the IRS caught up to him and came down on him. This has happened to a number of stars. It happened to Joe Louis. The IRS comes down on them with penalties and past payments years after they pass their peak earning power, and it breaks them. Stars are always the targets of fast-talking accountant-lawyer tax-type people who have ways for them to borrow tremendous amounts of money and write off the interest and this and that dodge, all of which have no purpose except to avoid taxes. And that's a red flag—you can't go into a business just to avoid taxes. It's got to be a real business.

When I started out, I remember, one of my first great benefactors was Kay Kyser, the bandleader. Kay really fretted under the stress of show business. He wasn't in good health anyway. So he always used to tell me that when he had his first million he was going to quit. He was the only person I ever knew who did it. Because after you have your first million, it's like your first peanut. You are only going to eat one peanut, but has anybody ever stopped with one? It just whets your appetite for more. When Kay retired and went to live in North Carolina with his million dollars, a million dollars was a lot of money. It sounds like a lot today, but of course a million dollars is no money anymore. If you live in a good style, it isn't a lot of money because of inflation, for one thing. Kay's million today, if he'd just put it away at 5 percent interest, or someplace that was very, very safe, would be worth about $300,000.

So you can't sit still. You either have to have your money earning a lot of money or you have got to be earning a lot of money yourself, because every year your money is worth about 8 to 10 percent less.

If I lost everything tomorrow I would look around for an opportunity to be a salesman of some kind. Probably my greatest asset isn't money, it's contacts. I can open almost any door anywhere in the United States. And if I didn't lose my money through something that was scandalous, those doors would still be open.

A lot depends on how you lose your money. If you lose it by investing in the cattle market, you've gone over Niagara Falls to the bottom. But you are still alive and still just as good a swimmer as you were before. So if I lost everything, I'd just dry myself off and start swimming again.

City of Greed

*We've had cases of guys just trying to win
their dinner . . . and they end up losing
$10,000.*

—JACK BINION

DON PAYNE

The Department of Health, Education and Welfare recently concluded a three-year study to determine why Americans gamble. The study's conclusion: "Gambling is inevitable."

Says Payne, "We could have saved the government $3 million. We know it's inevitable that people are going to gamble. We just prefer that they do it here."

Born in 1929, Payne is a genial, gray-haired man, a Rotarian with eight children. For the last fourteen years he's headed the Las Vegas News Bureau. He earns $27,000 a year plus expenses.

My job is to publicize Las Vegas and the surrounding area. The entertainment, the gambling, the area attractions like Boulder Dam—anything that would tend to give a person a reason to come to Las Vegas. I do that in any and every medium at my disposal. I have a staff of sixteen: four writers, nine photographers, two secretaries, and a file clerk. My annual budget is $300,000. Many of the hotel-casinos have their own publicists, but they are concerned with garnering space only for the hotel for which they work. My responsibility is the entire city of Las Vegas and southern Nevada.

The gross gambling revenue, which is the real barometer of the Las Vegas economy, exceeded $700 million last year. Our revenue was up about 10 percent.

When the recession hit a few years ago, some people here anticipated a drop in business. The exact opposite happened. Business increased, and I think the reason was that people decided they were going to have one last fling in Las Vegas. We've been through this before, but every year we do more dollar volume. People decided to have a last fling here in 1970, when the stock market broke. Every year since then, though the country's economy has been shaky, people have been having their last fling in Las Vegas.

The people of the United States look at Las Vegas as an escape hatch. The money they've set aside to spend in Las Vegas is sacred money, sacred to them because it's earmarked for only one purpose: pleasure.

We figure the average person visiting here, exclusive of gambling, spends $100 a day for room, meals, taxis, souvenirs, magazines, shaving cream, toothbrush, etcetera. I have no estimate of how much money the average person wins or loses at gambling. That depends on the individual.

I hold the theory that nobody goes home from Las Vegas a loser. They may go home with less money, but not too many people will yell about it. It's an ego thing. I think people want to say, Well, I showed them how to play 21 out in Las Vegas, I showed them how to shoot craps, or I hit a slot machine for a jackpot. That certainly isn't true in every case, but I think that for the most part there is a strong tendency for people to exercise that sort of psychology.

People critical of Las Vegas have called it a city of greed. I can't disagree with that, but then again General Motors is a company of greed; the free enterprise system is motivated by the greed syndrome. And in Las Vegas greed is a two-way street. We clock nine to ten million visitors a year, and it has to be greed that makes them think they can come to Las Vegas and win. I honestly don't think people come here feeling they are going to lose. You told me you played poker yesterday. Did you play to lose?

You are talking to a nongambler. Oh, I wouldn't say I never put a chip down, but if I do, it's done in a frivolous manner. If I gamble, it's just to be sociable. If friends happen to be playing a slot machine or they are at the tables, I'll drop a chip or two. But I don't, frankly, know much about gambling, and I don't intend to educate myself.

If you should ask if I can justify gambling on a moral basis, I would have to say I see nothing morally wrong with a person's wagering money if he does it knowing what the risks are. It's the same as going into business; it's the same as investing in the stock market; it's the same as crossing against a red light. Gambling is a calculated risk. Morality itself is like beauty. I expect it's something for each person to judge individually. Would you call the nine to ten million people who come here every year immoral?

When I first came to Las Vegas, I had a job working at a filling station, and I remember people coming into that station and attempting to get some cash for a watch or a razor or a car or a piece of luggage—anything. They had gambled more than they could afford to gamble and they needed some money to get home. But the incidence of that has declined noticeably over the years. I think the reason is that my office and the entire gambling industry here have encouraged people to manage their money better. We say, Don't gamble what you can't afford to lose. I can't remember the last time I even heard of somebody having to borrow money to get home. However, I would temper that by saying that the Western Union office here is crowded with people who are wiring home for money—and people who are wiring money home, too.

Nevada has the highest suicide rate in the nation, and it would be difficult not to make a correlation between suicide and gambling. But you also have to consider that Las Vegas has a very high transient population. On any given day we have 30,000 to 60,000 people here who are visitors. I'm not suggesting necessarily that people come here to commit suicide, but the possibility exists that they do come here with that last fling in mind and that they are going to make it or break it. And if they don't make it, you may have a suicidal situation.

We also have a very high crime rate in Las Vegas.* The reason for crime, usually, is money. A good number of the residents of the world look to Las Vegas much as the immigrants from Europe looked to the United States a hundred years ago. The old streets-are-paved-with-gold idea. The cash flows freer in Las Vegas than anywhere else. That is naturally going to attract the criminal looking for some illegal means to get money. I consider our crime rate a very serious situation.

Even though proponents of legalized gambling have traditionally maintained that it would reduce crime and taxes, that it would make a city self-supporting, I think that's unrealistic.

*The gambling mecca has the highest crime rate in the nation, according to FBI crime reports. The city's ratio of serious crimes, including robbery, burglary, larceny-theft and auto theft, is twice the national average.

On the other hand, gambling isn't without its blessings. To give you the chamber of commerce pitch, we do have some advantages. Nevada has the seventh highest income per capita in the nation.* We have no personal state income tax. In Las Vegas, our sales tax is only 3½ percent, and this city has 165 churches of all faiths, which is more churches per capita than any other city in the nation. We have no death tax, no inheritance tax, no corporate income tax; and we have what we call a free port law which eliminates an inventory tax.

` What really makes Las Vegas hum, and what in my opinion has made it as recession-proof as a city possibly can be, is the convention business we've developed in the last nineteen years. We have more than two hundred conventions a year here. What this has done is to even out the peaks and valleys that we used to experience with the straight tourist trade. We still draw 50 percent of our visitors from southern California, but the convention business has been a great shot in the arm. The American Association of whatever it happens to be will meet generally from October through May, which used to be our slack season. The Las Vegas Convention and Visitors Authority has staff offices in Washington and Chicago, and the convention sales staff based here is constantly traveling, anywhere from Hawaii to South America to Europe to Asia and all over the United States, to arrange sales meetings, seminars, expositions, association executive meetings, and that sort of thing. Their purpose is to sell Las Vegas, and I think if you would talk to them, you would find that Las Vegas is a very easy thing to sell.

This is a cash town, perhaps the last cash town in the country. Even though we honor all the credit cards, when you are playing at a table or a slot machine, you are dealing with hard currency. It's not at all unusual to see $100,000 or $200,000 lying on a table. It takes an enormous amount of loose cash to maintain this gambling atmosphere. Millions of dollars in cash changes hands in one casino in one eight-hour shift.

Everybody in Las Vegas, of course, has gambling stories. This one was told to me by a number of sources that I wouldn't question. It concerns a group of six Japanese industrialists who

*The first six: Alaska, Connecticut, New Jersey, Illinois, New York and Delaware.

came here without hotel reservations. They attempted to check into the Sahara, which said it didn't have any rooms. So they went to the Sands and found rooms there. They stayed less than a week and lost $3 million in cash. Needless to say, when the Sahara people found out they'd lost those high rollers, somebody's head rolled. Most hotels, even if they tell you the place is full, will usually save a few rooms for high rollers who may check in at the last moment without reservations, as the Japanese gentlemen did.

I would never advise anyone not to come to Las Vegas, not even those Japanese gentlemen or compulsive gamblers. If they need action, let them find it here.

For most visitors, Las Vegas is tremendous therapy. I happen to be a fisherman, which is my therapy—my psychiatrist's couch, if you will. I can pretty much cleanse my thinking processes with a few days of getting away from the telephones by going fishing. I think that a good number of people in American society do the same thing in Las Vegas. Whether they lose $20 or win $100 or lose $5,000 or whatever, it's a service charge they pay to cleanse their souls. In that context, I think a great many people look at Las Vegas as a therapeutic holiday. You can't play the stock market with a two-dollar roll of nickels, but you can play here with that amount. I know of a secretary who ran a quarter into $1,500.

What would happen if casino gambling were suddenly made illegal in Las Vegas? Well, you'd have a ghost town. You'd have nothing to attract the people. The greed would still be there, but the way to satisfy the greed would be gone.

JACK BINION

Benny Binion, a bootlegger-turned-gambler, opened the Horseshoe casino, a Las Vegas landmark, in the late forties.

"The Horseshoe is the most profitable place in downtown Las Vegas. Honestly, I couldn't offhand tell you what we gross, but we're making a decent living," says his son Jack Binion in his down-home Dallas drawl.

The forty-one-year-old casino owner is a balding man in a red shirt

and a brown suit. He wastes little money on overhead. His office above
the casino, located next to a forest of jutting water pipes, is nondescript.
Downstairs, the action roars. The place is so busy and the players so
involved in their games that no one notices the $1 million in $10,000
bills displayed in a glass case in a corner of the huge, sprawling room.

After you have a certain amount of money, a couple of million
maybe, you go on earning more just because of ego and prestige.
I'm in that position, thanks to the opportunity my father gave
me. Without him, I would be dealing 21 somewhere.

We've got a corner on the action downtown, just as I'm sure
some guy in ancient Rome had a lock on the slave market and
made himself a pile of money, too.

I still work a lot of hours. At one time I didn't do anything but
work. Now I take off and go skiing in the winter. But you have to
watch everything when you're in the gambling business. It's a
business that doesn't run itself. It's a unique business, and the
decisions are so big that they can get away from you awfully fast.
You are handling so much money in these gambling joints, you
become accustomed to big decisions. We beat a guy a week ago
for $98,000. But we got beat a while back by a guy who came in
here with $200,000 and won a quarter of a million.

Either my father or me is always in town, watching the store.
Security is a big word in the gambling business, and you pretty
well have to be here to keep your finger on things, because
nobody else has the incentive you're going to have to do the job.
When it's your own money that's involved, that gives you the
incentive to do the job in the right way and in the most profitable
way.

One thing our security people have to watch for is employees
who try to cheat the house. Some of them use what we call a
"sub," which is a pair of shorts sewn together at the bottoms to
form a pocket. They just drop the money into the pocket. It's the
simplest, most coldblooded and effective way of cheating. It
takes the most guts, too. To give you an example, we caught a
dealer just the other day who had over $600 in his sub.

Now, where you're really worried is when there's collusion
between a dealer and the people you've got watching him. See,
you've got a dealer, a boxman, a floor man, a pit boss. When you

are handling such tremendous amounts of cash, if they get together and steal a thousand a day, it isn't going to show.

One of the unique things about the gambling business is that there is absolutely no audit trail. The audit trail is a term used by accountants; it means being able to trace where the money is. In almost every other business, a guy has to alter the books to throw you off the audit trail. Okay, so we have no audit trail. Then how are we going to know where the money is and if anybody's stealing? Only by physically watching it. The only way to catch a guy stealing is to see him do it.

When we catch an employee cheating, we fire him, that's all. We don't press for restitution and we don't prosecute. We're a little old-fashioned—traditionally in the gambling business you don't try for restitution or have a crooked employee arrested. Now, these corporations that own the hotels on the Strip do arrest them, but it's awfully hard to get a conviction on this type of offense.

We handle over $1 million a day. We have twenty-four 21 tables, two wheels, a big six, and six crap tables, and we are out of space on slot machines. We have just 590 slots. Every night we literally win a ton of money on the slots; that's how much the change amounts to.

It's just impossible to say how many players we have in here during one day. I have no idea. But we're open twenty-four hours a day, seven days a week, and we're generally crowded.

We like good players. A good player is anybody with money, especially anybody with a lot of money. A guy who will lose $3,000 or $5,000 is a nice player. But I would rather have a guy who's going to come in every week and lose $100 than a player who comes in once a year and loses $3,000, $4,000, $5,000 at a clip. We like good, steady customers. In the gambling business you build up customers in the way a dentist or a restaurant builds a clientele. The same psychology goes into it. Why do people keep going to a certain dentist, a certain restaurant or bar or casino? To them the important thing is that they are known there. So we maintain a lot of personal contact, even though we operate on a pretty large scale. I think the fact that we know so many of our customers and treat them right is one of the reasons we've been so successful.

There's an old saw that says, "Peck like a bird and shit like an elephant." That applies to people who play systems. People who play systems are tough, because the system itself forces them to discipline themselves. Say a guy with a system comes in and wins $100. But he doesn't leave a $100 winner. He keeps playing. Then he starts losing, and he loses his winnings; and then he starts chasing his money, thinking he's going to get even. He winds up losing $500. In fact, we've had cases of guys just trying to win their dinner, trying to win a twenty-dollar bill, and they end up losing $10,000. A system player who chases his money or anybody who stands to win only a small amount but loses a very large amount is pecking like a bird and shitting like an elephant. On the other hand, there's another saying—"Take a toothpick and run it into a lumberyard." That just means someone with a small stake who hits it big, comparatively speaking. On occasion, I've seen a five-dollar bill run into $5,000.

I'm not a philanthropist, I'm a businessman. I'd like to make a profit every day, but it doesn't work that way. There are a lot of ups and downs in this business. That guy I mentioned who beat us for a quarter of a million, well, that just knocks the hell out of everything.

I figure my business is like a life insurance company. When you take out a life insurance policy, you are betting you are going to die and the insurance company is betting you won't. The players here are betting that they're going to win, and I'm betting they aren't. That's one of the unfortunate things about the gambling and insurance businesses. There's gotta be a winner and there's gotta be a loser.

Most of the time, of course, I'm the winner. But not always. People have won enough money in this casino to go off and start businesses. Naturally, they are in the minority. But it does happen. There was a fellow in here a while back who came into town and won $17,000 and bought a dry-cleaning business. I know another guy from Houston who bought a meat business and became very, very successful off the money he won shooting craps. I can't recall exactly how much he won from us, but it was a couple of hundred thousand dollars.

The Horseshoe is a gambler's joint. We offer the world's highest limit. We let a guy bet whatever he wants. A week ago there was a player in here who bet $125,000 on one roll of the dice. He lost.

A large number of the people who come in here are real gamblers, people who know the odds, who know what they're up against. They are coldblooded players. They are sophisticated players. The Strip deals more to a guy who's just out to have a good time. Up there they cater to tourists, and for them winning isn't necessarily the main thing. They're out to have fun.

If a guy walks in here with $1 million and wants to play against us, we're naturally going to cater to him. We'll give him a higher limit than he can get anywhere else. If he wants a private table, he'll get it. He'll get whatever he wants, because we feel we can make a profit from him.

It's awfully hard to say if that man with $1 million is going to win or lose. But it's really irrelevant whether he wins or loses. You have to remember that there are other gamblers playing at the same time. And every time $1,000 is bet in this casino, we make $14. That's the natural advantage the house has; it's a mathematical law. Fourteen dollars per $1,000 bet is the average percentage we figure on, and that's what keeps us in business. So we would make $14,000 off the guy with $1 million. Say he turns his $1 million over five times, winning and losing. We've still earned $70,000 from him, whether we beat him or not. It's the total action on the floor that counts, not one player, no matter how much he's betting.

It's sad to see people go broke. I have gambled myself, so I know the distress they are going through, the mental anguish they are suffering. By the same token—and I can't overemphasize this enough—gambling is a natural phenomenon. Gambling isn't anything that's evil in itself. It's too bad when it's overdone. We get a lot of compulsive gamblers in here. What are they looking for? An escape. It's the same as a guy who gets on narcotics or booze. He finds the real world so unbearable for some psychological reason that he escapes and keeps escaping to the point that he becomes a mummy.

In a sense, you could call me a pusher, because I am providing the facilities to gamblers. But how many people smoke marijuana and don't become addicted? How many drink without succumbing to addiction? And if I weren't supplying the facilities, someone else would be doing it.

Also, you have to remember that I'm adding excitement to their lives. You have to consider that gambling is a sedentary sport, especially for older people who can't be physically active anymore. Anybody can participate in gambling; you can sit on your rear end and you're a participant. And there's no skill involved in playing a slot machine. But you get the thrill of a sport anyway. Myself, I would rather ski than gamble. But the person in his sixties can't ski. So where I get a thrill from skiing, he gets a thrill from gambling.

People gamble for a number of reasons. It's a diversion. It's cheering for the home team to win. Gambling is child's play. And it's engrossing. It's a manufactured thrill. The outcome of a pair of dice rolling along a table has no significance; in itself, it's boring. But when people bet money on the outcome of that roll of the dice, you have accelerated the importance of that event. If you had $300 of your own money on the line, you damn sure would be more interested in the outcome of that event than whether California is going to sink into the ocean when the next earthquake hits.

Gambling is recreation, too. If you go to a movie or a theater, it only costs you so much. One of the unique things about gambling is that you may have to pay $20 or several thousand dollars to get your recreation.

People who gamble are looking for enthusiasm, excitement, a way to beat boredom. I would also say that gambling is an emotionally uplifting experience. I think that's what people want. From the time you make your play until the outcome of your bet, you are in an emotional frenzy. That's the actual feeling a gambler gets. You have induced this emotion, this enthusiasm, this thrill upon yourself by the turn of a card or a roll of the dice.

We have businessmen who come in here and try to use us as a banking tool. Say a guy's business is going bad and he needs $5,000. He comes out here with $500 and takes a shot at winning the $5,000. You get a lot of that. Most of the time he doesn't win the $5,000, he loses the $500. But sometimes he does come up a winner. Gambling isn't the best business tool in the world, but still it's used as such by many people.

I've heard many people say that money loses its reality in Las Vegas. It's true. Money becomes a game; it just becomes the way you keep score. You make a thousand, you lose a thousand, win a thousand, drop a thousand. It gets out of kilter. You forget that money can buy things other than a bet.

To sum it all up, I'd have to say we're not really in the gambling business. What we do is supply joy. Take these old ladies who play the slot machines. We have them pass out, faint, get hysterical and scream when they hit a jackpot. We have had quite a few wet on themselves. Hell, there's nothing I could do in my own life that would make me so happy I'd piss on myself.

VICKEY LAVENDER

Her hands form quick pyramids and pirouettes as she shuffles and snaps out the cards to the eager, fretful 21 players at the Golden Nugget casino.

At 32, Vickey Lavender has been a dealer for thirteen years. Born in Texarkana, Texas, she grew up in Utah. She has seventy-five hours of college credit at the University of Utah. Pretty, blue-eyed and soft-spoken, she's divorced from her bartender husband. She has no children.

She works the swing shift, from six in the evening until two o'clock in the morning, when the action is at its peak.

After I quit school, I drifted to Jackpot, Nevada, where I got a job working cocktails in a casino. One day they were short of dealers, and they asked if I wanted to learn the trade. They put me on a table and taught me how to shuffle. After forty-five minutes of lessons, they put me on a game. The next night they taught me how to handle the roulette wheel. And the following night I came in and they taught me craps. At the end of six months I was an experienced dealer, good enough to handle myself in any casino in Nevada.

I went to Carson City and stayed five months. Then I went down to Reno for a while before I came to Vegas. Vegas isn't as friendly a town as the other places I've worked in Nevada. The people are colder. People here are so worried about losing their money, you don't see too many smiles.

I work five shifts a week and earn $31 a shift and about $20 in tips. No, I've never had a pang of envy seeing hundreds of thousands of dollars on the tables while I earn about $250 a week. I just do my job and don't worry about other people's money. I guess the people who lose can afford to lose.

One of the biggest games I ever dealt was with a nice lady who bought the table and played by herself. When you buy the whole table, you can only play three places. That's the policy of this casino. The lady bet $2,000 at each place. And she played that way, betting $6,000 every hand for seven hours. She lost $70,000.

The biggest loser I ever played with was a gentleman who dropped $500,000 shooting craps. The odd thing was he was a very good player; he just never was able to shoot up a hand. He took his loss very well. Evidently he was one of those who could afford to lose. He has a garbage-collection business in San Francisco, and he comes here a couple of times a year to play. He generally loses $50,000, $100,000, or more at one time.

If I had that much money I wouldn't gamble with it, because I know all the odds. The odds are scary. The only way you can win is luck, I don't care what anybody tells you. I've busted more people with systems than I can count. If you happen to be in the right place at the right time under the right circumstances, you'll win. But it's all chance.

I think most people gamble because they want something for nothing. Have you ever watched people gambling? They do strange things. A lot of them get drunk and are oblivious to everything around them. Some lose their tempers. You never know how people are going to react when their money is in jeopardy.

I have a set rule to handle people if they get really grumpy and start cursing. I try to joke with them. But some people come in in a nasty mood and then they start drinking, which makes them even nastier. If I can't joke with them, I try to ignore them. If that doesn't do any good, I insult them back. And if that doesn't work, I call for security and have them thrown out. With some people, when their money's at stake, you can't straighten them out, no matter what you do.

One night a young kid came in here celebrating his twenty-first birthday. I was on a 21 table, and I beat him to where he was broke. He hadn't lost that much—a little over $200—but to him it was a lot of money, the same as $200,000 to somebody else. It's all relative. The kid had too much to drink, and like most people he blamed me for losing. So he just threw his drink in my face. I lost *my* temper. I grabbed a crap stick from a nearby table and beat him with it clear to the front door. If he had stopped running, I would have killed him.

Another guy stabbed me in the hand. I still have a four-inch scar from that episode. The guy sat at the 21 table and played nothing but $100 chips. He never said a word, never asked for a drink, never yelled about the cards, never threw the cards, never showed any emotion whatsoever. When he had lost $2,700, he said he didn't want to play anymore. Then he reached into his pocket and came down on me with a knife. They called the cops, who put him in jail. I testified at his trial; he got two years.

I lost my temper one other time. This guy was $3,500 ahead, which in a game with a $50 limit is a lot of money. I was running hot that night, so they moved me to his table to play with him. I was supposed to beat him, and I was doing it very well. The gentleman suddenly picked up his drink and poured it on the cards. Have you ever seen a Bloody Mary on green felt? Revolting. You can't clean it up. The layout was ruined. They wiped up the table and brought me a new deck. We resumed playing, and he did it again, poured his drink over the cards. I was getting hotter by the minute. My jaws were locking tight. So they cleaned up the table a second time, and we started to play again. The first hand out, the guy spilled his drink for the third time. I said, "That's it!" I reached over, grabbed him by his shirt, and pulled him across the table. He ended up on the floor, crawling on his hands and knees. I was beating him with my fists. Security finally pulled me off him. Then the pit boss sent me to the bar to cool down.

Sometimes the things that happen are just plain hilarious. One night I was dealing craps to an Idaho dirt farmer. He was yelling and screaming and jumping around while he threw the dice. At one point in the game he was yelling so much and he was so excited that he spit his false teeth right out on the table. The other dealer at the table was seventy-one years old. He just took his own false teeth out, set them right next to the farmer's and said, "Shoot, you're faded."

I was at the wheel one night when the sky caved in. Those mirrors above the tables are one-way. This guy named Peter was a very heavy man. He must have weighed three hundred pounds. One night his walkway above the casino gave out under his bulk, and suddenly it started raining glass all over the wheel. There was no way you could clean up that layout with all the glass that was on it. Pete just looked down, with his leg hanging through the sky, and said, "Vickey, I guess you better close the game."

If you have a bad night, you don't get chewed out by management for losing. They just take it as part of the risk of running a gambling house. They never say anything when I win, and they never say anything when I lose. They can't and hang that shingle out front that says gambling casino.

We're seeing a lot more women gambling since the onset of the women's liberation movement, which I think is a lot of crap. The only part I agree with is that if we do the same job we should get the same wages. You see these liberated women turning up at the tables braless and in see-through blouses. They like to play against a male dealer, thinking that will distract him. Of course, it doesn't work. Nothing ever distracts a good dealer, and there are only good dealers in this casino.

I don't have any savings at all. In fact, I'm in debt. My whole savings account went down the tubes when my mother had a heart attack. She was in the hospital under intensive care for two weeks, and it cost me $7,800. And I still have $2,300 to pay off.

Living in Las Vegas isn't cheap. My apartment costs me $450 a month. It's a good thing I don't gamble. I couldn't afford to, though many dealers do gamble when they're not on shift, and they're always in hock.

There's no way I'd change my life. I like the gambling business, or I wouldn't have stayed in it this long. I like the life-style. I like the constant excitement. I can't imagine being a secretary, walking in at nine in the morning and leaving at five. Sitting behind a typewriter, the most exciting thing you're going to get is a busy signal on the telephone.

Some customers like to play against me whenever they come in. They consider me their lucky dealer. I don't know why, since I usually beat them.

I look at the faces of the people I play with. When people are gambling they look happy or unhappy, depending on whether they are winning or losing. But even though the vast majority of them lose, they must like to gamble. If they didn't, they wouldn't keep coming back to buck the tiger.

AL R.

Al is a member of Gamblers Anonymous, and one of the rules of GA is that names can't be publicly revealed.

Fifty-one years old, he's a chunky, brown-eyed man with three children. He's been in the wholesale plumbing supplies business for thirty-two years and lives in a spotless Mediterranean-style home with a red tile roof and a lawn gushing ivy and purple bougainvillea.

I started gambling in Detroit, my hometown, when I was fifteen years old. We pitched pennies, matched pennies, nickels, dimes and quarters. We even used to bet on how many peanuts in a bag.

When I reached my twenties, I was into big stuff—big dice games and high-stakes poker. Gambling was against the law in Detroit, but you could always find a game, and a big one.

I was lucky in business, unlucky in gambling. By the time I was thirty-three years old, I'd taken a bath for $160,000. Everything that I had of value was lost gambling—my business, my house, my car. My wife, God knows why, stuck with me; any other wife would have left me.

I was a compulsive gambler, but I wasn't aware of it at the time. We decided to move to California and make a clean start. We hit Los Angeles in 1959, with $1,000.

I didn't gamble for ten years, except I would play a little poker at a friend's house once a week. During those ten years, I built up my business to the point where it was going pretty good. By not gambling I had bought a very nice $53,000 home, my wife had an Imperial, I had a Cadillac, and my two daughters each had a car. I was making money and saving money. Everything was fine. Everything was wonderful. I had plenty of money, and we did what we wanted to do with our money when we wanted to do it.

Then I discovered Vegas. My brother-in-law took me there for the first time. The latent instinct to gamble big returned immediately. That first trip I played baccarat at the Sands. At first I couldn't do anything wrong. I was enjoying myself; it felt like old times. I'd long since forgotten that I'd lost a huge amount of money gambling. All I knew was that it felt fine sitting at that table. I had more than enough money to gamble, and I was sure I couldn't get hurt very badly, even if I lost. I was also sure I could walk away from Vegas whenever I wanted.

I was hitting them real good in that baccarat game. I was $2,500 ahead at one point. The mark of a compulsive gambler is that he never quits. He keeps playing until he's busted.

After three or four hours at the table, I got up to eat a sandwich. Then I went back to the table. My luck went up and down all night. Finally, the game closed at three o'clock in the morning, and I was $300 ahead. Our plane didn't leave until 6:15 A.M., so I had time. I went over to a crap table and lost the $300 right away. Then I lost $2,500 of my own money at blackjack. I went to the cage and got credit for $500 and returned to the blackjack table. I started winning, and I felt invincible. It was getting near time to catch the plane, so I started betting $200 a hand. And I kept hitting blackjack. I let the money ride, and I was playing hands for $400, $800, $1,200. I was hitting them all. I was up about $9,000. But then I lost some of it back. I came out $5,100 ahead, though. The only reason I left the casino was that I had several very important customers to see that day. When I got home, I gave my winnings to my wife and told her, "Go out and buy anything you want."

I made the next trip to Vegas, a week later, by myself. I hit them for $1,800 at craps. I wondered how long this had been going on. By now, I was hooked on Vegas. I didn't want to gamble anyplace else. And Vegas was being good to me—I'd already won nearly $7,000.

On my third trip, the downward slide began. I lost $3,000 in cash and $8,000 in markers. When the Sands wouldn't give me any more credit, I went to the Dunes and got $3,000 worth of credit. I lost that too. Then I went to the Tropicana and got $5,000 in credit, and lost it. The Aladdin and the Sahara gave me $10,000 in credit altogether, and I dropped that. The trip cost me $29,000.

I kept going back to Vegas every chance I got, and I kept

losing. At the end of a year, I'd gone through my $75,000 savings account. Then I raided my wife's account, withdrawing $25,000. I left that money in Vegas too.

Now I began taking money wherever I could. I was writing bum checks. It was angles and lies and tricks. I even sold some bonds I had bought for my kids, which raised a couple of thousand. Then I found my wife's jewels, and hocked those for $5,000.

We began to run short of household money, and I told my wife that business was bad. She still didn't know I was gambling again. I told myself that the reason I kept going back to Vegas was to get even. If I could get even, I'd quit.

I always kept at least $100,000 worth of inventory in my business. To raise more money, I began selling off the inventory—at fire-sale prices—and not replacing it. Then I began ordering more inventory on credit, $50,000 worth, and I sold that cheap, too, and gambled it all away in Vegas.

At the end of four years, I'd lost more than $400,000. My business and my life were in ashes. I had a terrible down feeling. What was I going to do? How could I ever replace that money? My life was wrecked. I was drowning in guilt and self-pity. When I would take my eleven-year-old son shopping and he would see something he wanted, a new bike, say, I couldn't buy it for him.

I thought of committing suicide many times. When I would go up into the mountains to see some of my customers, on the way down I would say to myself, Boy, how easy it would be to just turn the wrong way and go off this mountain and not have anything to worry about anymore. But then I would figure that would destroy my wife and kids. All I would do is leave them a lot of financial problems.

I didn't have the guts as yet to tell my wife about my gambling. It was always one more trip to Vegas—to get even.

In Vegas I was a big shot. The hotels comped my room. I had comps all over town. I never paid for anything except chips. Cigars they gave me by the box. As much free liquor as I wanted. I was offered girls. You know, whatever I wanted, just name it. I could go to any of the shows I wanted to on the house, but I was too busy gambling to see a show. Once I noticed a young couple at my table who were betting $2 a hand. I asked them how long they'd been married, and they said they were on their honeymoon. I said, "How would you like to have dinner and see a nice show on me?" Their eyes lit up, and I arranged for them to go to the Totie Fields show and have dinner at no charge.

I wouldn't leave the tables, not even to eat. I'd sit and play into the morning. When I got hungry, I'd have the girl bring me a pitcher of orange juice and a sandwich. But I usually didn't eat the sandwich. Losing all that money made me too nervous to eat.

My gambling got so bad that whenever I was visiting my customers and found myself near an airport—Ontario, San Diego, Palm Springs, Los Angeles—I'd grab a flight for Vegas. Sometimes I'd leave at five in the morning, go up and gamble and lose and be home by seven-thirty at night.

My wife would ask me worriedly, "How much business did you do today?"

I'd show her phony invoices for $600, $1,000, $1,900.

"Where are the checks?" she'd ask.

"Everything's charged—the checks will be in by the tenth of the month." Then she found out about everything. She waited for the checks to come in, and when they didn't arrive, she knew. "You're gambling again!" she said, and started to cry.

I told her the whole story. Besides all the money I'd lost, I was in debt for $100,000, to finance companies, to my suppliers, to friends, to the casinos.

I thought my wife was going to have a heart attack. We talked about it all night, and I promised her I would stop gambling. But I wasn't quite ready.

Two months later I went to Vegas again and gambled at the MGM Grand. I got $3,000 in credit and lost it. At five-thirty or six o'clock in the morning I had $87 in my pocket, and I decided then and there I wasn't going to go home. I had caused my family enough problems. I was just going to fly as far as $87 would take me and start a new life for myself. But I wasn't optimistic about succeeding in a new life. Maybe this time I'd really kill myself.

I decided to call my wife to say goodbye.

"I'm sitting in the lobby of the MGM Hotel," I said when she came on the line. "I'm going somewhere, anyplace; I don't know where yet. I won't ever see you and the kids again."

"Come on home and talk it over," she said. "Then if you still want to go, you are free to go. But let's just talk it over one more time."

I was surprised she wanted to talk. Even though I had stopped gambling for two months before this last trip, things weren't right at home. There were big money worries. I had to borrow from my wife's brother to cover the bum checks I had out. And we had to borrow just to eat and pay the mortgage. It had gotten so bad that every time I came into the house, the kids would walk away from me, like I was some kind of an animal with a disease. They had a right to feel that way, because I was hurting their mother. We had been married for twenty-six years, and we'd been a very close-knit family until Vegas started competing for my attention. Though I couldn't blame them, I was very deeply wounded when my kids lost their respect for me.

"I need help," I told my wife on the phone.

"Just come home, Al; just come home."

When I got there she said she'd already called Gamblers Anonymous and there was a meeting the next night. I could get all the help I needed at GA, she said, but I was skeptical.

I went to the GA meeting, which was being held at a church. We sat outside in the car and saw people walking in the door. I saw people shaking hands with each other. It all looked friendly enough, but I wasn't sure if I wanted to go in or not. To tell the truth, I'd rather be back in Vegas.

"You need this," my wife said. "Maybe they can help."

"All right, I'll try."

I walked in there and introduced myself to the secretary, who in turn introduced me to everybody else in the room. There must have been forty or fifty people there.

The meeting was an eye-opener. I didn't realize there were so many compulsive gamblers.* I didn't realize I had the disease until it was my turn to talk. I got up and began my speech by saying, "My name is Al R. and I'm a compulsive gambler." Soon I was telling them my story.

---

*GA has chapters throughout the United States, England, Canada and Australia. Unfortunately, its worldwide membership is only about 10,000. In the United States alone, there are more than nine million men and women who gamble compulsively.

That was July 17, 1974. I haven't gambled at all since then. GA teaches you that the first step to a cure is admitting and recognizing that you are a compulsive gambler. Then you just follow their program, including the buddy system. A couple of times I got the urge to go to Vegas, but I'd call a friend from GA and he'd talk me out of it.

A lawyer who was also a member of my GA chapter helped me straighten out my financial affairs. It took two years, but I was in a basically sound, basically good business. There was plenty of money to be made so long as I didn't gamble. I paid back every penny I owed, and I'm free of debt now. I just bought a new Granada and I have $15,000 in the bank, so you see what can be done when GA teaches you how not to gamble.

At GA, we never talk about why we became compulsive gamblers. Nobody really knows why he became a confirmed gambler. There are a lot of theories—the urge to get something for nothing, the idea of punishing yourself . . . some even think gambling is a substitute for sex. I don't know what the answer is in my own case. If I had to guess, I'd say I gambled because I thought I could get money without working, without having all the problems of running a money-making business.

There's no way to predict who is and who is not going to become a compulsive gambler. Some people claim it's heredity. But my father didn't gamble; nobody else in my family was what I'd call a gambler. I was raised in a conventional lower-middle-class home where money was important, where it was a sin to throw money away on a thing like gambling. Anyway, as they teach at GA, trying to learn why you became a compulsive gambler is a waste of time. It's enough that you've stopped.

As far as Vegas is concerned, I don't think it's a good thing for the country. If it hadn't been there, I wouldn't have gambled and had all the misery I did. True, nobody dragged me there kicking and screaming. But God, they make it so easy for you in that town to gamble away everything you have; not only money, but your marriage, your kids, your decency, even your life sometimes.

Now the mere thought of Vegas makes me sick. I think someone ought to put a time bomb in the center of the town and blow the damn place to smithereens.

Color Money Pink

You can't mix money and sex.

—DARLENE THOMAS

BETTY BINDER

More than thirty million Americans belong to credit unions. Eight hundred of them are members of the Los Angeles Feminist Federal Credit Union, a burgeoning enterprise founded in August 1975 largely through the efforts of Ms. Binder, an ardent, pragmatic feminist who puts in a sixty-hour week wrestling with the financial problems of her sisters in the women's movement.

Dressed in yellow slacks and a black sweater, she smiles readily as she declares that she is the credit union's unpaid, volunteer president. "I'm ineligible for unemployment, so I support myself through savings."

From New Rochelle, New York, she has an M.A. in political science, earned at Columbia University.

When I was going through my divorce, one of the things I faced was credit discrimination. I came to realize that it wasn't adequate for women just to bang down doors one by one to try to get credit cards and loans. I felt something else had to be done, something on an organizational level.

It was just about that time that credit unions were being organized by feminists in other parts of the country, chiefly Detroit, which was the first one. I contacted several women in the Detroit credit union; they told me there were other women in Los Angeles interested in organizing a similar unit here. So a few of us got together and began building this financial clearinghouse. I was elected president and have held the office since we were founded.

Membership is open to men as well as women. In fact, we have three male members to whom we've loaned money. The credit union is composed entirely of feminists, but there are male feminists as well as female feminists. Feminism, in my mind, means adequate and equal rights for women, the right of women to do whatever they want with their lives in a financial way or in any other way. The man who believes that is a feminist.

Clearly, there isn't equal pay for equal work for women in this country.* Fifty percent of the women to whom we loan money earn less than $9,000 a year, so that tells you something about salary discrimination. I do a lot of financial counseling with women who come here to apply for loans. We talk about why they haven't been able to get a loan at the corner bank. We talk about how much they are earning. One of the things that emerges again and again is that they may be one of three women working in a large company, or perhaps the only woman in their particular capacity in a smaller company. And they've had to fight to get that job, and it may have taken them years to get where they are. One woman who is an officer in this credit union had a tremendous banking career ahead of her, except that she saw the writing on the wall. She knew there was going to be a limit as to how high she could go. So she left before she reached that limit, because she realized she couldn't possibly accomplish her goals or fulfill herself by staying where she was.

Many stereotypes about women are perpetuated as a way of preventing them from succeeding financially. Some of them are very subtle and some very blatant. Even a woman who is able to fight back successfully against these sterotypes must face conditions designed to prevent her from succeeding.

I know a woman who's been an engineer for years at a major company. Male management at the company knew that because the firm was getting federal assistance, they would have to promote her to supervisor. The result was that they changed the ground rules by which a supervisor could be promoted. They required, all of a sudden, a new, rigorous management course which involved six months of intensive training. She tried to take the course and qualify. When they realized that she was serious

---

*"The average woman worker earns less than three-fifths of what a man does, even when both work full-time year 'round," a recent survey by the U.S. Census Bureau concluded. Families headed by males had a median income of $14,186 compared with female-head-of-household salaries totaling about $6,700, the Bureau said, adding: Among clerical workers, earnings of women average about 60 percent of men's earnings; sales workers, about 40 percent; women managers, officials and proprietors, slightly more than 50 percent of men's earnings in equivalent situations.

and that indeed she wanted to take the course, they eliminated the position. They reorganized the department so she couldn't possibly assume the supervisory position. That kind of stuff still goes on, and I think it's going to get worse before it gets better.

The point will come, and perhaps it already has, where we are going to have a lot more qualified women than there are jobs. Take, for example, the number of women who are being graduated from law schools. A lot of these women are going to come to grief because they won't be hired by established law firms. Men will get preference, if there are jobs at all. Some women may have to start their own firms, but that's pretty tough to do when you are fresh out of law school.

Much of the stereotyped male chauvinism really comes from the training and conditioning men have received. They believe their role is to maintain control and power over the economic system. They are reluctant to face the reality that sooner or later they must surrender some of that economic power to women.

In the credit community, there is a tremendous resistance by men to change. The feeling is that it has always been this way; it has been good for us—why should we give it up? Why should we change if we don't have to? We had to struggle to get here; let women struggle, too; let's make it difficult for them. There is a lot of that.

It will only change when government regulatory agencies genuinely become advocates of affirmative action for women. It will only change if the women's movement keeps pushing. Where the laws have been changed in some states, with passage of equal opportunity legislation and equal credits acts, what happens is an interesting dynamic. Partly because of the fear of prosecution and partly because of a genuine desire to obey the laws, there tends to be something built into the fabric of the laws which allows some of the men who've resisted to see that there are advantages to complying with the new ethic. I think that's beginning to happen in the credit field, but it will take several more years for total compliance and total fairness to women.

Already there are some creditors who believe that women are good credit risks. I also think there are some creditors who are beginning to come around to the point of view that they have been denying themselves a lot of income, a lot of earnings, because women haven't been able to obtain, say, mortgage loans or credit cards on an equal basis with men. It's beginning to occur to them that the economy has been in rough shape for years. Why cut our nose off to spite our face? It's about time we provided ourselves with a little more money in the balance sheet. I think this ethic will in fact become more of a reality in the next few years. It will become more acceptable, and with it we will have credit equality.

Meanwhile, there's still plenty of credit discrimination. I consistently talk to women who've been refused credit because they supposedly do not have the stability of income that men do, or they don't have the income to qualify for the same credit that a man can get. The offenders are all the institutions who give credit—banks, savings and loans, credit card companies, department stores, finance companies.

Even the government is an offender. Until five years ago, less than 1 percent of all Small Business Administration loans went to women. The percentage now is somewhere between 4 and 5 percent. That's a considerable increase, so you could validly say that there's been an upsurge in credit for women and that there isn't so much discrimination. But the overall percentage is still small. I know women who've applied for loans to the SBA and have had to really battle in order to get them. I know other women who've been flatly refused solely on sexist grounds.

Take the financing of a home as another example. Although 90 to 95 percent of the realtors are women, most of their buyers are men. An increasing number of single or divorced women, however, want to purchase homes. They've come to the realization that real estate is an exceedingly good investment, that there probably is no better investment than equity in a house. They also realize that if you keep renting, you are throwing money down a rathole, and you never get out. To service this clientele, an increasing number of feminists are becoming realtors. They encourage women to buy homes and help them fight the battle to get them financed. As of now, most women buyers are those who happen to be in good financial shape. The day is a long way off when the middle-income woman can walk into a savings and loan or a bank and get a mortgage loan readily.

We have somewhat in excess of $100,000 in this credit union. That may not seem like much, but we are talking about a lot of women who don't have a lot of money who've chosen to deposit what they have with us.

We loan money to women who don't qualify elsewhere but who we think are good risks. We wanted to prove that we could do that, and we've proved it. Our default rate on loans is negligible.

The staff of five other volunteers and myself have talked to and counseled well over 2,500 women since we began operating. The largest single block are women who need assistance in just establishing credit. We instruct them in how to obtain a credit card, tell them why they should have a credit card—very basic and practical stuff like that.

The second category has to do with women who've come through a divorce or who are in a transitional period in their lives. Perhaps they are ready to graduate from college and don't feel that they are getting adequate financial advice from anyone. The best time to establish credit is while you are in college, but most students, through ignorance, lassitude or because they don't think they can get it, do not apply for a BankAmericard or a Master Charge or any other credit card. Nobody has ever explained to them what credit is. Suddenly they are thrown out into the world with no credit and very little income, and they find it extremely difficult to cope. Then they also find that they need lots of assistance because they aren't accustomed to financial planning.

The divorced woman is in much the same situation. Many women coming out of a divorce haven't protected themselves. They may have been married twenty or twenty-five years and never so much as thought of getting a credit card in their own name. When the divorce is pending, they get scared. They don't know where their next dime is coming from. It's threatening for them to have to go out and deal with the job market. We are counseling more and more of these women, because they have no place else to go.

I also do a lot of counseling with women who want to establish their own businesses. They are developing goals and need assistance. They need practical advice on financing, loans, inventory control, record keeping, you name it.

There's a strange irony in all of this, because it's the woman who handles the checkbook in most homes. I find repeatedly that the average woman I meet knows down to the last penny where everything goes. Rarely have I talked to a woman who didn't know the price of everything at the supermarket. And in fact they formulate the household budget. But at the same time in our culture there is a lot of sexist conditioning of women about money. The same woman who balances the family budget will tell me that she knows nothing about money. I have heard that more times than I can count. She's been conditioned to believe that she really doesn't have the capacity to do anything more than go out and shop, and that she doesn't have the capacity to make important monetary decisions on her own.

I think the feminist movement, especially the credit unions, is beginning to get across to women that this isn't true. We are showing women that they can invest money, showing them how to make money with money, encouraging them to go into business, encouraging them to walk into E. F. Hutton and feel comfortable with that broker sitting across the desk.

But there still is an incredible amount of ignorance on the part of women about money. I'm convinced that a lot of it has developed as a way to keep women powerless. Too many women simply don't have the vaguest idea how to apply for a simple loan, how to manage money; too many have been led to believe that they are incapable of handling money.

Many of our loan requests are for the purchase of cars or car repairs. Occasionally we give a vacation loan or lend a woman money so that she can buy clothing for her children. We have made loans to cover medical bills, to buy a stereo or some other small luxury, to take job-improvement courses. We loaned money to one woman so she could purchase camera equipment which allowed her to change jobs and become a photographer at a higher salary than her previous job paid. And of course we finance women who want to open small businesses.

We make a number of second and third loans. One woman, for instance, got her first loan six months ago to buy a wardrobe.

Then she wanted a loan to buy a car so she'd have mobility and the option for a better job.

Those are very typical of the kind of loans we make. The overwhelming majority are for very basic needs.

Our largest loan was for $5,000, to the woman I just mentioned who needed a car. That car enabled her to get an awfully good job, and she is really on her way now. We have given a lot of loans from $300 to $600, and we have an increasing number of loans out for $750 to maybe $1,500. Our smallest loan was for $5, to a woman who wanted to purchase supplies in order to go to a beauty school.

I often counsel with women who come in and say they want a loan. In reality, what they need is counseling assistance. Maybe their real need is a feminist attorney who can help get them a divorce settlement so they don't lose everything.

First and foremost, I am supportive. It may take hours of my time to work through a woman's financial problems. But many times I see tremendous results. Often they are immediate. When the woman leaves my office, the weight of the world has been lifted off her shoulders. She realizes she isn't alone, which is very crucial. And she has an understanding of her capability, which is worth a great deal, because society often says to a woman, You are nothing; therefore you are worthless. A lot of women feel that way; they are on a real guilt trip.

What they learn here is really an eye-opener, because most creditors will not take the time to explain equal credit opportunities. The most important thing a woman learns here is that she is at the beginning of a process of growing. She goes out of here with a tremendous feeling of competence, knowing that she is going to have an impact on a credit manager, that she can ask him for credit without fear. Even if he gets a little hostile or bureaucratic, she can tell him, "This is what the law says," and she'll hear him say, "Yes, ma'am!" and he does what she wants. This is a sense of power, a sense of self. And that fundamentally is what counseling and our credit union are all about.

There are several ways women can fight credit discrimination. Ideally, those means should be correlated. One is on the individual level. A woman has to be assertive whenever she finds credit discrimination. Number two, there has to be collective action, which is why we have a credit union of our own. Number three is the fight to end job discrimination as well as credit discrimination; the two really intertwine. Only when we succeed in fighting employment bias in a very basic way are we going to succeed in fighting credit discrimination.

On the scale of feminist values, I would place knowledge of money very high. Feminists must have the capability of planning their own financial lives. Without knowledge of money, how is a woman going to assert the power to obtain control over her own life?

DARLENE THOMAS

"I grew up, I must admit, where there was a great deal of money, but no one made much of a fuss about it. There was always more than enough money for whatever I wanted to do."

Darlene is a divorced, attractive, long-legged, tawny-haired daughter of a socialite lawyer. A graduate of Wellesley, she lives alone in a $900-a-month Manhattan apartment. The living room has an Aubusson rug, antique French furniture, paintings, sculpture, and lots of plants. "I live in surroundings I have created myself, an atmosphere in which I am comfortable."

She is a partner in a public relations firm that specializes in industrial accounts.

Women are still in that stage where they are considered inexpensive labor. Though it's not quite as bad as it used to be, even a woman who graduates from college today is expected to know how to type and have all those other menial secretarial skills. A man, on the other hand, who graduates from college doesn't have to start his career as a typist or secretary. He is allowed, he is expected, to go out there immediately and do something important.

I never learned how to type. I refused. To this day when someone comes into the office and hands me a piece of paper— people are forever walking into the office and asking me to type something—I say, "No!" I just look at them and say, "I don't type." That mystifies them. If I don't type, they wonder what I'm doing in the office. What other possible reason could I have for being around? It's surprising and discouraging how much of that still goes on.

I hate it when somebody assumes I am working *for* my partner. I work *with* him. The distinction is very important.

This business doesn't earn enough money to support my life-style. I supplement my earnings through savings and a trust fund. I become terribly uncomfortable when people find out my father is a millionaire and that I have money. People think that if a woman has money, there's no reason for her to earn any more. That really disgusts me.

I walk around in a mink coat, and sometimes it helps and sometimes it's a detriment. But if a man runs around in a Rolls-Royce, everybody says that's fine. He *should* be earning a great deal of money, because he has to keep up the Rolls; he has to keep up the apartment in New York and the house in Connecticut. It just so happens that I have a Rolls, a New York apartment and a house in Connecticut. Therefore, the attitude is that I shouldn't be working, I shouldn't be trying to earn more money. I don't have a need to work; I'm a dabbler; I'm somehow replacing a man in the labor force; I have no worth as a person who is trying to achieve.

The feeling is that a man who works for a corporation has to earn money to support his house, his wife, his children, and everything else. A woman, with or without money, is relegated to the back of the line, and she gets whatever is left over. That's true even for single women who must support themselves.

We are living in a male-oriented society, and men resent a woman who has any kind of capability, unless she sits back and is very deferential to what a man wants done and how he wants it done. Most men do not want to work with women who are their equals. When there's a conference with a group of men in my office, I find myself moving out from behind my desk and sitting on the floor in the lowest chair in the room. I do that because I've found that my physical presence behind my desk becomes psychologically debilitating to men. And as soon as I open my mouth, I incur hostility. Everyone thinks I should be serving coffee. Why am I the one who is expected to serve coffee, serve sandwiches and go call the delicatessen to send it up? The men at the conference are just as capable of doing it as I am.

Invariably, I do the ordering and the serving because it makes things easier. But sometimes I just sit there dumbly, pretending I can't hear when somebody says, "Darlene, why don't you get us some coffee and sandwiches." There are times I just won't do it. The mere request is infuriating.

Then, of course, there's the sex thing. The vice-president of public relations at a very large and important company offered me a trip to Europe in exchange for his firm's account. He put it right on the line: "I'll pay for the tickets and pick up all the expenses, and of course we'll spend every night in bed." That was a horrifying feeling, because you realize that for x number of days someone you don't know wants to share your bed and body. I don't see how any woman could go to bed with a man under those circumstances.

I am incapable of using sex to advance myself professionally. I resent the very idea. You can't mix money and sex. I know women who've tried it, and they have gotten into enormous fights and enormous trouble as a result.

A woman who gets into bed to advance herself in her job is a bigger whore than a prostitute who asks $100 up front. You can't bargain about money in the middle of making love. Money and sex are totally separate and apart; they don't belong together. If you put them together, then you are being cheated, and you end up with nothing anyway.

If a woman chooses to advance herself that way, I think she's going to have a very short career. If your whole career is based on how well you perform in bed, or whether you are willing to perform in bed, it always ends badly.

A gal came up to me about a month and a half ago to ask me what she should do about a proposition. She'd gone to one of the networks and a guy asked her to go to bed with him. In return, he'd give her a job. I threw the book at her, because it was so insane. I mean, if she wants to go to bed with somebody, go ahead, but forget the job. Sure, you can get a job that way, but you won't keep it very long.

I also find that when I'm after an account, a lot of male

executives will hem and haw around for a long time. There will be endless excuses for endless lunches and meetings, and inevitably the talk gets around to sex. I've been propositioned under those circumstances I don't know how many times. The result is that a lot of my time is wasted. I find it very difficult to get the idea across to these men that I'm interested in getting the account, not getting into bed. When I finally make the point, I'm called a "ballbreaker." I'm supposed to be one of the biggest ballbreakers in New York. The first time anyone said that to my face I was flabbergasted. Because I don't want to go to bed with just any man, because I do want his business, I'm a ballbreaker.

The president of another very large corporation wanted to give me his account if I'd go to bed with him. He offered me everything he could possibly think of offering, including a long-term contract which would have meant $250,000 in business.

I explained to him that under no circumstances do I ever mix sex and money and under no circumstances was I going to bed with him, even if the account had been worth $250 million. I told him that it had nothing to do with him as such, that there was nothing personal in it. It was just something I didn't do. I told him that if he wanted to hire me it had to be for my professional competence.

Of course I didn't get the account. Now, a man doesn't have to go through that routine of being propositioned.

I can't imagine getting into bed with someone who expects something from me other than me. And it's not just because I happen to have money. I wouldn't do it if I were a waitress or unemployed or penniless.

I've always considered money in itself meaningless, though it can be used as a lever for power. You can buy people with money, unfortunately. You can buy impressive things with money. If I wear my mink coat when I go to the butcher, I get a better cut of meat. I can walk into any department store in New York if I'm wearing mink and easily get a credit card. Those are small but perfect examples of money as power. It's how ingenious you can be with money and the façade that money can create for you that often matters. You have to play games with money, and I can be good at that.

Before I was married, I'd picked out a pattern of china that I came to hate after I'd had it for quite a while. I decided I just couldn't stand that china. I put myself together in what I call my morning diamonds and my blond beaver coat with a ranch mink collar and I went to the store where the china had been purchased and asked the manager if he'd allow me to return it.

"How long have you had it?" he asked.

"A year."

"We only allow the return of china if it's been out under six months."

There was no way in the world he was going to take it back. And I just kept hating that $50-a-place-setting china.

So I finally looked at him and I began to lie.

"I must tell you," I said, "that my husband is a physician and he despises the china. And cook won't even use it."

"In that case," he said, "why don't you have someone bring it in tomorrow; or, if you wish, we'll pick it up."

"I'll have someone bring it in."

The next day I had my husband put on a car coat and a cap, and he walked into the store carrying all these boxes with the china in them. I followed him in, still in my morning diamonds and whatever coat I was wearing.

"My chauffeur has the china I want to return," I said.

Instantly the manager accepted it back. I opened a charge account immediately, and he credited all this china to my account. Then I leisurely rummaged through the china department and bought another pattern.

Obviously the manager thought, This woman has money, and she is going to spend a lot of it in the store if I pacify her and take back the china.

The women's movement has been a godsend, because it has given women more of an opportunity to earn money, and it has given women a certain amount of self-respect. And I think it has given us the goal of equal pay for equal work. Someday that will happen. Men who hold out against it are defeating themselves, because there is nothing so imprisoning as intolerance. If a man wants to lock himself into that kind of prison, I feel sorry for him.

Too many women are still at the point where they can hide

behind a husband or children or a house. Society says that's fine. But a man can't do that, because he has to produce; he has to be something; he is judged by the work he does.

Without realizing it, a lot of men have sold themselves for money. They are castrated because they have put themselves into a financial bind. There are many, many such men. This type of man is married to a woman he can't abide. He's tied to two children he probably didn't want. He's bound to a house he likely can't afford. He's been doing everything society says he should do: you must have a wife, you must have two children, you must have a house in the suburbs, and you must work hard and support all of this. It becomes a horror of a relationship when the man is snagged in this sort of dilemma. If he's lucky, he gets out. Or his wife gets out. But if they aren't lucky, they are joined together for life, hating each other, hating the fact that there isn't enough money, hating the way they live.

Too many men are still married to women who are incapable of doing anything except having babies and living in Scarsdale, women who go out to country clubs and run up all kinds of bills. And the husband is out there, in a job he probably hates, supporting all this. What could be more tedious and frustrating, more unfulfilling, more unrewarding? The greatest thing about women's liberation is that by allowing a woman equal pay for equal work, the man is freed of those obligations. Most men have yet to understand that.

There's another aspect to this. A woman will always be a woman. When a working woman comes home, she wants to be very feminine. I know I reach a point where I must turn my head off; I can't possibly cope with the business world for another moment. I want to forget about business. I don't want to make any more decisions. I don't want to think about money. I want to get back to what I basically am, which is a lady who likes to cook and likes to wear pretty clothes.

I enjoy being feminine, I like having a wardrobe, I enjoy serving a man, I enjoy cooking. But when I am told that I must do this automatically for all men, that's when I become angry and just sit back dumbly.

We're all of us in a prison still, men as well as women.

LYNN ROBBINS

She smiles. "You're talking to another happy hooker." Lynn Robbins's ambience is a lovely, tasteful $750-a-month apartment in Westwood, near UCLA, on the gold coast West Side of Los Angeles. Sinatra is on the stereo. Thirty-five years old, she's just had a face-lift. "It cost $2,000, but it was worth it. Be good to yourself and the business will be good to you, I always say." Blond, she wears her hair in the lion-mane style of Farrah Fawcett-Majors. "What else do you want to know? My life is an open book, practically. I have thirty-eight-inch tits and wear a D cup. Don't think that hasn't come in handy for hustling."

I grew up in the Midwest, in a small, pleasant college town that had a population of about 10,000. I lost my virginity, voluntarily, at fifteen. At a party when I was seventeen a man offered me $100 to sleep with him. Jesus, I'd never seen a hundred bucks in one place. I thought, Why not?

After that, I pulled back from selling it, for the sake of my parents. It was too small a town and they would have heard.

I went to a free state university for two years, majoring in liberal arts. I was always pretty attractive, and I kept getting propositioned. I was giving it away free; then for kicks I started asking guys to pay for it—nothing big, $15. It was easy money, and somehow there was an extra thrill in getting paid for doing something I didn't particularly enjoy but didn't mind doing. How long has this been going on? I asked myself. As long as there's been a world.

I was nineteen and going nowhere in college, so I dropped out. My father worked for the railroad and my mother kept house. I had three older sisters, and by this time they were all married and had babies. I saw that they were already trapped in a dull life, and I wanted no part of that.

Though I wasn't trained for anything, I wanted to make my own way. And I wanted to make as much money as possible. I like comfort; I like beautiful things, and they cost money.

I borrowed $300 from my father—which I paid back—and came out here. I started by working the streets in Hollywood. These guys would pull up in everything from Volkswagens to Cads. In those days I was charging $20 a throw. The guy also had to pay $8 for the hotel.

I could see there was no future working the streets. The cops hassled you. And the crazies and the weirdos, you have no idea. I wanted to get into the upper echelons of the business. I was young and pretty, and I thought, Why should I be selling it for $20 when there are girls who are merchandising the same product for $100 or more?

But to get to the top rung of the business, I had to have better clothes and a nice apartment. I needed fast money, lots of it. So I got the idea of working motels. I just knocked on the doors at the motels, and if there was a guy in the room alone or two guys, I just asked them if they were lonely. You'd be amazed how many lonely guys I ran into or guys who weren't averse to a new chicken in the coop. As long as they had the twenty-five bucks I was asking, to put it plainly, I fucked them or did whatever else they wanted, within limits. Pretty soon I was making $200 a day for a couple of quick hours' work.

Then I decided it was time to graduate. My clothes were better now; my makeup was done carefully. I was getting my nails and hair done in Beverly Hills. I moved up to the hotels in Beverly Hills. I'd just sit at the bar and wait. Shit, they sidled up like I was the prize in a contest. Those guys in Beverly Hills were no different from the ones in the cheap motels in Hollywood. They just paid better and smelled a little better. The tab for me now was fifty bucks.

Pretty soon I had all the right clothes, I had a white Thunderbird, and I had about $10,000 in cash. I got this apartment, which was $300 a month when I first moved in. Inflation's eating me up, too; my rent has more than doubled. But I want to stay here because a corporation owns the building and nobody bothers me.

I've built up my clientele over the years, and now I've got as good and profitable a trick book as there is. Most of the time I bring guys here. If they don't want to come here, I arrange to rent a room at a good hotel. I've never used a pimp; there's no percentage in that, and I feel sorry for girls in the business who go that route.

I've been in the business now for about fifteen years, and my assets aren't spectacular. I've saved $45,000. I'm going to stay in the business until I have to get married. There's one special guy. He knows what I do, and he's told me repeatedly that he'll marry me whenever I want. He owns a fancy restaurant in Los Angeles, near the Biltmore Hotel. He's prepared, he says, to sell out when we get married. Then the idea is to go someplace, Chicago or New York, where no one knows us and start over again.

The only trouble is, I'm not sure if I love the guy. Love is a very curious emotion. I don't know if I'm capable of loving only one man. What I do is often called "making love," and I'm paid for that. So, in my mind, love equals money. And I still resist the idea of getting married. Why should I have to leave here and start over again? I'm not ashamed of what I do, except in the case of my family. Also, I like my life-style. I can't think of a better way to live.

Basically, I'm a loner. I probably won't ever get married. When I get too old for the business, I'll buy General Motors. Seriously, I'll invest in some kind of business. Hopefully, I'll have a comfortable old age.

I'm sure nobody in my family back home knows what I do. They have their own problems. I tell them I'm a model, and they either believe it or choose to believe it. I send each of my sisters $100 at Christmastime and send something to my parents.

I have no regrets about leaving home and getting into this life. My sisters sold out for a lot less than I did. The way I look at it, a wife is nothing more than a legal hooker. A wife sells out cheap. A wife sells out for financial security, but how many wives really have financial security? Maybe there are some wives who really love their husbands. And whose husbands love them. But why would all these guys be coming to me if they were happy at home?

I also tell the Internal Revenue Department that I'm a model. I can't admit to them what I do. My income runs between $15,000 and $25,000 a year, all in cash. I have to declare some income, so I put down that I earn $10,000 a year. I pay the government $1,500 a year in income taxes and also I have to pay the Social Security tax.

I don't feel that I'm exploited financially by society or by men. What I do is a straight commercial proposition. It's capitalism at its purest. I have a product that I sell to whoever wants to buy it.

Maybe you can argue that society did force me into the role I play. We didn't have much at home when I was growing up, but there was enough. I had a shot at college; it didn't take. I couldn't be a nuclear scientist, so I became what I am. But it was my choice; nothing and no one forced that choice on me. That's why I say I'm a happy hooker.

I can walk away from the business anytime I want, but I don't choose to, at least not yet.

Women's lib is a good thing, I guess. Women should have equal pay for equal work. But let's be honest. Most women don't earn as much as men. Maybe they will fifty years from now, but I can't wait to find out.

I keep reading and hearing that we have a more permissive society so far as sex is concerned. It makes me laugh. Things haven't changed that much. There are still plenty of guys ready to pay to go to bed with me. That's always been true, even in the Bible, and it's always going to stay true.

Even though more girls are giving it away gratis, it hasn't hurt me. I only work five days a week, from Wednesday through Sunday, and I turn a lot of business down.

The sort of business I turn down is from the freaks. Christ, am I ever tired of the freaks. Just the other day a guy called and offered me $500 if he could handcuff me and beat the shit out of me. No way. I'd never permit myself to be handcuffed or tied to a bed; you lose control of the situation that way. I had another guy offer me $2,000 to spend a week on his boat. He wanted to watch, only watch, while three other guys made love to me. I said no. I've done gang-banging, but I try to avoid it now. Some things I just won't do for money.

When a guy calls me on the phone, I put everything up front. I ask him what he wants. I tell him the price. If he wants to rip off a quickie, I charge him $100. All night is $200.

Most guys pay up without messing around. But I've had knives and guns pulled on me by guys who wanted their money back. When you are in a situation like that, you don't argue. I give them back their goddamned money. It doesn't pay to get killed for a hundred bucks.

The secret in this business is volume. When volume is high, say, on a Friday night, I can handle three or four tricks. Wednesdays and Thursdays usually are bummers. But you make up for it, money-wise, on Friday, Saturday and Sunday nights.

Sometimes you hit an unexpected bonanza from guys who aren't exactly weirdos, but who are different. One guy paid me $1,000 to give him a blow job on the ride from his house to the airport. Another guy sends me $200 every time I talk to him on the telephone. He calls about once a week and I talk dirty to him for an hour or so. He holds his cock in his hand while I talk to him and gets it off. For that, he pays me. It's harmless, and it's good money for an hour on the phone.

You'd be surprised at some of the guys I do business with. I've got a Catholic priest who I meet once a month in a hotel. I've fucked two governors and three mayors who were in town for conventions, and more corporation executives, $200,000-a-year men, than you can imagine.

The most money I ever made from one trick was with a guy who took me to Acapulco for two weeks a couple of years ago. He paid me $5,000. And it ended up with a marriage proposal. He's okay, but not for marriage. I still see him every couple of weeks professionally. He stays the night and pays me my fee, $200, plus a $50 tip. I make as much in one night as a secretary makes in two weeks.

I've said I was happy in the business. To tell the God's honest truth, I'm not. I don't think any hooker can be happy. But I also don't think anyone can be happy who just does something only for money. I've never given in to booze or drugs. I drink sparingly and I don't use shit, except a joint now and then if a guy who's staying the night insists.

The point I'm trying to make is that with everybody using booze and shit, nobody seems to be happy. Everyone's hung up on money, just like I am.

My greatest fears are poverty and boredom. To me, life isn't worth living if you can't have the luxuries, a nice apartment, a big car, a smashing wardrobe. I think I'm enjoying my life as much as anyone is enjoying life.

BERTIE WILLIAMS

Born in Wolfe City, Texas sixty-two years ago, Bertie Williams spent her early married life on a farm in Okemah, Oklahoma. Brown-eyed and stocky, she's now a maid-housekeeper at a forty-seven-room motel on the outskirts of Los Angeles.

I had to pick a hundred pounds of cotton a day when I was seven years old for my daddy. I went to school until the fourth grade, and I was married at fifteen. I never have been sick a day in my life. Never had time for it. If you keep aworkin', you don't get sick.

We came to California in 19 and 41, with no money, after my husband had one of his feet cut off. He got an ulcer sore on his toe and lost part of his foot and part of his leg. He has been invalided and unable to work ever since. Now he's got sugar diabetes and is in a wheelchair.

I have four children. I put them through school and all doing maid work. My oldest daughter is forty-one and I got a son that's thirty-nine; then I got twin boys thirty-five. The oldest boy, he went over to Pierce College for a while; now he's a highway patrolman. After he got married, why, he went to Glendale College and got his degree. He went to school for eight years after he got married. My twins just do factory work, and my other daughter is married.

I commenced being a maid when my children were going to school. I'm proud of the work I do.

When I first came to California in 19 and 54—I was raised on the farm, so I didn't have any experience—I went out to hunt for a job. I was thirty-eight years old when I come down to this part of the country. Everywhere I'd go they would say, Have you got any experience? Well, how could you have experience at anything if you never did work at it? So I just got tired of walking around trying to find a job. I went down to the agency and I got my first maid's job and went to work. I knew a lot of women then that worked at factories, and I made more money at the time than they did.

When I started maid work, I worked six hours a day and made

$1 an hour. I wouldn't speak of the tips you get in this business. You don't get enough tips for nothing. Not that I expect people to tip me, because I get paid my wages. I make around $5,000 a year in wages, so it's a good job. It's a clean job. I like it.

All these years, I could have used more money but I have always had plenty to eat and plenty to wear, so that pays me all right. I never did want more than I could get. I don't really think too much about money, if I have everything I need, which I do.

I don't resent people who have more money than I do. I guess they got more money because they were better managers and had a better start than I had. That's all I can say about that.

My dad was a Texas farmer, and there were five children in the family. We didn't have much, but we never wanted. I'm a lot better off than my daddy was, though. I'm asittin' in this old house here that's worth $35,000. We give $18,000 for it about sixteen years ago.

I have worked for four motels in this town. I worked for fifteen years at the Olive Manor as a maid and a housekeeper. I said I didn't want to be the housekeeper anymore because there was so much demanding of you. So I went out and worked as a maid at a motel for about three years. But I couldn't make no money that way, so I went back to housekeeping.

When you are a maid in the motel business you have just your own rooms to study about. But a housekeeper, you have got to study about all the rooms, watch over the other girls you work with. You got to do a lot of different things. I take care of the laundry and tell them when to order supplies. I see to the washing. We wash a lot of things, and being the housekeeper like I am now means there's a lot more work to do than just being a maid.

I prefer, though, to be just a working maid. I'm a working maid at the motel now. I mean, I have my section of rooms, too. But there's also the housekeeping chores. I work in the girls' places on their days off, and that way I know just about how things are going without running around and inspecting. I hate that inspecting. They put me on that too much and I'll quit. I won't do that. I hate going around and inspecting in the corners and rubbing white gloves over the headboards—all that stuff. I just hate it, and so I'd rather just treat the girls like I like to be treated myself.

I'm the housekeeper over four maids, all of them Mexican. When I started motel work, I worked only with white people. I wouldn't work with nobody but just white people, but you can't get white people to do it anymore. I think they would rather draw welfare than to work. I know that's so, because I have been trying to hire whites for twenty years now. I used to work with them all the time. So they have just let them take over, and I think it's terrible. Me, I've never had a thing given to me, and I wouldn't take welfare.

Some of these girls just almost demand tips from the guests. That's not nice, because the guests are paying for their rooms, so I don't think it's correct that the girls want tips. They are getting paid their wages. I don't go for that.

The girls work five days a week. I work six days a week, eight hours a day.

I'm at work by seven in the morning. I come in and get started on the rooms. We try to get to our check-outs first. And we just go through a routine, doing whatever has to be done to the rooms. That's about all there is to it. I clean the bathroom, vacuum, clean windows, dust. It's hard work, but I always liked to do it. I always said that you had to do things you like to do. And be good at anything you like to do. I am good at it.

Some people leave their rooms real sloppy. You step into a room and you don't know what to do, pull out your hair or run. But there is an awful lot of nice people, too. I have found that out. They'll even leave me a tip on occasion—$1, $2, sometimes as much as $5.

Where I work is a good motel. I wouldn't work at some motels. I wouldn't work at a motel that doesn't have a good name. I've always worked at a nice motel, triple A, most of them.

I feel real proud of what I do. There ain't anything else I'd like to do that I know of.

I've heard about women kicking up a fuss, wanting their rights and all. I don't pay no attention to that because I've always had my liberation or whatever they call it. I've always had my freedom, in the matter of money and every other way.

I have raised four beautiful children, all of them just great. I have got seven grandchildren. My husband, while I'm at work, he takes care of himself. He is real good. The only thing I have to do for him is to feed him and wash his clothes. He keeps house for me a lot, even though he's in the wheelchair.

I'm going to work until I'm sixty-five. Then I'm going to retire on Social Security and make $3,000 a year doing maid's work. The law says you can make that much and take your Social Security.

I'll only be aworkin' part-time, doing what I do best. It's good for anybody to work, no matter how old they get to be. But I see people getting lazier all the time. You can't find nobody to work very much anymore, American people.

Some folks look down on maid's work, I know that all right. I think people that don't feel that maid work is very nice or is good work ought to go out and look at the world a little bit or look at themselves a little better. They ought to see what is going on in the world, see the type of jobs most people have and the kind of wages most people make.

The kind of work I do is honest work, and it's clean work to a certain extent. But there is a lot of jobs that are not very clean that people do. I worked some in a cannery, and I will take motel work to cannery work anytime. I told my husband when I left the cannery work that if I had to stay there another minute I was going back over the hill. That is the nastiest work I ever got into.

I pay a little over $200 a year to the federal government for income taxes. I go home with about $100 a week. I buy food and clothes and everything else that I need, and I save a little, too. Every so often I save up till I get to a $1,000, and then I put it on the house or something. The new cupboards in the house cost $1,000. The house ain't paid for yet. We still give $152 for it every month.

So I have less than $300 a month to spend, but my husband gets Social Security of $267 a month. He is 77, a lot older than me.

High prices is getting worse all the time, but it hasn't hurt me too bad. We just have to go along with it, I guess.

I don't have any regrets about spending all these years doing my maid work. I wouldn't change a thing. I am a very happy person. I wouldn't trade places with a millionaire. I make the best of what there is. Life is for people to enjoy, and that's about all I can say about that.

Shelter

Lending money on a house is the only business
I know that generates profit at the beginning,
the middle and the end of a transaction.

—DAVID ATHENS

DAVID ATHENS

David Athens was born in Philadelphia and became a southern California real estate broker in 1960, after a career as a disc jockey, announcer and newsman. "Then I got tired of the entertainment business–too insecure. Homes and property had always appealed to me. So I studied real estate and got my license." Prosperous now, he drives an Audi, supports three children in college, and lives in a $145,000 home he purchased in 1962 for $33,000.

My first year as a broker I made about $14,000, which was considerably less than I'd made in show business, but I could see a brighter future. Although now I'm wondering if my future is really that bright.

My show business connections helped me. I was able to utilize those connections, and success in the field came rather rapidly. After two years, I became sales manager. Soon I was offered a deal to buy in as a partner, which I accepted. It cost me $10,000 for a piece of the business. So now I sell property, oversee a sales force of thirty-five, and share in the profits of the business. All in all, my average income in the last ten years has been $40,000 a year, through good years and bad years. What it will be ten years from now, or next year, I have no idea. Maybe I traded one insecure career for another that might turn out to be more insecure.

In the seventeen years I've been in real estate, there have been incredible changes. Much, much higher interest rates and rapid, unreal inflationary prices for houses.

The fault lies primarily with lending institutions, the savings and loan outfits, the banks and the insurance companies, which are gutting the public.

Lending money on a house is the only business I know that

generates profit at the beginning, the middle and the end of a transaction. First off, the institutions get a loan origination fee, which is what you pay in the beginning for the privilege of getting the loan. Some of them charge up to 3 and 4 percent of the total loan. Normally, it's 1 percent. If you are borrowing $30,000, they charge you $300, what they call 1 point, plus $50 which they add for paperwork. So right away you are in a minus position, paying an extra $350 on your $30,000 loan. I've never thought that fee was legitimate. I can't see that it's warranted. I forget when this actually started, but the charge used to be $3 per $1,000. In other words, they could initiate a $30,000 loan for $90. Now it's almost four times as much. In the case of institutions that charge 4 percent, the same $30,000 loan bleeds $1,400. It's pure avarice—the institutions provide no service that justifies the fee. One reason they get away with it is that so many people want loans, and they can pick and choose, just skim the cream. The borrower is in a horrible position—either he pays or he doesn't get the loan.

The institutions get their money in the middle from the interest you pay on the loan. And they get it at the end by means of a pay-off penalty, which is usually a charge of six months' interest on the unpaid balance. I sold a house for $86,000, and the pay-off penalty was $2,400—a totally unnecessary charge. Why should a man be penalized for paying his debt back to the savings and loan? The man who paid the penalty was ramrodded—with that $2,400 he could have bought a late-model used car for his teen-age daughter or taken a vacation with his wife in Hawaii.

I'm a guy who is in the business of selling homes, and maybe I shouldn't knock the process. But reforms are needed. If we ever get the reforms, everybody will make more money by selling more houses.

People have no idea what it costs to own a home just in terms of the loan. Let's take a figure. You borrow $40,000 over a twenty-five-year period at 8 percent, an interest rate we no longer have. By the time you're finished, you've paid back $98,000. A $98,000 return on a loan of $40,000 is pretty damned good. I'm sure it compares favorably with the rate charged by Mafia loan sharks. It's to laugh—these men who run our lending institutions are considered respectable businessmen.

There's also another insidious factor here. In my opinion, it's a denial of the free-enterprise system. Theoretically, a real estate broker should be free to shop for a loan for his buyer. He should be able to call half a dozen lending institutions and get a rate that varies. But what happens when you call those half a dozen institutions? The interest rate at all of them never varies by more than ¼ of a point, if that. You can call New York or Chicago for money, and it's the same thing. I ask you, is that free enterprise? Why shouldn't the rate at one institution be 5 percent, 7 percent at another, 9 percent at a third? Why is it always exactly 9½ percent, no matter where you call? To me it's collusion, monopoly, price-fixing, and why the federal government doesn't do something about it beats me.

Like so many things, it's a legal ripoff. It's condoned for the simple reason that there is no overall agency that says to these institutions, You cannot set the interest rate here; you cannot set your loan payoff here; you cannot set your point system here. There is no state or federal governing body that rides herd on these abuses. For the consumer, there is no one to complain to. It's laissez-faire at its worst, as bad as it was in the nineteenth century, when Rockefeller and the other financial buccaneers could operate as they wished, in free-for-all fashion and without any governmental supervision.

If we didn't have these venal lending practices, the prices of homes would drop. A lending institution can make a very handsome profit loaning money at 5 or 6 percent. The rates now, which got up to 11 percent in 1974, are a disgrace.

People must deal with the lending institutions—how many of us can go out and pay cash for a house? Still and all, it's preferable to buy a house in comparison to renting an apartment. When you rent, you are merely buying someone else's property for him, and you don't get the deductions the government allows for interest. You also lose the appreciation, the increased value of your home, which has gone up historically over the years. Owning a home also allows you to build an equity, so I still maintain that private home ownership is the best way for an individual to live. Owning property has proven to be one of the best investments in the world today, though I think it is obtained at a cost that is unnecessarily high.

The commission our office charges is 6 percent of the selling price of the home. It's been 6 percent for thirteen years. But it's getting harder and harder to hold that line. Some brokers in southern California and in other parts of the country have raised their commission to 7 percent, and I can understand it. In our case, the cost of doing business, our overhead, has risen 20 percent in the last thirteen years. Some of the slack is made up because now we are selling more expensive homes; therefore, we are deriving more income. The best way for brokers to increase their income is not to raise commissions, but to increase volume. You can't keep bumping commissions.

The average guy who comes into our shop and says he wants to buy a home goes into a state of shock when you throw some of these prices at him. Usually, too, he's got a haunted feeling about his job. He's insecure. He has the specter behind him that he may not have his present income next week or next year. He asks, Can I afford to take the chance of committing myself for thirty years?

The health of the real estate business is closely allied to the overall economy, to the unemployment rate, to the fact that so many are insecure, to interest rates and inflation. I don't see these problems being solved quickly. I don't even really see that these problems are being worked on. We are going to have to face these problems for a long time.

I don't see this as a failure of the American system. I think it's a failure of the people in power to control the financial institutions. I think this country and a lot of the world are being controlled by multinational companies who tell whole countries what to do, and by savings and loan outfits and banks. Basically what we have is what I term a "bank economy." Every possible advantage accrues to the banks and the other lenders, and the guy who finds himself on the short end is the middle-of-the-road guy who has to knuckle under to the lenders. There is no way out for him.

It's astonishing how little has changed since Franklin Roosevelt said in the thirties, "I see one-third of a nation ill-housed, ill-clothed and ill-fed." You still have that situation. You have it in every city and state in the country. True, people are making more money today; wages and salaries are higher than during the Depression. But they are paying out those dollars for their ordinary living expenses, so they are fundamentally in the same position they were in when they were making less money. They haven't gained anything.

I'm not even sure that most people can truly afford the houses they are buying. I haven't seen a great many foreclosures around here yet. But if the economy doesn't improve, I don't know what will happen to these people in unemployment situations when mortgage payments come due. I know foreclosure rates are up at an alarming rate in places like Detroit and Cleveland, where you have unemployment of 8, 9 percent. What do these people do? They are not making out now, so how do they retain their homes?

Another expense that's shocking is the replacement cost of anything on an existing house. As an example, my neighbors just had a fire, and they've had to redo their whole house. What they paid $25,000 for a few years ago cost them more than $50,000 to replace. During the fire, I stopped a fireman who was about to break in the front door. I told him, "For God's sake, don't knock that door down. It's a beautiful old door."

Luckily my neighbor managed to find the key. Just for the heck of it, we checked out what it would have cost to replace that door if it had been broken down: $600. A few years ago a solid oak door like that could have been bought for less than $100.

Oddly enough, it's easier to sell an expensive home. The more expensive the home, the easier it is to sell, because you are dealing with a wealthier buyer, a more sophisticated buyer, a qualified buyer, a man for whom a few thousand one way or another isn't really important if he gets emotionally involved in the house and wants to buy it. In a lower-priced home, the deal may get down to maybe the difference of paying added interest of $16 a month. That can really bother the buyer. That hurts him. That makes him think, I don't know if I can do that; it's almost $200 a year more. Maybe I can't really afford it.

Fortunately, I sell mostly expensive homes, though those have their problems, too. In 1974 there was a credit crunch. The lending institutions said they didn't have any money to lend. That brought our business to a grinding halt. At that particular time Redd Foxx was a client of mine, and he wanted to buy the

William Holden house. The price was $300,000. It could have been bought five or six years before for $140,000. Redd was willing to put up $100,000 in cash on condition he could get a $200,000 loan. But there was no institution willing to lend him $200,000, under any circumstances.

"What's the matter?" Redd asked me. "Is it because I'm black and I want to move into a white neighborhood?"

That feeling was a fleeting thing, said in anger more than anything else. I told him, "We tried twenty-one different lending agencies, and they all said no. They didn't know if you were black or white or green."

That's another example of the control the lending agencies have. Why should money suddenly dry up simultaneously at different lending agencies? And if a guy like Redd Foxx can't get a house with a down payment of $100,000, what about the guy who has only a few thousand to put down? In a few instances I have sold the same house several times. One house I sold back in 1963 for $90,000. Three years later I resold it for $115,000. Two years ago I sold it again for $165,000. Now it's worth more than $200,000. So in fourteen years the value of the house has more than doubled. It's insanity. I might add that none of the buyers or sellers have done anything to improve the property.

Homeowners also have to contend with a continual rise in property taxes. In my area, property taxes have jumped 100 percent. It's unfair. It's more than unfair; that kind of increase is madness. Here the county is taking one element of the population, homeowners, and taxing them punishingly on the basis of the fact that they own property. Though the homeowner may have no children in school, his property taxes go to pay for the education of other people's children. And the person who rents an apartment may have three children in school, and he pays no property taxes. The apartment dweller gets a free ride. What kind of a system is that?

It's an outrageous thing to realize that 50 percent of our young people are destined never to have their own homes. That's a sad commentary on our economy and our times. It's really unbelievable that even couples with an income of more than $20,000 a year can't afford a home. Twenty thousand a year was once a lot of money, and one of the rewards of earning that much was that you could buy a home. No more. Even under the terms of a Veterans Administration or FHA loan, it's tough for a couple to qualify, because those government agencies are charging 9 percent interest plus 3½ to 4 points. You want to hear a more shocking case? I know a young couple who between them make $50,000 a year. But they pay 44 percent of their salaries in income taxes. So they pay a very high rent for an apartment, $500 a month. What the hell's wrong with us if a couple making that kind of money can't get a house? If they can't, what chance do the people in the barrios and the ghettos have, people who are making $5,000, $8,000, $10,000 a year?

So there are young people in our society today who are saying fuck the American Dream. It's empty and shallow for us. The Dream is meaningless, because a part of the Dream was having a house, and we can't afford one. I can put myself in the position of such young people. They are paying through the nose for a car, for gasoline, paying exorbitant taxes. Everywhere they turn they are being ground under. I think this is the thing we should be worried about: we should worry about these young people who are trying to cope in this housing market and in this economy.

Another thing we should worry about is the social unrest that's coming because of a lack of housing. You are going to find millions and millions of people who can't afford a house and at the same time can't afford rental housing. So what do they do? What they do is this: they turn to the federal government and say, Find us a place to live. But the federal government won't be able to find living quarters for all those people, and that will lead to social unrest, maybe to a revolution.

This country, if it doesn't meet the housing crisis, could go up in flames. We're already seeing the result in the inner cities. More people are crowding into less space. They are tumbling over one another, and it causes hot tempers, frustration and crime. And many of these people are unemployed and have nowhere to turn. This is where crime begins. You get somebody who all of a sudden gets to the place where he wonders where he's going to get next month's rent and he's a potential criminal.

I wish I had more hope, but it just isn't there.

RAYMOND GAFFNEY

The $400 billion savings and loan industry finances the purchase of 80 percent of the homes bought in America. Of that staggering amount, $2.25 billion are the assets of a thirty-five-office savings and loan association in Los Angeles where Gaffney is a vice-president and branch manager. He earns $500 a week. A portly man of fifty-six, he has been in the S&L industry since 1955. He wears brown slacks, a light green shirt and a tan jacket.

Our only business is lending money for mortgages. Our current interest rate is 8¾ percent. Ninety percent of the loans we make come in at that figure, but there are some for which we charge more. If we wished, we could get as much as 12 percent, but there is a higher risk involved on a loan like that, so we try to stay away from it, though sometimes we're tempted. There are some people and some properties we wouldn't touch at any price, even if they agreed to pay 30 percent. Maybe the house is a bad investment, or the buyer is a poor credit risk.

There is no fixed interest rate in the savings and loan business—the marketplace dictates the price at which money is loaned. However, you'll find that the rates at all S&L associations are exactly the same. If we charged 9 percent, for example, and everybody else was charging 8¾, we wouldn't get any loans. Conversely, if everybody else charged 9 percent and we charged 8¾, we would get all the loans. So the marketplace just keeps us all in line. We have to charge the same as other associations, otherwise we wouldn't get any business at all.

The rates charged by S&Ls don't collide with the American idea of free enterprise and competition. There is no collusion. I've heard it suggested that one S&L might charge 9 percent, another 7 percent, another 5 percent. But that wouldn't work. As I said, the S&L charging the lowest rate would get all the business.

There's another factor. The only source of money we have is what the depositors leave with us. We just don't go out and float a bond issue and get a couple of million dollars and loan it to people.

Okay, now the maximum rate which we are permitted to pay is determined by law. It is called Regulation Q, and it applies to banks and to savings and loans. The maximum we can pay on a passbook account is 5¼ percent. If we wanted to pay 20 percent, it wouldn't make any difference. By law, 5¼ percent is the maximum rate we can pay. There are exceptions for long-term accounts. If you leave your money in for a year, for example, we can give you 6½ percent on accounts over $1,000. But the law says we can't give you 6¾ percent, no matter who you are or how much you deposit, or how badly we want to. That policy, that law is determined by the federal government.

So, naturally, every association pays depositors the maximum allowed under the law. So it is true that we all pay the same interest rate on money our customers give us, as well as charging the same interest rate on the money we loan. The S&L industry is powerless to change that system.

You must also remember that S&Ls make very little profit. We're not like, say, the cosmetics industry, where there is a terrific profit margin. Over the life of a mortgage, the borrower will pay back to us more than twice the amount of the loan. That sounds as if we're making a huge profit. But don't forget that while we're collecting interest from the borrower, we are paying interest every day to the people from whom we are getting the money. We are only a middleman and a collection agency. We don't create anything. We don't manufacture anything. We don't fabricate anything. We don't do anything except act as a third party between the customer and the borrower.

We are paying out interest on a great deal of money all the time. If you left money with us in a long-term account at 7¾ percent, it would double in nine years. That is in effect an 11 percent interest rate. We are paying much more than 5½ percent on a great deal of our money. We are paying 6½ to 11 percent on millions and millions of the dollars our customers deposit with us. Actually, the 5½ percent rate on passbook accounts is becoming a minor part of the business. If a customer wants a passbook account, where he's constantly putting money in and taking money out, he should use a commercial bank account. Since our loans are long-range, up to thirty years, we

also want long-range deposits. But to get the long-range deposits, we have to pay a higher interest rate. The higher the interest
rate we pay, the less profit we make.

Another factor that drives down our profit is the cost of
money, which is between 6½ and 7 percent. Now this is just the
cost of money, the interest we have to pay on money when we
borrow from commercial banks or the Federal Home Loan bank.
We are not talking about salaries or the cost of doing business.
Suppose the cost of doing business is 1 or 1¼ percent. Now we
are up to at least 8 percent before we can talk about profit. Then
you have to allow for taxes and other overhead and fixed costs,
so the profit of a savings and loan is considerably less than 1
percent. Most people think it's way up in the billions, which it
isn't.

In all candor, I should mention that S&Ls do participate in a
mild rip-off in persuading customers to deposit their money with
us. We all advertise that interest is compounded daily. It's a
gimmick invented—I don't know—maybe twenty years ago, and
it sounds good: daily interest you can count every night, with a
computer compounding it. People rather naïvely think, Oh boy,
I'm going to get rich if I take my money over to a savings and
loan. Unless you have a lot of money on deposit, it doesn't really
make any difference. If you have, say, $500 in a savings and loan
and you leave it there for twenty years, the difference under
compound interest would be forty-five cents or so.

The latest income statistics tell us that at today's prices only
one in four American families can afford to buy a home. That's a
darn shame. It's unfortunate. But it has nothing to do with
savings and loans. Oh, to a small extent it does, because interest
rates are higher. But when I look back ten years, the interest
rates then were somewhere around 6¾ or 7 percent, so interest
rates haven't gone up a great deal. It isn't the interest rate that
makes the difference in the high price of housing; it's the fact
that it costs more to build a house today than it did years ago. It's
also due to the fact that we have run out of choice land. I keep
asking a builder I know, "Why don't you build cluster houses? I
would buy one right now." And he says, "There's no land."

Another thing that has driven prices up, of course, is the
unbelievable rise in labor costs. It is just plain ridiculous. Do you
know that a man who mixes cement—I am not talking about a

bricklayer, I am talking about a guy who mixes cement; who just takes a bag of cement, pours it into a trough, puts water in it and sand and mixes it up—makes more money than I do? Worse than that is the price of common labor. Where a guy puts bricks in a hod and carries them up to the bricklayer. He doesn't lay the bricks, he carries the bricks, and he also makes more money than I do.*

The labor unions have taken the attitude that this guy's human, so why shouldn't he live in a house as good as mine? Well, there are a lot of reasons why he shouldn't live in a house as good as mine. First of all, he is not worth it; he is not contributing anything. And yet he expects to live in a fancy house in a fancy neighborhood.

That sort of thing just kills incentive for people like me and other professionals. Did I go to college for four years so I could earn less than a common laborer? Why, say, should a guy spend a lot of time learning to be an electrical engineer when just a plain electrician can make thirty bucks an hour? You figure thirty bucks an hour times 40 hours is $1,200 a week. Just a plain old electrician who screws the plugs in your wall makes almost $5,000 a month. It's imbecilic. And that's why houses are as expensive as they are. I am sure you can remember the days when an M.D. didn't make $5,000 a month. Five thousand a month before World War II was what a highly specialized brain surgeon might make. Today an electrician makes the same amount for screwing a plug in your wall.

Statistics also project that the price for a typical home will be a cool $78,000 three years from now. That's probably the way it's going to be. You see, even if a contractor can find land, he's a prisoner of the building trade unions.

Labor contracts are negotiated for three or four years hence, with an increase in every year. No contract is negotiated for four to six months, which is about how long it takes to build a house. The thing is programmed out as far into the future as the unions

---

*Including fringe benefits (vacation pay, medical insurance and employer contribution to a pension fund), a cement mason earns $15.14 an hour. Counting his fringe benefits, a laborer who carries bricks on a construction site earns $11.20 an hour. Assuming a 40-hour week and employment fifty-two weeks a year, the mason earns $31,491.20 a year. The annual wage for a brick carrier figures out to $23,296.00.

can manage. Every year of the contract, the builder knows he's going to have to pay more and more for labor. As a consequence, the price of the house goes up.

And there's nothing that's going to make the price of land go down, even where it is available. And the price of building materials is bound to go up, too, because materials are produced by people in other unions that have the same kind of contracts the building trades do. As a result, there is no way the price of homes will ever go down.

Even if the interest rate of S&Ls was 40 percent, that has nothing to do with the cost of the house. When you go to buy a house, the salesman says, "This house is selling for $75,000." The cost of the house has nothing to do with the cost of financing. That's what it cost to put that house in that spot. Only after you buy the house do you start talking about what it is going to cost to finance it. But the financing doesn't contribute to the purchase price of the house.

I don't foresee S&L interest rates declining. They'll probably move up rather than go down. In our industry, every six months an employee doing the same type of work and doing the same amount of work expects a raise. How that came about is beyond me. But if you hire a teller, for example, and she is doing the job for $600 a month, six months from now she wants more money, even though she isn't producing more. If she doesn't get the raise, she quits. We have a lot of that. So every time we give a raise, our cost of operation goes up. That teller, if she's good, will get two $25-a-week raises a year. It's the same with all the other employees.

I would be perfectly happy to work at my job for $200 a month if prices were what they were in 1930. I would live better than I do now. I think I used to live better just prior to the Second World War than I do now, though I make probably ten times more in actual dollars. Nobody seems to realize that just getting a raise from $8 an hour to $10 an hour really doesn't do you any good. There is just something economically wrong with that. The minute someone gets a raise, his employer adds the increased labor cost to the price of what he is selling or manufacturing.

Families whose income is less than $20,000 a year are just

going to have to settle for apartment living. That's a shame, and I hate to see it. Forgetting unions, forgetting everything else, the price of houses keeps going up because more and more people are pressing into the cities. The housing industry isn't like the automobile industry. If you sell 7 million cars this year, you very likely can sell 7 million next year. Or maybe 10 million. Not with houses. There's no way we can make more land on which to build them. Thus, existing houses as well as new housing becomes more expensive every year as the demand for them by more people increases.

Where is it all going to end? God knows. I moved into my condominium two years ago and paid $60,000 for it. Two friends of mine just moved into the condominium next door to me, and for the identical thing they paid $81,000.

I don't see how the young people who are coming along now, just graduating from school, are ever going to get started. If you bought your house years ago, you're in good shape, except for the increase in property taxes. But the poor guy who gets out of school nowadays who is twenty-two or twenty-three years old and goes to buy a $60,000 house, which is a pretty minimal house these days, has to come up with a $12,000 down payment, 20 percent of the purchase price. Well, he could save the $12,000 if he could live for about a year without eating or without paying rent or buying clothes. But the guy has to support his wife, and he has to live someplace and eat, so in the very time of his life when he is making the least amount of money, he is supposed to be saving $12,000 to get into this crummy little house which is probably worth $25,000.

The people who are coming along now are just up a creek. That's all there is to it.

JOY D'AMATO

Joy's husband Vince is a foreman for a company in Los Angeles whose only business is painting homes. "Like they always say, I'm just a housewife." They've been married three years and have a two-year-old son.

"What's this country coming to when a man making $300 a week can't afford to buy a house?" That's what Vince keeps asking himself.

We have $1,550 in savings, which isn't enough for the down payment on the house we want to buy, a house in the $40,000 to $50,000 range. We saw just the place we wanted last week. But when we figured it out, with the mortgage, taxes and insurance, it would come out to a cost of more than $600 a month. We couldn't afford that much; it would mean spending more than half of Vince's take-home just to keep us in that house.

We're in this trap, but we're going to have to do something. I've talked to three real estate brokers, and they all say we'd better buy now, because prices for homes are going even higher. But how can we buy now when we don't have the down payment and the savings and loan won't lend us money?

Money has led to tension between Vince and me—this business of trying to figure out where it all goes. We had our little arguments before, but never like now, never like over money.

The other night when we were going over the bills, I said to Vince, "What really worries me is that you don't have any insurance."

"Don't start on that," he said. "You don't know what money is. You spend $55 every time you go to the supermarket, and it's too much. I could do the shopping myself and spend less. You throw away $10 just for stupid junk to clean the floor."

I understand Vince's frustration. The company he works for isn't making as much profit as it used to. He's worried about his job. Too many people nowadays are turning to do-it-yourself paint jobs, and that hurts the professionals.

He got a $50 raise last year, which put him at top union scale. But even with the raise it's not enough to cover the rise of everything we buy, and it's not enough for the house we want.

Until six months ago we were renting an apartment for $220 a month. The manager kicked us out because we bought a dog. So we decided to rent this house because it has three bedrooms and a backyard for the baby and the dog. Even getting this place was a rat race. We snapped it up for $300 a month while three other couples were poking around looking at it at the same time.

We don't want to buy a cheap house. It would cost too much for upkeep, and it wouldn't satisfy our sense of quality.

Vince has pride. He says, "I'm proud of myself. I know I make darned good money, more than most schoolteachers. We deserve better than we've got. I've worked full-time since I was fourteen years old, and we're entitled to a bigger piece of cake than we're eating."

After taxes Vince brings home $980 a month.* We're better off than most, and yet we aren't. We aren't because we can't afford a decent house. It doesn't make sense. The only way I see others have made it is that they bought a house years ago. We're stuck.

We're not starving and we're not short of most luxuries. We have all our living room furniture bought and paid for, $900 worth. We paid $500 for a stereo. I have an Amana Frost Free in the kitchen. But we won't feel we're taking part in the good life until we get the house we want.

Since we've been married, we've taken only two three-day vacations, one to Palm Springs, one to Lake Tahoe. But there won't be any more vacation trips, not for a long time, the way things are going.

My food bill has more than doubled in the last year. I've switched from sirloin to tacos. We used to go to a good restaurant for dinner once a week. Now it's a pizza joint. We used to splurge once a month and go to a movie. But with the babysitter, dinner and the price of the tickets, it came out to $25 for the evening. So we stay home and watch television.

Vince's only extravagance is the $50 a month he spends for breakfast at the coffee shop. He gets up at four in the morning and leaves before I'm out of bed. But that isn't really extravagance when you figure he skips lunch.

Vince is after me all the time to quit smoking. He says I blow $20 a month into the air. He's right, I guess. I really should quit. That would give us $240 more a year.

But I save a lot by making the baby's clothes. I taught myself to

---

*This is $126 more than the median income for Los Angeles County families, according to U.S. Labor Department statistics.

sew on an old machine my mother gave me. Relatives and friends have given us all the baby's toys; and that's a saving.

By the time we finish spending for everything each month, we're in the hole. We're going deeper into the hole every month. Rent, food, utilities, gasoline and the rest of it costs about $125 more than Vince brings home. The way it's going, we'll have to move down, not up. What do people do who earn less than Vince?

When we first got married, we plunged into the credit-card game. For a time we were charging everything we could. Then we realized we were paying very high interest for the credit, at least 18 percent a month. I went to work as a waitress before the baby came. I averaged about $125 a week with tips. We had a $3,500 credit debt, mostly for the furniture and a '70 Pontiac. We stayed home for seven months, never went out once, and made double and triple payments. We took every penny and paid everybody off. Now we pay cash for everything. The only money we want to borrow is for the house, and that isn't happening.

I want to go back to work, but Vince says not until the baby is older, if then. He's old-fashioned. It's his pride; he thinks he should be able to support his wife and baby on what he makes.

We're both good Catholics, but we don't go to church anymore. We can't afford to give to the church, and we'd be too embarrassed if we were there and didn't give. Vince and I wanted four kids. But with the money situation the way it is, there's no way. I'm on the Pill, and I feel guilty about it. I know the Pope's against it, but what can we do?

I was named for that part of the Bible that says, "Joy cometh in the morning." We're both only twenty-four years old, and I wonder how much joy is ahead of us; what the morning is going to be like a year, five years, fifteen years from now. Holy Mother of God . . . sometimes I get so frightened of the future I could scream.

JUNE PETERSON

"My husband calls me a slumlord." If she is, June Peterson belies the stereotype. Her manner and speech are soft, almost sexy. Mrs. Peterson is an attractive blue-eyed blonde in her forties, the mother of two teen-age girls. She owns a five-unit Los Angeles apartment building in a modest neighborhood.

Saying I'm a slumlord is ridiculous. People with a low income must have someplace to live. When I bought the building in 1963, my rent for two of the one-bedrooms was $60 a month; I charged $65 a month for two other one-bedrooms and $75 for the two-bedroom. Now the rents are, respectively, $95, $120 and $125. Those are still truly remarkable prices in this day and age. Some months I break even, some months I take a loss, some months I make a profit.

I bought the building for $6,000 down. The total purchase price was $30,000. My mortgage payments are $200 a month. I went into property as an investment for retirement. Also as a tax shelter. My husband was making $15,000 a year as a television writer. That was taxed as ordinary income, and we needed an investment that we could depreciate.

I was a real novice. I had never owned any kind of property, and I was led to believe that I would have money rolling in. Naturally, this seemed like a good thing to me—profit plus tax advantages.

But I wasn't told about the property taxes that came due twice a year. The taxes then were $480 a year. They've since doubled. Nor was I told that roofs leak, that faucets constantly drip and run up your water bill, and that the cost of maintenance can be astronomical if you let things get out of hand.

At first I rented to families with children. I thought the property lent itself to families more than to single people. But I haven't rented to couples with kids in years. I found out the hard way, after I had to pay thousands in repair bills, including a fire set by a ten-year-old, that children aren't commercial.

Nor was I told, unfortunately, that many tenants run down a building. They have no respect for property, especially low-income people who've never owned property. I've had it all—besides the fire, tenants have destroyed kitchens and bathrooms, broken windows, left hoses running. They even stole my garbage cans.

The property was too small to have a manager, so I had to worry about everything myself. For the first few years, I wasn't sure if we were going to make it. Making it became particularly important when shortly after I bought the building my husband became ill and was unable to work. With such a situation, every penny counted.

One evening, just about dark, I went up there to collect the rent from a couple of tenants who were late and to take the change out of the coin box in the laundry room. When I walked into the laundry room, two fellows were there, acting strange. They pulled the door shut and I opened it. I didn't recognize them, so I said, "What are you doing in here?"

One of them answered, "Oh, we're hiding from our wives."

"I know what you're doing. You've got my coin box."

They were both young men, nineteen or twenty years old. It looked as if they were getting ready to run.

"Stop," I said. "Stop immediately or I'll scream."

They both stopped. Now, I was in there all by myself with these two boys, and I was vulnerable. But I wasn't about to let them get away with my coin box. One of the boys reached into this black leather jacket he was wearing. I didn't think anything about it at the time. It was only later that I got scared. When he reached in, he could have pulled out a gun or a knife. Fortunately, what came out of his jacket was my coin box, which he gave to me. They must have been amateurs—they looked frightened. One said, "Lady, give us five minutes before you call the police." I didn't bother—none of my tenants had a phone anyway. All I cared about was that I had my money back.

There was about $25 in the coin box. My husband was howling mad at me, saying I was insane to risk my life for that small amount of money. But at that moment $25 was very important, because I had a lot of debts that month. Even when he reached into his leather jacket, all I could think of was, That's my money and I worked hard for it, and nobody is going to take it away from me.

You have to learn to qualify people when you are renting. That's the first thing you learn; either you learn it or you go broke. If someone comes to you and he must have the apartment that moment—he must move in that instant—there has to be a reason. He's probably been kicked out of the place where he's living now and he's probably a deadbeat. If he pays in cash, it's always good, but many times deadbeats will pay the first month's rent right on the spot, and that's the last rent you will ever see from them.

I've never had a black tenant, but that's only because no black ever tried to rent an apartment. I've had Mexican people; I've had Indian people; I had a Chinese couple one time who were fine tenants, probably better than many of my white tenants.

In the beginning my biggest problem was that I sympathized with people and their problems. If anyone gave me a hard-luck story I'd fall for it. They didn't have the rent because they had to fix the kids' teeth or their mother was ill. I remember one time this family who'd lived there for maybe a year and a half didn't have the rent. That month my taxes were due, and I desperately needed the money. The woman told me she didn't have the rent because she'd given it to a sister to pay *her* rent.

That's the moment I began to learn that when you are renting, particularly low-income property, you get the rent first. If you don't get it, the furniture man will get it, a sister will get it, somebody will get it, but you won't get it.

I know the landlord has a lousy image, but I think it's unjustified. More often, it's the tenants who deserve the lousy image. They tear up and damage your property. They don't own it, you see, so they don't really take care of it. They have the mistaken belief that landlords are earning so much money that they can afford, for instance, to paint the whole place when the tenants move in. I've had tenants who banged nails in the walls for bookshelves or pictures. When they leave, the walls have holes in them, and it's expensive to repair them. Tenants do just about anything they please.

Landlords have a bad reputation in part because certain organized tenant groups have said an apartment is the tenant's home; he should be allowed to decorate it as his home; and the landlord doesn't have the right to say what can be done and what cannot be done to his property. I think that's completely wrong. You own the property. Your sweat, blood and tears have gone into buying the place. You have gone heavily into debt when you bought the place. You've put the work into the place. Tenants are only renting something from you, and they should be considerate. They should treat the property with respect.

Landlords provide an essential service to the community, and I think more landlords would probably take better care of their property if they had better renters and if they had a better profit margin.

In addition to my taxes doubling, the cost of labor has skyrocketed. I've had to learn to do an awful lot of the work myself. I found that I usually could do it better and cheaper. For instance, a leaky faucet may need a part that costs less than fifty cents. You call in a plumber and he charges you $15. So I learned to do it myself in ten or fifteen minutes. You have no idea how many $15 plumbing charges I've saved.

Sometimes when there's a vacancy I paint one wall so that when the tenant comes in he smells fresh paint. He thinks the whole place has been painted. I don't think that's necessarily taking advantage, because you can't paint a complete apartment every time a tenant moves in when you have a large turnover, as I've had.

You become a landlord, after all, to make a few dollars. Most other businesses show a greater profit margin than rental property. For instance, the markup on a dress is anywhere from 50 to 75 percent. It's nothing like that in property, and you are a sitting duck for all the increases in taxes, water, and the cost of labor.

But there are advantages to owning property. The biggest one is that the government legally allows you to take depreciation. I'm able to write off $1,800 a year, which saves us a considerable amount in federal taxes. That's the major reason a person buys property.

There are very few good investments for the average person. You have to be rich to go into oil, and you have to be crazy to risk it in cattle unless you have a lot of money. Crops and the stock market are also too hazardous for me. I'm a very conservative person, and, I might add here, it's getting so you have to be almost crazy to get into the rental business now, not only because of the damage people do to your property and the headaches they cause you, but because taxes eat up your profit. The costs of owning a property are rising faster than the rents.

And you always have to contend with people who run out on you, owing rent. I have had people who, when I go to collect the rent on the first of the month, say they are going to pay it on Friday, payday, and there are several boxes around, and you say, "Why all the boxes—are you going to move?" And they say, "No, this stuff belongs to a relative who's coming to stay with us," or some other simple-minded, transparent lie.

Sometimes you see them at eight P.M., and by nine P.M. they are gone, especially when you have furnished units, which mine are. All in all, I've lost between $2,000 and $3,000 from skippers.

I once had a family with five children, and every time I would go to get the rent, I'd see the kids running around half-dressed and chewing on chicken bones. I would get a hard-luck story about how the husband hadn't been paid or how he'd lost his job. The last time, I carried them for two months. Then they skipped out on me. I came to find out that the husband was an alcoholic, and that's where the rent money was going—for liquor.

When people don't pay the rent, the landlord is supposedly protected by small claims court, assuming you can find them and drag them into court. But it is trouble to go to court and get the judgment. So you are merely wasting your time. One year I was in small claims court five times, and I only collected once on a judgment.

Then there are the fights. I was called in the middle of the night once by a neighbor because there was a knife fight taking place on my property. I had to run up there and call the police. By the time they arrived, one of the men in the fight was dead.

Almost every Friday and Saturday night there are fights, with guns, knives, brass knuckles, clubs. You wonder about people who take their lives so lightly. Maybe poor people don't care about their lives as much as wealthier people do. That sounds like an unkind thing to say, but based on my experience, it seems true to me.

Being a landlord makes you a student of money and a student of human nature. As a landlord you see the seamy side of people. Now I have great empathy with policemen, who also see the seamy side of people. When you're a landlord, your faith in human beings takes a nose dive. You see all the pimples, and you lose all your fairy-tale dreams about people.

And being a landlord doesn't automatically assure you a profit. I know people who've gone broke in property. One woman I know bought a ten-unit building about the time I bought mine. She paid $20,000 down, and ten years later she walked away with $2,000. She didn't know how to operate the property. She had different managers who robbed her blind. She didn't take into consideration the fact that her second mortgage was coming due. She never put time or feeling into owning that property. She treated it as though she had money in the stock market: you put it in and forget it for a period of time, you never go near it, and you don't have to touch it.

I blame real estate brokers who sell property without giving the buyer any real knowledge of what he's getting into. In other words, selling a person the idea that this is an easy way to make money, without hassle. The brokers don't inform the buyers about the costs of running the property; they don't tell them they must allow for unexpected expenses; they don't tell them a lot of very important things.

Take my case. You have a unit that is earning $555 a month and your payment is $200. Right away you think, I have $355 to spend. But you forget about the insurance and the taxes and upkeep, and there are many jobs I can't do myself. All that comes out of the $355. Unless a person has experience or learns fast, you are going to go under.

I've just closed a deal to sell my building. The selling price is $42,000, a $12,000 profit on my purchase price. But there's more to it than that. On our original down payment of $6,000, we earned much more. I estimate we saved about $13,000 in income taxes. Also, I'm going to carry a $35,000 first mortgage at 9 percent interest that comes due in five years. Meantime, the buyer pays me $350 a month. At the end of the five years, there is a balloon payment of $28,000. So, taking everything into consideration, I would say that on our investment of $6,000 we will earn a total of approximately $75,000. And when I say earn it, I mean *I* have earned it. My husband never lifted a finger to help me, not once in the thirteen years we owned the building.

With the profit, and despite all the troubles of owning income property, I plan to buy another building, but carefully. Your greatest fortunes always have something to do with land, whether it is gold, oil, mineral rights, improvements on the land, air rights, whatever. Whoever owns land can become rich. Property is still a gamble, but to me it's a better gamble than anything else.

Whatever Happened to Society?

Money is just paper.
—SUSAN HARTUNIAN

JODY JACOBS

"Society changes, Fletcher, but not much," author Gregory McDonald said in his riveting suspense novel, Fletch. *"It does not die. It oozes. It changes its shape, its structure, its leaders and its entertainments. There is always a Society. As long as the instinct for power beats in the breasts of men and women, there will be a restricted clawing called Society."*

Ms. Jacobs, the good-humored, powerful Society Editor of the Los Angeles Times, *a post she's held since 1971, after working fourteen years for* Women's Wear Daily, *puts it this way: "Everything has changed. A couple of decades ago people didn't do the things they do now. Young society men didn't run around town in Levis and go to school wearing whatever they felt like wearing. There were a lot more rules then than now. Women used to wear gloves and hats to certain affairs. But nowadays fashion rules have relaxed, and social decorum is much looser and more casual except for some of the remaining grande dames, though even some of their children don't stick to the code."*

What has not essentially changed, Ms. Jacobs avers, is that money is still the prime requirement for entrance into society.

Society remains a privileged class. They are privileged by the amount of money they have, by the amount of leisure they have. But what is really interesting, what *has* changed significantly, is that people who have made money in their own lifetimes, moneyed celebrities, and a lot of wealthy people who spend a lot of time helping others are now allowed into society; in fact, they are courted.

It's difficult if not impossible to separate money and society. On the other hand, losing your money doesn't necessarily mean you're dropped. If you have good friends, they are still going to invite you. You are still going to see them and they will remain your friends. Some people who are impressed only by money or to whom money means a great deal are going to drop you, but real people are going to hang on.

I think it's very difficult for those in society who do lose their money. Someone who has grown up with a great deal of money and privilege finds it hard to adjust to poverty or relative poverty. They don't have the frame of reference for realizing that there are children who can't go to school because they don't have clothes.

You can be taken into society, if you're lucky, if you have one hit book or one hit record or one hit movie. But you must have other things going for you. Magnetism or charisma helps, and so does being a marvelous guest at a party, one the hostess can depend on to spark the proceedings.

There's been a resurgence in attention among society for authors. They've become social lions, and it's rather nice, a pleasant change from hairdressers, royalty, the French and fashion designers.

The late James Jones, who was here promoting a book, was given a dazzling party by the Malibu Colony. The same night he was given a dinner party by agent Irving Lazar in Beverly Hills. Norman Mailer doesn't come out here very often, but I think that anybody with that kind of a reputation would be swamped by invitations and could go out, virtually nonstop, to lunches, cocktails, dinners.

People want to be seen with famous writers. Maybe that doesn't apply to old society, which isn't tuned in to the literary world or to the movies or to music. However, even these people would be thrilled to go to a party and find a Rubinstein or a Beverly Sills. A person like that adds a lot to a party.

Many hostesses have their antenna out for anybody who is a celebrity, a worthwhile one. Jackie Onassis is certainly the kind of woman any hostess who prides herself on giving stimulating parties would want to invite.

Another way of entering society is to get involved with the right causes. Charity, more than ever, is a benchmark of society.

Sometimes the pressure on me is very strong from hostesses to attend charity parties. I oblige whenever I can, but there are evenings when I'm invited to four or five parties. Deciding which invitations to accept, without offending anyone, is a matter of delicate balance.

Most of the pressure in regard to charity affairs results from the fact that the women sponsoring them are aware that advance publicity will help them sell tickets, or they feel that my appearance adds an extra little incentive to get the guests they want. They figure that the female guests have spent a great deal of money on the tickets and on their hair and clothes and makeup and whatnot and they want to be recognized for it. And one way of getting recognized is to have their name mentioned in the paper.

Some charity parties are genuinely motivated. They are sponsored by women who really have the desire to do something for less fortunate people. But sometimes those parties can be no more than a time-filling enterprise for wealthy women who perhaps are bored.

You can always tell if a benefit is genuinely motivated. If women are unhappy with the coverage, it's usually because names have been slighted. Somebody doesn't get recognition for the amount of work she's done. But women who are totally dedicated get their satisfaction from whatever good the money does that they've raised. For these women, coverage is not so important.

One thing that I am sometimes embarrassed about when I go to cover a big charity event that has a lot of press present is that a few reporters immediately knock it. No matter how happy the occasion is or how beneficial the affair is to other people, they knock it because of the money thing. I find it destructive to criticize a worthwhile money-raising event because reporters have less money than the guests. That's sheer jealousy.

I don't think society people talk about money more than other people do. It's still considered bad form to mention how much you've spent on anything. And it's considered crude among most people to ask how much something costs. If it's your best friend, certainly you might discuss money and the price of things.

I hear women talking about the cost of something that has had a startling rise, maybe a restaurant that has doubled its prices, or a furrier whose price has increased tremendously, or a designer who used to make dresses that sold for $150 and now suddenly is making clothes that start at $600. They will talk about money under such circumstances, or they will talk about money as it relates to real estate, about somebody who has just traded a house or sold a house and gone into a condominium. During the energy crisis, everyone was talking about the high price of gasoline. Quite a few people were leaving their big cars at home and driving little cars.

During the recession there seemed to be just as many parties, the restaurants seemed to be just as crowded, and such luxury items as jewelry seemed to be in circulation as much as ever. I think some society people cut down on things that were not so obvious—not taking as many trips, for example. But on the whole I don't think people with great amounts of money were affected very much unless they had unusually large holdings in the stock market or were heavily invested in a troubled industry.

Incidentally, speaking of things that are off-limits, women who flash a lot of jewelry are considered a little gauche. It may be beautiful jewelry that looks right for the occasion, but sometimes you see too much on one woman. There are some women for whom jewelry is part of them; they love it. If they didn't have the money to buy jewels, they would be wearing dime-store diamonds, and wearing as many. There's no explaining to these women that they would look better if they took off a piece or two. They feel that since they have it, they're entitled to wear it.

I have no way of knowing if it's true, as the stories go, that Jackie Onassis spends $100,000 a year on her wardrobe. I know there are women here who spend $20,000 a year on clothes. That's fine, if they can afford it. But a clever woman needn't spend that much. There are society women who've bought very good designer clothes and have established a certain style of their own, and they don't have to change their clothes with the winds of fashion.

I don't envy millionaires. I cover society as an observer, as a reporter, and I am adequately paid for my work. I find that there are some millionaires who are happy. Others just happen to like being unhappy. I meet a lot of people with money who are unhappy in spite of everything they have. I find a lot of rich people who have enormous problems that I would not like to have, but who overcome them because they are happy spirits. They have personal problems, marital difficulties, or perhaps children who are incurably ill or were born deformed, or children who marry people they don't approve of and maybe drift away.

For these people, obviously, money hasn't solved all their problems. There are lots of things you can't buy with money. Yet Scott Fitzgerald was right when he said the rich are different from you and me. I find the biggest difference among those who have been raised in an overprotective atmosphere and are insulated from the real world. Money for them has become a cushion, and they are robbed of experiencing all the pleasures of a variegated world."

SUSAN HARTUNIAN

The daughter of a wealthy land developer, Susan wears a slim gold chain around her neck with the word "sexy" attached to it. She's a hazel-eyed blonde, somewhat shy, much given to giggling.

Susan is an eighteen-year-old debutante whose coming-out party is only a few months off. She lives in the San Fernando Valley. "I'm not a typical debutante," she says. "You ought to be talking to someone from Bel Air or Beverly Hills or San Marino (the richest per capita enclave in southern California)."

After being presented to society, she'll enter the University of Colorado, where "I plan to study everything because I haven't decided what I am going to do with my life."

I went to Westlake, an expensive private school in West Los Angeles. Shirley Temple Black went there, too. When she was there, you sort of had to be someone to get in. All of a sudden it is now based mostly on the scholastic and intellectual abilities of the girls—at least that's what they say. The headmaster told us he wanted a complete cross-section of girls from all parts of Los Angeles. He said that he hoped there would no longer be such a thing as the stereotyped Westlake girl—you know, the snob type of kid, the spoiled brat who has a nice car and everything.

Though it's not so prevalent, there are still a lot of girls like that who go to the school. It hasn't changed that much, and the parents don't realize what kind of children their daughters are.

The reason I'm a debutante, the reason I'm coming out, is mainly that it's traditional. My oldest sister was not presented, and she regretted it. She simply wasn't interested at the time.

Being a debutante used to be mainly a social thing. I don't know how it is in the East, but out here it's mostly connected with charity. I know that many, many years ago in the South, people just formed some type of organization and sponsored a ball for their daughters' coming out. It was just spending a lot of money to be presented.

The girls I know are supposed to earn the right to be presented. You are expected to work for the National Charity League, but most of the girls go through without doing any work. A lot of them try to fly through by doing as little as possible.

Some of the mothers plunk their daughters into the organization. Their mothers want them to come out. The girls don't care. They are not interested; they just go through the motions for their mothers. They say, I am just doing this for mother, so why should I work when I can get by without it? Working with crippled children really upsets some of the girls. And others just don't want to waste their time; they have better things to do. A few of the girls have their grandmothers make creative things for them, dolls and stuff, and they send them in and get credit. Then they go and work with the handicapped children one day a week or so and get the rest of their hours.

A few do work. In each of the last six years, I've devoted over a hundred hours to charity. I spent last summer at a camp for crippled children—you know, taking their braces off, helping them dress, helping them get into the water, teaching them to swim, playing with them—all different kinds of projects.

I don't think I'm selfish or spoiled, though I've never thought about it much. Until recently I honestly didn't know that it cost money for me to be in this thing. I rarely think about money.

Also, I don't think it's fair to call the other girls spoiled, because they aren't really doing it for themselves. It's not like saying, "Daddy, I want this, I want that, and, Daddy, I want my debut." They are doing it for their parents. That's not being spoiled.

There are only fifteen or sixteen girls in my group. I'm not sure why there are so few. Maybe there have always been that few, I don't know. But it is true that there just aren't that many girls making their debut anymore. A lot of them drop out along the line, too. They just get sick of doing the work.

The biggest adventure I've had was going to Nicaragua. It had nothing to do with being a debutante, but they gave me credit in hours for doing it.

One day in school a lady came and talked about Amigos de las Americas. It's a goodwill program between North and South America. I like to travel, so I just signed up. The training was once a week for three hours a night for six months. We had to study the language, we got some medical training, first aid, everything.

I arrived in this tiny village, San Pedro de Lovago, and I helped the only doctor in the area immunize the young and old against smallpox, polio and tetanus. Then we got on horses to go to the next town with our guides. A flood hit and the horses got mired down, so we had to struggle on foot through the mud. Because of the flood, we couldn't immunize as many as we'd hoped.

I was used to seeing poverty. I'd traveled before, to Europe, Guatemala, Mexico and Hawaii. I guess someone from here who didn't know and had never really seen how poor people live would maybe be shocked by it. Some people go down there and just can't believe it and they can't take it. At first, you do notice the poverty a lot, but after a few days it is just ordinary. You don't think anything of it. I didn't really notice it.

Most people say they are glad to get home from a place like Nicaragua. I didn't want to come home, because I'd got used to it, and the people were really nice. They do everything for you. They clean your room and your clothes, they make your food, they bring you flowers, they paint your fingernails. I hate nail polish—I never wear it at home—but I always had to have it on. Every time I'd finally get it off, another little girl would come and paint my nails again. When we left, they dressed up and gave us some real nice things, clothes and stuff.

A trip like that does make you realize how lucky you are. I want to do more traveling. I'll probably get married someday, and I definitely want to work. I don't want to settle down and marry and depend on my husband. I don't want to depend on anybody, ever. I want to have my own career and make my own money, and then if I marry, fine. But I want to have my own thing, too. I don't want my life to just be taking care of children.

It won't matter how much my husband earns—I never think about that. I'm going to get married for my emotional feelings. Money has no emotional feelings. Money is just paper.

I just don't care that much about money. Maybe it's because if I ever wanted money when I was little, I knew it would be there. But I never think about it now. I mean, money doesn't mean anything to me. Sometimes I'll be walking out the door of the house and all of a sudden I'll think, Gee, I need money to do something I want to do today. My father or mother gives it to me. Lots of times I just forget about it and walk out of the house without any money.

I don't get an allowance. If my dad thinks to give me money, then I just try to use what he gives me for a while, till he thinks to give me money again if I haven't asked him. Every once in a while he'll ask, "Do you need money?" and he just gives it to me. I don't like to ask for it, but he gets mad if I haven't asked for it.

I have no idea how much it has cost my parents for me to be a debutante. The main expense I think is for the gown and the party. The gowns run anywhere from $200 to $300 up to $700. I'd say the average is about $500, which is what my folks will probably spend. The evening of the ball my family will buy a table. That will cost about $800. The proceeds go to the crippled children.

I think I've earned the right to shine at the ball, but I don't think there really is such a thing as society. People are trying to get into something that isn't really there. They're trying to make themselves feel more important than others, trying to make themselves special or different or something better. But I don't think society is really there—do you know what I'm saying?

I never think of myself as being part of society, of that system. The only time I feel a part of it is when someone asks, "How much money do you have?" or "What kind of cars do you and your family drive?" When I say what kind of cars we drive, people just give you weird looks, and they must think something like, There goes a spoiled brat. But the kind of cars we drive doesn't mean anything to me. I have a Mercedes. Each of my three brothers has an expensive car—a Mercedes, a Ferrari and a Porsche. My sister has a Ford Granada and my mother drives a Merc station wagon. But my dad doesn't have a nice car; he has a Barracuda.

I think my father works too hard, and it seems to me his whole life is devoted to making money so that we can keep on having what we have. But we don't need all this stuff that he gives us. He wastes money on things we don't really need.

I don't think he should work so hard. He lives to give us things and likes to give us money so that we can have what we want. I don't think he should do that. For example, the cars. He doesn't have a nice car, but he makes sure that we have really nice cars. His car never runs, but just because he cares for us he gives us better cars than he has.

I think Dad should take care of himself. He doesn't take care of his health or anything, and I think that's really bad. I wish he would care more for himself and let us manage more on our own and not have us depend on him for so much. He just wants us to have everything. I don't think we should have everything. I don't want him to do that for us anymore. I don't like it.

HERNANDO COURTRIGHT

A houseboy ushers a visitor in through the double doors of the seventh-floor apartment of one of the world's best-known, most distinguished hoteliers.

Courtright, a diminutive, dapper man, believes in elegant living for his guests and himself. His crystal-chandeliered living room has one wall festooned with floor-to-ceiling mirrors. A pantry, a sun-drenched dining room, two bedrooms and a den-office complete the living quarters of the 75-year-old Beverly Wilshire Hotel proprietor whose Irish grandmother told him repeatedly in childhood: "The main thing in life is to go out and make money."

He took her advice. After college, he joined the Bank of America, *rising swiftly to a vice-presidency. In 1953, he headed a syndicate which bought and refurbished the Beverly Hills Hotel cum storied Polo Lounge. After selling it for a profit of $8 million, he became president of Century City, a $1 billion office building and apartment complex built on the backlot of Twentieth Century–Fox.*

In 1962, he bought the Beverly Wilshire, which has become, under Courtright's watchful eye, one of the world's finest hotels. The $40 million yellow-awninged carrara marble leviathan that bestrides Wilshire Boulevard is composed of two wings, separated by a private street (to discourage picketing of controversial guests). The top four floors are devoted to apartments.

Courtright warms quickly to his three favorite subjects—money, society and his hotel.

The original settlers of Los Angeles were not necessarily important people. A few of them came from families with background, but most were common soldiers, given so many acres of ground for their service to Spain and Mexico. The people who started Los Angeles were similar to those who settled San Francisco. Almost all the money in San Francisco came from Irish miners who hit there in '49, went up into the hills, struck it rich, came back down and built society.

In the four hundred years since Los Angeles was discovered, the network of those first families has become weakened considerably by the influx of others. The families have married outside society, married people who weren't always rich. Modern southern California was primarily settled by middle-westerners from Iowa, Kansas and Ohio. And so there has been a great dilution of the original families, though I think those original families, whose descendants compose a sort of underground society—you never see their names in the newspapers—still have quite a bit of stature and quite an aura around them.

Of course, society has always been kind of a reflection of money. A man like Vanderbilt or Rockefeller, those people in the last century, where they originated from I don't know. They were robber barons who became very important people; they were businessmen who came from ordinary backgrounds and made a lot of money. And having a lot of money made them very important.

Society starts with your father or your grandfather or your

great-grandfather, or you can go six to eight generations back. It doesn't start with *you*. European society developed much the same as society here. They were a bunch of brigands to start with, and they became the duke of this and the count of that because they were strong and created a domain of their own.

I respect European royalty, because the nobility has been over there now eight or ten or fifteen generations. And during that period it has been nurtured by good education, position, and all the other benefits of money. Most of them sort of show it. Not all of them, but most. We get quite a few here. The majority of them are booked in like anyone else, and act like anyone else. But I think that eight to fifteen generations of power creates certain things in people—taste, elegance, sophistication.

Having money doesn't automatically mean you appreciate elegance. Elegance is the epitome of good taste, and good taste is a matter of aesthetics. I think that's something you have to learn by experience, by observation, with the help of your family and your teachers. Having money helps, of course, because if you go down and buy a suit or a dress, you are more apt to come away with something that fits pretty well than if you didn't have money.

Generally speaking, people with money aren't apt to be as big tippers as people who are on the make. Very often wealthy people are simply tight. A lot of people who do very well still have their first quarter. I see nothing wrong with it. Whether that makes them wealthy or not, I don't know. Some people are spenders and some are not. Some people are givers and some are takers, so far as money and everything else in life is concerned.

I grew up on a ranch in the foothills outside Coeur d'Alene, Idaho. We had a little circular sawmill, cattle and horses. My father was a cavalry officer in the Army. His parents were well off, his mother particularly. But his father was a lawyer who went through most of my grandmother's money. Ours wasn't much of a ranch, but when I was growing up we were never in want. The ranch didn't make any money to speak of, but we had four or five cowpunchers and a Chinese cook. Everyone had a Chinese cook in those days—that was before Hearst got his yellow-peril thing going.

I never forgot the advice my grandmother gave me, so when I

graduated from college I went to work for A. P. Giannini at the Bank of America, which got me into the hotel business. When the Beverly Hills Hotel became moribund and the mortgage payments were flagging, it became a pink-stucco elephant. The bank put me in charge of it, and I tried, unsuccessfully, to find a buyer. So I had to run it. Among the backers I brought in were Irene Dunne, Loretta Young, and Loretta's husband (then), Tom Lewis. I spruced the place up and created the Polo Lounge, and we were then able to sell it at a substantial profit.

Even though I became involved in Century City, I never lost interest in the hotel business. The Beverly Wilshire was in trouble, too, and I bought it with the idea of turning the goddamned thing around. I think that's happened.

It has become *the* hotel for society. The reason in part is its central location in Beverly Hills, the hot part of town, so far as commercial real estate is concerned. Also, we try to operate it as a European-style hotel, with a little more finesse than commercial hotels like the Century Plaza and the Beverly Hilton, which are, as you know, convention hotels. We don't take conventions.

The socially prominent, diplomats, heads of government all come here. During the bicentennial, we had everyone from King Hussein to the Emperor of Japan, and three or four Scandinavian monarchs. Some of it just happened, and some of it we promoted through the State Department.

Our style of operation is a social style of operation. We are geared to give special, personalized service. For Hirohito, the soup was served as he wanted it, tepid. His chicken was deboned, and even his grapes were individually peeled. The King of Tonga, who weighs four hundred pounds, sent out a late-night call for thirty hamburgers. Though the kitchen was formally closed, we supplied them. When Queen Margrethe of Denmark arrived, we flooded the hotel with daisies, her favorite flower.

The Beverly Wilshire is a refuge for society. Many social functions are held here, but there is a distinction between society and social functions. Not all the people who attend social functions are members of society.

Society has been sort of played down in the last ten or fifteen years by newspapers and magazines. One reason, I think, is that society was always being discussed by columnists who were repetitious. The same names—a relatively narrow group—kept coming up all the time, and you got sick of it after a while. Also, society often became a matter of notoriety. People who were merely famous or scandalous began to be identified as members of society. That's why there is so little real society remaining in this country—or the world, for that matter.

I know princes and princesses who don't use their titles. They call themselves Mr. and Mrs., just like anybody else. Why? Because in this day and age of anti-elegance, they think titles sound pretentious. Perhaps, too, they're a little ashamed of being a prince or princess. Also, if you use a title, the price of everything goes up three- or fourfold—not here of course, but at other places.

Titled people are also afraid of kidnapping, even in this country. I'm not sure all of them could pay, say, a $1 million ransom. And you really don't score any extra points anymore for being titled, except maybe in the society columns and among a small group of people who are impressed with a title, people whose idea of royalty comes from the movies. But all those who carry a royal title aren't necessarily rich and charming. Sometimes they're rich and not charming. Sometimes they're charming and not rich. Sometimes they are neither.

Royalty's not using their titles is another small nail in the coffin of society. I don't think we're ever going to get to the place where we'll see a resurgence of society, see people respected solely because they were accidentally born rich and with a name that's several hundred years old.

This is the age of the common man, isn't it? And for the most part that's a good thing. We still have a tradition and an atmosphere in this country where being born poor isn't necessarily a handicap to wealth. My life is an illustration of that. If I had been born in Europe in the Middle Ages, I certainly wouldn't have risen to the position of owning a hotel.

Yet, through it all, there is still what I like to call "a silent society." It doesn't throw money around, doesn't flaunt money, and doesn't discuss money under any circumstances. These survivors—this silent society—number perhaps a few thousand. Their life-style is the quintessence of understatement. They are the quietly rich, and their names seldom if ever appear in the newspapers. They are secure within themselves; they know they have enough money to travel as they wish, live as they wish, do anything they want. They don't have to work. They don't even have to have their names associated with a fashionable charity. They are not publicity seekers, not even indirectly. Money, of course, gives them that power. Money gives them the freedom to be royally independent. Money gives them freedom to do any damn thing they please.

I don't envy such people; I think life is empty without work. I've worked very hard all my life, and I don't regret it. I still work, though it's been suggested that I retire. If I retired, I could live in luxury and comfort to the end of my life. But that would be an empty life for me.

Past and present, I've taken a deep interest in this hotel. Years ago we projected our thinking here to the kind of expensive things that we thought people would want. And we were right: our most expensive rooms have turned out to be our most highly occupied rooms.

The profit on our apartments is figured on a square-foot basis, a dollar and a half or a dollar sixty per square foot. We have some that go for $300 a day, a couple that are priced at $500 a day. The cost usually depends on how many bedrooms you hook onto the suite.

What happens to this hotel if there's a depression? It all depends on the type of depression. There are different types. Sometimes a depression affects the middle class, sometimes the lower class; at the same time, it may not affect the upper class. That was the situation in this country a few years ago when we had a recession. Strangely enough, that recession didn't hit people with money. We found that the upper class still had money to spend.

If there's a general recession or a deep depression, naturally everyone suffers. Fewer Cadillacs are sold. Fewer expensive clothes are sold. Fewer jewels are sold. People can't afford to pay those prices.

But I'm doubtful that we'll ever see the kind of depression we saw in the thirties. There's too much welfare, too many government handouts. And the labor unions have the economy by the throat. They'll use all their influence and power to keep a depression from happening.

CAROLINE LEONETTI AHMANSON

One of the world's richest women is the widow of Howard Ahmanson, California's first billionaire. Ahmanson, who died in 1968 of a heart attack at the age of sixty-one, made his fortune in insurance and banking and as the owner of Home Savings and Loan, the largest such institution in the nation, with assets of more than $8 billion.

Born in San Francisco, Mrs. Ahmanson is poised, elegant, slender, brown-eyed. She is an indefatigable businesswoman and philanthropist whose commercial and cultural affiliations cover two single-spaced typewritten pages.

Among her involvements: board of directors, Walt Disney Productions; the only female director of the Federal Reserve Bank of San Francisco; and president of Caroline Leonetti, Ltd., a women's center for self-improvement. Former President Nixon appointed her to the National Council on the Humanities and the Peace Corps National Advisory Council. She's a member of the board of trustees of the Los Angeles County Museum of Art and the Los Angeles Music Center. Ronald Reagan, while governor, named her to the California Arts Commission.

Her personal staff includes two full-time secretaries and a butler who serves coffee to a visitor in a commodious sienna-brown apartment in an exclusive section of Los Angeles.

The West has a whole different vision of society compared to the East. Here, it's not just your name that gets you into society, because names are still being built in California. We don't have bluebloods, a social four hundred, as such. A name or just having money means less in society here than in a place like Palm Beach. More than in any other area, society in California is a meritocracy. If you go to any so-called society party, which now usually involves some kind of charity, you will find people there who might not necessarily have a famous name, but who have money earned through talent. They are achievers.

That label "society" is so passé. It has no meaning for me. My own interests straddle so many areas in the local and world communities that I never think of myself as a member of society. That's too confining a term.

It's not important to me to be mentioned in the society pages of the newspapers. I'm flattered whenever it's noted that I attended some function or party, but I really couldn't care less. Years ago, from a business point of view, perhaps it was important in a way, because it was a form of advertisement. But I no longer need that kind of advertisement. Given a choice, I would rather hire someone to keep my name out of the paper than to get it in. That's what Howard Hughes did, but the people he hired hardly did much of a job. I don't object to publicity, but I don't do the things I do because of publicity.

I didn't come from a wealthy family. I came from an Italian family that had a cultural heritage. Both my father and my mother were born in Italy but were brought to the United States when they were babies. They always had an interest in the performing and visual arts. They weren't rich, though they became very comfortable in time with a great deal of hard work. My father was in the garment business, but he never had wealth as we count wealth today.

Thrift was a habit inculcated in me during childhood. But it was a special kind of thrift. I was taught, for example, never to buy anything that was second-best. It was better, I learned, to have one ensemble made of good fabric rather than to have a number made of inferior fabrics. Although thrift was always important, it didn't pertain if money was going to be spent on, say, opera tickets. It was a matter of saving up for the better things in life.

I vividly remember my first bank account as a six-year-old girl. It was with the Bank of Italy, before it became the Bank of America. Every Friday I deposited the ten cents my mother had put in my hanky and pinned on my dress. The dime wasn't part of my allowance; it was considered part of my education in learning how to be thrifty and learning the importance of saving money.

That habit of thrift remains with me today. As a matter of fact, my husband, who didn't come from an extremely wealthy background either, was a man who watched his spending, too. He could spend a tremendous amount of money on certain things, but he was very careful when it came to what he considered unnecessary expenditures. He didn't buy things merely to buy things.

I started my self-improvement school out of personal necessity. In junior high I began to gain weight, and I began to have personal self-doubt problems about my physical self, never from the mental point of view. I was tall for my age. I had grown to my full height, five feet six inches, which isn't tall now but at that time was considered very tall. So I became very self-conscious. The fact that I was taller than all of the girls and taller than most of the boys in my class triggered a complex in me. I was afraid to stand up in class and speak aloud. And I began to suffer a little bit of a speech impediment, particularly if I had to read aloud. I would hesitate and almost stutter.

My mother, who was a typical Titian-style Italian beauty, very petite, with lovely red hair and green eyes, realized this was a growing problem, and she encouraged me to do something about my physical self. At that time there was no one place you could go to work on your figure and your makeup and your style and your clothes to give you self-confidence. This was before the birth of the so-called charm schools. So I had to learn to do all those things by myself.

By the time I reached high school, I was studying nutrition. I began to study fashion and the rest of it. As I achieved for myself, finding which were the best makeup and clothes for me, other people began asking me how to do the same thing for them. At the University of California at Berkeley, in order to have extra money, I worked at a department store. I became their campus representative, which was the greatest training imaginable for self-confidence as well as a marvelous introduction to the business world. Then I won a scholarship to the California School of Design, and before I realized it I was doing commercial work while I was still in school. It was very exciting to me.

I then started my self-improvement school at the age of twenty-two. It's still there on Sunset Boulevard, and being run very capably by my daughter Margo. Over the years it became quite successful, though there were many occasions when I had to worry about making the mortgage payment and meeting my payroll on the first and the fifteenth of the month.

By the time I met my husband I was very comfortable, financially speaking. I owned several properties, and the school continued to earn money. I met Mr. Ahmanson through personal friends who suggested that there might be something that both of us might appreciate by getting to know each other. We were actually married for three and a half years, and had known each other for about three years before that.

The assumption is that when a woman meets a wealthy man, she is attracted primarily if not solely by his money. But I had been divorced for seventeen years and never intended to remarry. I had raised my daughter and educated her well, and I had a flourishing business. I had a life of my own choosing. I could take time off when I wished, and I traveled a great deal. I had a position in the community which I enjoyed. I felt that my life was as I wanted it.

So meeting Mr. Ahmanson at that point in life was right for me. It was one of those happy things that were right for both of us. Naturally, I was impressed by his enormous wealth and success—who wouldn't be?—but I was financially independent, and I married him because he was a remarkable man.

Obviously, he was a financial genius. He was an extremely complicated human being, but he was still very simple. He loved family life; he loved simple things and took great joy from them. Although he did not have much formal training in music, he could play any instrument. He could just pick it up and play it and enjoy it tremendously. He took a great interest in the performing arts. And he read a great deal, often all through the night, because he was an insomniac.

He wasn't after money per se. It was just that the things he did happened to make a great deal of money. He did everything with intensity. He had a great drive for perfection, in business and at play. He used to wake up every morning and say that somehow he was going to try to better the world that day. So his goal wasn't just money.

He always said he loved champs—he didn't care what they did. If the man was a barber, he had to be the best barber in the world. He respected anyone in any position provided that person did his best at whatever he was doing. His highest compliment was to call a person a champ. He was also very competitive. For instance, he loved to sail boats, and he always had to win. As a matter of fact, he usually did. After he won in one boat, he would rent the sister boat in the race and win again, to show that it wasn't just the boat, it was the skipper. And businesswise, of course, he was extremely competitive, and that was the reason he was so successful.

Even in school he was way ahead of himself. He carried on his father's insurance business and formed his own company while he was still working his way through college. He had literally become a millionaire by the time he was twenty-one.

He sold a great deal of insurance to savings and loan institutions, which is how he actually got into that business. He'd encouraged other people to buy Home, but no one seemed interested. So he bought it himself. It was his great vision in everything he did that also helped make him successful.

He was concerned about serving more people. The savings and loan company to him was a way of allowing more people to own homes. In insurance, he made the rates less expensive so more people could afford to buy policies. All of his financial success was working with what he called the little people, trying to get them into private homes and insurance and into the habit of saving.

Before his death, he saw the fulfillment of the Music Center. He contributed a great deal of money for its building, and they named one of the theaters for him. He donated over $2 million to the Los Angeles County Museum of Art and contributed heavily to the building fund of USC, where he was a trustee. So he had given a great deal of his wealth back to the community.

I always point him out as the absolute ideal capitalist when I talk to my foreign friends, particularly those from Communist countries. I tell them that we have wonderful men and women in the United States who've become very successful through hard work. Mr. Ahmanson was a perfect example of someone who came from a small community in the Middle West and worked very hard to develop his tremendous empire through his genius and vision. But then he wanted to give back to the community, and he did.

His philosophy meshed with mine. Even when I was struggling with the school, I was trying to give back. At that time it wasn't money, because I didn't have that much extra to give, although I gave whatever I could afford. But I gave my time and whatever abilities I had. I started a charm clinic on the east side of town, and I worked in a number of schools there that weren't as privileged as those on the west side.

One of the things that money has allowed me to do is become a director of Walt Disney Productions. I attend the board meetings and the annual stockholders' meetings, which offers me a wonderful opportunity to meet the people who've invested in the company. Almost half of them are children whose parents have bought stock for them in Disney. It's all very exciting. I kind of act as an ambassador-at-large for Disney, because to me the Disney films and Disneyland and Disney World spell Americana. When I entertain international guests—for instance, the minister of culture of the Soviet Union or the ambassador from the People's Republic of China—the first thing they say they want to do is go to Disneyland. And so Disneyland has become a very interesting way for me to show off America. I feel the same way about the Disney films, because I am very family-oriented and very oriented to children. I love what the Disney people do in their films. Thus, my participation in the company is not only from a business point of view, but also from a community point of view.

Two years ago I was appointed to the Federal Reserve Bank in San Francisco, which is the money manager and financial headquarters for the twelve western states, with $19.5 billion in assets. I am very vocal. When they put me on a board, they know they will hear from me. The Federal Reserve system actually balances the economy of our country. Even many businessmen don't understand the Fed and how important it is. It prints the money and mints the coins autonomously and yet in connection with the Treasury Department. What causes our inflation problem is that Congress overspends, which forces the Fed to print more and more money, and that gets us into deeper and deeper deficits.

There are seven of us on the board, including three bankers, one of whom represents the large banks, one who represents the medium-size banks, and one representing small banks. I represent business, and my job is to supply information about what is happening in the Los Angeles economy, whether it's the price of real estate or the price of food in the supermarkets.

Though I take pleasure in travel, most of my traveling these days isn't for enjoyment. When I traveled with Mr. Ahmanson it was just more of a vacation and an interest in seeing other places. But now my interest is to help transcend the boundaries of nationalism and open a line of communication with people. That's why I went to China twice, in 1973 and 1975.

I saw the same thing in China that I saw in the Soviet Union, Egypt and Israel. For the most part I talked with women, and wherever they're from they all have the same desires. They all want peace; they want their families to have enough food, to have meaningful work, a decent place to live, and a chance to enjoy some of the cultural things, the fine things, in life.

As I looked around in China, I found that they are trying to accomplish these things. Their very first line of priority, of course, has been to feed everybody. So there is a great effort made to raise enough rice and wheat. They are trying to educate their people. I was amazed to see how clean the place was. They are working at improving health services for people, though they still don't have enough doctors.

I was very impressed with what I saw. Now, mind you, I agree entirely with the Shanghai Communique, which said both of our countries recognize that we have different forms of government, different economic philosophies, but that neither of us would impose its will on the other, that we would respect each other as people and would try to improve our cultural exchange. It was in that spirit that I visited China.

How does it feel to be very, very rich? I don't know, because it was a matter of growing into it, not becoming overnight rich. I grew up in the Depression years, but I was never aware of the Depression. I was never aware of it because my father was always in business for himself and so he was never out of a job. Maybe he had difficulties with his business, but I never knew it. There was never any question about food; there was never any question about clothes. So I never really knew anything other than having good food, good clothes; having the opportunity to do the things I wanted to do, to have the education I wanted. Although if I wanted extra money I worked for it, and was happy to do it.

Before I became Mrs. Howard Ahmanson I had overcome those worries about the first and the fifteenth of the month. The early years were a struggle, but I'd made it. I had achieved that part of my life. But obviously I wasn't in the financial condition that I find myself in now. However, I can only wear one dress at a time, and I don't dress any differently now than I did before I married Mr. Ahmanson. Certainly it's more comfortable to be able to spend more money when you want to. It gives you a feeling of liberation. The only worries you have are your own family's health.

I have a very strong philosophy about how money should be used. I feel sorry for people who just spend their lives accumulating money for no other purpose than to accumulate mounds of bankbooks and greenbacks.

The only important thing about money is what money can do. If your directions and values are good, the money is used in positive and effective ways. It is used to improve the cultural life of the community, to improve education, as Mr. Ahmanson used his money.

The highest value of money is to utilize it for improving the quality of all our lives and giving it back through contributions to charity and worthwhile causes to those who were responsible for your receiving the money in the first place. It's a matter of *noblesse oblige.*

Ghettos

*The brothers here that would kill you for a
quarter are decent human beings.*

—STUART BAYLESS

STUART BAYLESS

A $125-a-week mechanic's helper, he wears an Afro, a beard and dark sunglasses even when he's indoors. The garage where he works is located in the heart of Watts, abutting the still-existing ruins of the 1965 six-day riot which left thirty-four dead and 1,032 injured and caused $40 million in property damage.

I was twenty-two years old when the revolt came in the black community. It was caused by racism, by economic exploitation, discrimination in education and housing, and unemployment. We were—and are—living in a place where there's high prices for all goods and services. We pay more for food, shelter and clothing than anybody else. We are screwed on the price of everything that's necessary for survival.

My participation in the rebellion was direct. Yeah, I threw a few Molotov cocktails at stores owned by whites. I was damn careful not to hurt a business owned by a brother.

The revolt broke out because the whites fuck your mind, body, soul and spirit. They rule you from the womb to the tomb. And it's not any better now than it was in 1965.

The Watts rebellion started in the neighborhood where I grew up, at 116th and Avalon. I saw the first pictures of it on the news that night. I recognized some of the people that were on television, because they were friends and relatives and family and people from my own neighborhood. That's what got me involved. I was mad. I went out into the street that night and things were hopping in my mind. My whole life turned around, my whole direction; my energy started flowing on a different course. But first I had to throw the Molotov cocktails some of the brothers gave me. It felt damn good.

In the rebellion there was a togetherness, a unity among our people, a single purpose. And that purpose was to overturn the economic and social exploitation of black people.

Was the rebellion worth the lives of thirty-four people? Absolutely. Everybody knows that freedom isn't free.

The rebellion was a big economic uprising. In other words, we were saying, We're not going to take this shit anymore. We don't want to be charged double for everything. We are sick of all the liquor stores owned by rich white men. It was saying, If I can't afford to buy a color television set, I'm damn well going to take one.

What I earn is not what I need. It's barely enough to live off. I was born and raised in this Watts ghetto and I'm what I'm supposed to be, a loser. I'm not far from the back end of some truck emptying garbage cans. My probation officer tells me I'm a loser. I'm on probation for smoking some marijuana—would you believe it? Also, a little scuffle I got into—you know what I mean. I live in a tough neighborhood.

What is my philosophy of money? It's in the Bible, in Ecclesiastes 10:19: "A feast is made for laughter, and wine maketh merry: but money answereth all things."

Money answers all things, all right, but how much you have depends on what you want to do to get it. Most of the brothers in the ghetto do whatever they can to get money. Life's a struggle here. Life's a struggle in black communities all over America. It's really rough here; you have no idea. We've been saying that a long, long time, but nobody pays any attention.

The whole thing is about making it. White people up there making $40,000, $50,000 or $60,000 a year. They got everything under the sun, all they could possibly want materially. What the fuck are they complaining about? Why don't they get their shit together and start helping people here who haven't got a damn thing? Why don't they give some of their bread to the ghetto? If they don't, we're going to have to go back to primitivism, where the strongest rule and the strongest survive.

It's serious what's going on here. People selling drugs and everything else that will make a dollar. It's real serious out there in the streets.

Drugs are running wild in this community. I know what I'm talking about. People are taking drugs to forget about the rent, to forget that their babies need some shoes and food. They are taking Valiums and red devils and smoking angel dust like there's no tomorrow. Just so they can forget about the money they don't have for the things they can't afford. And the kind of life-style they can't have for themselves and their children. They are out there just waiting for death to come along, death or old age or the county check, whichever comes first.

Everybody's trying to get out the best way they know. Some go to school to get an education to become a minister or whatever works. Just to get away from this, because this is hell on earth, and behind it all is the dollar. People breaking into their own mothers' homes, robbing their aunts, their grandmothers—that's what's going on. Look at the bars on people's windows all over the place. Everybody scared to walk the streets. People in Watts are robbing each other, and what are they getting? I mean, how the hell are you going to get anything from another poor person? What are you getting even if you take a goddamn Social Security or welfare check? Two or three fucking hundred dollars.

You got brothers out in these streets, sixteen and seventeen years old, don't more care a fuck if they take my life or your life. They'd take your fucking life because you didn't have 25 cents for a bottle of wine or 50 cents for a pack of cigarettes. I mean you ought to have had it.

I don't want you to misunderstand what I'm saying. The brothers here that would kill you for a quarter are decent human beings. They rob and kill because of necessity and anger. Even Jesus had a little righteous anger once in a while. Goddamn it, I would kill you for a quarter if I really needed your quarter. Don't feel too bad about dying for a quarter, people have died for less.

Life is hell without money; it's a damn struggle, a real downer. If you want to know what it's really like, why don't you spend three days down here? Don't bring any money. Don't bring one dime. No credit cards. They don't take credit cards in the ghetto. Get a feel of what it's all about. Feel what it's like to be in a struggle. Feel what it's like not to have any money. Maybe in three days you'll get hungry enough to steal or kill.

This is a white man's country, and it's a proven fact that it's easier for a white man than a black man to make money. The opportunities in the United States of America are painted white. There's a sign out there that says, No Blacks Need Apply.

I used to book horses, I used to sell drugs to make a buck. I could do it again. But that's not where I'm at right now. Sometimes I think I ought to sell drugs again, sell women again, book horses, do whatever I have to do to make more money. I made about $200 to $250 a week selling drugs. I was just dealing grass, no hard stuff. If you work real hard at it, you can make $300 to $500 a week selling grass.

The pimps don't make as much money in Watts as the drug dealers. The dealers have the silk and mohair suits, those flashing diamonds and gold, and they are the ones driving the big cars. Push cocaine: that's the way to make it big in this ghetto.

I went through all that, and I don't want that trip anymore. I mean, after 1965 I had a whole different view of life. I'm not ashamed of what I did pre-1965. It's just that since then I've become more aware. I have three children of my own and I don't want them to go the way their father did. But there are lots of brothers today who are where I was fifteen or eighteen years ago. I was exposed to a brother who lived next door to me who came home one day with a white woman and a big Cadillac. He didn't get those things being a brain surgeon. You know what I mean.

I have all kinds of brothers who do all kinds of things. I know brothers who are motivation specialists, job counselors, and drug dealers and pimps. I go to a party and I meet all of them, and it's always the same. First thing you hear a brother saying is, "Got anything?" or "Want to go do one?" That means, Do you want to get high on dust? or whatever they have in their pocket. Socially, that's the whole bit.

Most people in the ghetto are caught in a Peter-to-Paul situation. That's the one constant, how to put off the bill collectors. Once you get paid, you have to figure which bill you didn't pay last week or last month; who is breathing hardest on you. And that's the bill you pay. But I think it's a basic law among my people to pay off their indebtedness. White America doesn't have a monopoly on high morals and high standards. Those standards are universal.

The reason you find so many black women supporting households in the ghetto is because there are more black women than black men. We lost too many brothers in Vietnam and America's other wars. As a result, the women are burdened with the responsibilities of money. It's also a fact that black women outlive their men, like white women outlive white men.

Even if I had the chance, I wouldn't live in Beverly Hills. Sure, I live in the midst of all this horror, with drugs and robbery and murder. Sammy Davis, Jr. seems to have adjusted okay to Beverly Hills, but I would be lost there. I wouldn't know what to do in that world or how to act. I would probably come back here every day.

We are a wealthy community in terms of our potential. We are black gold. We are talented, dedicated, energetic, forceful. The bottom line is that we as black people are as human as any other people on the planet earth. We are just as creative, committed, law-abiding and virtuous as anybody else. And we could come into our own if we had more money.

In Watts, everybody talks about money all the time, every day. "If I had it" . . . "I need it" . . . "I want it" . . . "I am going to get it" . . . "I need this" . . . "I need that" . . . "I have got to get some money." It's a constant, it's there all the time. It's that way for me, too. I got some things I've got to do. I have kids that I have to take care of as well as myself. I've got lots of needs.

Money is one of the natural resources of man that's necessary for basic survival. It's just that simple. Money is like the sun and the air and the trees. I don't know why it got that way. One day there won't be any money. One day it will all be credit cards, and then after that everybody will have what they want. Money will just be issued out to you. That day has got to come or we're going to have the damnedest revolution this country ever saw. It'll make Watts '65 look like a fish fry.

Most people in Watts make $3,000 to $5,000 a year. That's the economics of America. That's the way the pie is cut up. But with $3,000 to $5,000 a year, too many of us in the ghetto are dying a slow death. And we want to stop dying.

Take me, for example. I'm close to dying. Right now I have $32 in the bank. If I miss a paycheck or lose my job, what do you think I'm going to do? I'm going to kill you for that quarter we were talking about.

ROBERTO SUAREZ

The East Los Angeles barrio is 128 years old, and looks it.

California became part of Mexico in 1822, after Mexico won its independence from Spain. The United States went to war with Mexico in 1846. Two years later the Mexicans were defeated and surrendered their claim to California, which became a state in 1850.

In Los Angeles, the dominant Mexican population was shunted into a corner of the city that hasn't changed much in more than a century. The once high-living grandees lost their ranchos and became dirt-poor. Pio Pico, a large landowner before the war, ended as a tamale peddler.

Defeat still hangs in the air in the barrio, which is plagued by drugs, alcohol, poverty, and the highest per capita crime rate in Los Angeles. The buildings are small, worn, neglected monuments to yesterday, with flaking stucco and a jungle of graffiti. Young children urinate on the sidewalks. Black-and-white police cars seemingly are everywhere, though the officers allow the prostitutes to ply their trade unmolested.

Sandwiched into the legal population of the barrio, which is about one million, are an estimated 50,000 illegal aliens. Suarez (not his real name) is one of them.

A short, dark, wiry and shy man, he lives in a $55-a-month hotel room. He works as a busboy, putting in forty-eight hours a week, for which he earns $115.20. His day off is Monday. On Mondays he works as a loader at a warehouse for $2.40 an hour.

There was no chance for me in Mexico, or for my wife and seven children. Now, since I came to the States six years ago, things are better. I send $200 a month home practically every month. In Mexico, that is much money.

I have not seen my family in six years, since I came here. I have been without a woman for six years. A woman costs money, and I have no money to spend for such things.

Except for the money, life in Mexico is better than in the States. There we do not have so much trouble, so much killing. In the alley across the street last month, some Chicanos spilled gasoline on a man. They asked him for his money. When he said no, they threw a match at him. The man burned to death. There was nobody to help him. I would have helped him, but I didn't hear about it until later. In the pockets of the man who burned to death the police found $14. In Mexico, I have never heard of such a thing, setting fire to a man for money.

There is much in this barrio that is terrible. The men drink too much, and some of them sell their wives as whores to make money so they can drink more and maybe eat a little. The young people cannot find work. So they drink also and take drugs. They kill each other for a little bit of drugs.

Always I live in fear here. Every day and every night for six years I have been afraid. If the police catch me, I must go back to Mazatlan. There is no work there, so how will I support my family? What would I do?

The police come to the barrio sometimes and take people away. They must go back to Mexico. So far I have not been caught, but I fear being caught. Why should the rich Americans want to send me back across the border? I hurt no one. We have fifteen busboys at the restaurant. All are from Mexico. The Americans do not wish to be busboys. For us, it is good work. The money we make does much good; it saves our lives and the lives of our families. What is money for, if it is not for saving lives, for the buying of a little food, a little clothing and a little shelter? America does not miss the money I earn.

For three years I saved money to come to the States. The coyote who smuggles you across the border costs much money. He charged me $200. When I was in Tijuana, just across the border from California, I stayed overnight with fifteen or twenty others in a small barn. Those people had paid the coyote much money, too. One of the people, a girl no more than fifteen years old, was raped by the coyote. We all watched, but we were afraid to do anything.

As I crossed into California, I was hit on the head with a rock. When I woke up, all my money was gone . . . $40. Maybe it was a miracle that I wasn't killed. Maybe it was a miracle that whoever robbed me left me my shoes. I had to come to Los Angeles on foot. It took me a day and a half.

I came to the barrio hungry and without money. I found a man I knew from Mazatlan, and he introduced me to a man who got me the job in the restaurant as a busboy. For finding me this job, I had to pay the man $250 from my wages. But I didn't mind too much. It is a good job; it is good work in the restaurant. It allows me to survive and allows my family at home to survive.

I receive my meals free, and I take home the extra bread and other food from the tables for people in this hotel. I have been told that I could sell the food because people in this place are so hungry. But I would not do that. One man that I feed some scraps whenever I can is seventy-five years old. He is too old to work and he has nothing. No one cares for him, so I feed him.

Because I am not a citizen here in the States, I can do very little. When I am not working, I stay in my room all the time. I stay in my room so I won't attract attention, and because going out of my room means I have to spend money.

I have a little television set. I watch much television, and it's good because it helps me learn English. I have no telephone. I have three pair of shoes. I have no suit, only two pair of pants and four shirts. I live on $125 a month. How? It is easy when you do nothing but work and stay in the room.

From my pay at the restaurant, there is money taken away for taxes and Social Security. Sometimes that makes me think I am a citizen. Sometimes I dream I am an American citizen. That is my greatest wish. That and having my wife and children come to the States. I think maybe I will go to a man who says he can make me and my family citizens in the States. He says it will cost $1,000.*

Here in America things are strange. Your poor people are rich; the poor are very rich when you compare them with the poor in Mexico. When you have no money in America, the government sends you money. In Mexico, the government does not send you money when you don't have any. Even the garbage is rich in America. Once I found a good shirt in a garbage can.

In the restaurant, I see the rich people of America leave much food on their plates. They ask for a bag for the meat they do not finish. The dogs eat better here than many people in Mexico.

On television I see the rich houses that Americans have. I too wish for a house—not a large, rich house, but enough room for

*The man apparently is a self-styled illegal "immigration consultant." A number of them operate in the barrio. But police and immigration authorities are cracking down. One of them was sentenced to state prison for one to ten years for taking money from illegal aliens under the pretense that he could legalize their status.

myself and my family. But I don't think it is possible for a busboy.

I would like to go to school here and learn more. I would like to better myself. Someday I would like to open my own little restaurant. But I fear going to school. There will be papers and questions.

I write to my children that they should study hard and learn to read and write well. That way perhaps they will earn money and not be as poor as their father.

I think that if there was no America I would have starved to death years ago. Starved to death or become a criminal. I think that it is very necessary that rich people care a little bit for poor people. I think that in America you do care for poor people. I like America very much. If I had my family here and we were all citizens, I would like America 100 percent.

FRED GABOURIE

Gabourie is a Seneca Indian and a Los Angeles municipal court judge whose salary is $43,000 a year. The phone call from Governor Edmund G. Brown, Jr., offering him the appointment couldn't have been more of a surprise. "I was amazed," he says. "I nearly fell off my chair."

Perhaps the most astonishing thing about his elevation to the bench—so far as he knows, he's the only Indian in the country serving as a judge—is that he didn't become a lawyer until he was forty-one years old. Assuming judicial robes has entailed a cut in income—he earned upwards of $60,000 a year as a lawyer in private practice.

Gabourie, a youngish-looking fifty-six, with strong brown eyes and jet-black hair, helped mediate the terms that concluded the seventy-two-day occupation of Wounded Knee, South Dakota in 1973 by militants of the American Indian Movement (AIM).

After attending grammar school at the Six Nations reservation in Ontario, Canada, he moved with his parents to Los Angeles, which today has the largest concentration of Indians in the nation, between 60,000 and 75,000.

My father was a full-blooded Seneca. My mother was French, German and part Indian. We lived in Hollywood for a while, way up in the mountains.

My father worked for the movie studios as a stunt man. He did pictures with Buster Keaton and Roy Rogers. When stunting was slack, he did construction work and made sort of a haphazard living. We had a few fairly good years, but a lot of thin ones. There were occasions when we didn't have all the food we wanted. I had a gun from the time I was six years old, and I'd go out and hunt rabbits, deer, quail. I used to go down to the beach and fish a lot, too. We had a little house, and my mother raised a lot of vegetables. We rented that place for a few dollars a month. How times change. Now I have a house I built myself for $10,000. On today's market it's worth $80,000.

My family moved around a great deal; we also lived in Venice and all over Los Angeles. One house was a little old cabin near Santa Monica and Western with a two-holer.* We even had to pump our own water.

Hell, when I was a kid, if you wanted a skateboard, you made it yourself. And we didn't have supervised recreation; we played on the nearest vacant lot.

No matter where we lived, we weren't accepted in the community, except, of course, by other Indian families. Whites never bothered with us and we never bothered with them. The Indian families in the neighborhood sort of stuck together. In that sense, I was brought up in a ghetto. But it hasn't changed much. Most of the Indians who live in Los Angeles cluster together in small or large groups. They do have a strong tendency to ghettoize themselves.

My father never told me to be a lawyer. When I was a kid, I was a bum. I'd work to get money occasionally, pulling weeds, cleaning swimming pools, and then as a grip for MGM. I bounced around all the studios and got into carpentry, then special effects. For a while I worked as a stunt man. A lot of times I just took off and hitchhiked around the country. I bummed my way cross country six times.

By the time I had started to study law, my father was dead. I went to the Southwestern School of Law in Los Angeles and graduated in 1963. I had started to become involved with the Indian community, very deeply involved, and the more I saw— things that agitated a person, like wholesale economic dis-

*An outhouse.

crimination—the more I thought, Hell, I'm going to be a lawyer and see if I can help my people.

Things were so bad for Indians that in many ways we were slaves. What bothered me most was that Indians didn't have a piece of the action. There was no opportunity for us. Indians weren't getting jobs. Just about every Indian I knew was out of work most of the time. Even in the movie industry they were hiring Mexicans and Italians to do Indian parts. And Indians weren't getting the education other people were getting. Indians lived in low-rent slums, with their kids growing up without any of the most basic advantages that society is supposed to offer to everyone.

Sometimes people argue that other minorities—the Irish and the Jews, for example—were downtrodden and yet carved a place for themselves in America. But you have to understand that no group of people has been as oppressed as the Indian. They talk about putting Japanese in concentration camps during World War II. Well, we had them beat by a hundred years. What the hell were the reservations if they weren't concentration camps?

Indians on the reservations were brought up with a strong feeling of paternalism. The government was supposed to do everything for us. If something went wrong, an Indian complained to the Bureau of Indian Affairs. Take an Irishman or a Hungarian or the other minorities who came to this country—they were encouraged to work. Not us. That tradition wasn't inculcated in us. The government gave us just enough to get by, often just enough so that we wouldn't starve to death, but never enough to lift us out of the most grinding, humiliating kind of poverty.

Let me tell you something—when you live in a ghetto, which is what all Indian reservations are—there isn't even any percentage in stealing. Who are you going to steal from? Everybody is as poor or poorer than you are.

Most of the reservations aren't the great vast hunting and fishing areas that you've read about. It just isn't that way, and it hasn't been that way for years. If you go hunting, you have to have something to shoot at. If you go fishing, you have to have something to catch. Well, the game and fish aren't there.

The schools on the reservation have traditionally been bad.

Until quite recently, there were places on some reservations where there were no schools. My mom didn't go to school at all. My dad got just a few years of schooling. Coming from a background with so many disadvantages, you can't expect the majority of Indians to be part of the American middle class.

I came along at the beginning of an era when things were changing slightly, although I doubt if I would have become a lawyer, much less a judge, if I'd stayed on the reservation.

Blacks were the first niggers. Mexicans were the second niggers. Now Indians are the niggers.

The occupation of Wounded Knee brought the attention of the American people to the problems of Indians. Sure, there was violence. I don't condone violence, yet AIM had to do something outlandish. How the hell do you get the attention of 215 million people? How do you get the attention of the power structure in Washington? Are you supposed to write a letter to the *New York Times?* Nobody's going to read it. Writing a letter to the editor of the *New York Times* is like pissing in the ocean; it's not going to lower or raise the water level one bit.

So Dennis Banks and Russell Means and the other AIM leaders took over Wounded Knee and said, Listen, America, you have to pay attention. We're the first Americans and we don't have jobs, and without jobs there's no money except what the government doles out. But we don't want to be on the dole; we want to be independent. We're tired of government handouts anyway.

The community of Wounded Knee itself offers a good example of what Indian people were up against. There was one trading post. If you didn't do business there, that meant you had to go all the way to Kyle or Porcupine or Pine Ridge. A lot of people didn't have money for gas. If you have no gas, you walk. And Pine Ridge was seventeen miles away, no matter how you walked.

The Bureau let this situation grow and grow and grow. A boil finally became a festering sore. A few people on the Pine Ridge reservation, the tribal council and their friends, were cutting a fat hog. For the rest, subsistence; nothing more. They had to pay through the nose for heat and electricity. A lot of families still heat their houses on Pine Ridge with firewood. And since there were no jobs, they lived at the pleasure of the government. Some families still don't have inside toilets. My God, that's the way I lived as a kid forty years ago.

Some good came out of Wounded Knee. It proved to be a small start. Instead of a white-owned trading post, the Sioux are trying to form their own co-op. So are the Navahos in Arizona and New Mexico. Co-ops offer the Indian a chance to get a fair price for his wares.

On the Navaho reservation, the trading posts keep Indian checks that don't belong to them. They overcharge the Navahos for the things they buy and give them less than fair market value for their jewelry, silverwork and rugs. The trading posts try to force a barter situation, and they are quite successful at it. They urge the Navahos to take groceries in exchange for their hand-iwork. But there are two prices in the trading posts, one for white tourists, another for Indians. If coffee is going for $3 or $4 a pound for the tourist, the price is $5 or $6 for the Navaho. But the Navahos are stuck. They have no dough and no place else to go. That's why the co-op movement is very, very important.

I think the Bureau has finally realized that Indians are not dumb, unsophisticated, unaware people. They know when they are being ripped off.

Since Wounded Knee, the Bureau has built some new houses and expanded health facilities on several reservations. They've improved the schools a little. More young Indians are getting college scholarships. Unfortunately, not all Indians are taking advantage of the new opportunities. When you're oppressed so long, sometimes you can't get out of the rut of poverty.

There's another problem. There are a lot of skilled plumbers and carpenters and welders who live on the reservations. But in the towns contiguous to the reservations, they won't hire Indian people. Or, if they do hire them, they expect them to work for less money than white men.

I don't know who has the toughest time, the Indians who live on the reservation ghettos or the Indians who live in the urban ghettos. There are more job opportunities in the cities if you have a mind to work. Now, I don't mean that Indians are lazy; I don't mean that at all. I mean it's difficult for them to compete in an urban setting. They are not accustomed to competition. The paternalism of the reservation is still too recent a memory.

Imagine how difficult it would be for an urbanite to be

dumped into the middle of the Arizona desert and forced to go out and hunt and make his own way. He isn't used to it; he doesn't know how to survive. That's the same problem urban Indians have.

Also, they find themselves in the cities with no money or little money and they cluster together in these honky-tonk bars. They see a honky-tonk and they say, Hell, that's the place I belong. They have a very poor self-image.

Though most Indians in the cities are doing badly, there are many young Indians on and off the reservations who are doing better than their parents or any of their ancestors. They're taking advantage of the opportunities they have to become lawyers, doctors, computer technicians, any of the high-paying professions and jobs.

I'd say that 95 percent of the cases that come to my court have financial overtones. You get people who are at the tail end of the financial ladder, Indian and non-Indian. Most of them aren't working, or if they are working they don't make much money, usually just the minimum wage.

The biggest problem I see among Indians who reach my court is drinking. They drink to forget they're poor and to forget the problems that come from being poor. They do things that may seem at the time to be almost humorous but end up being serious crimes—burglaries, thefts, stealing cars, rape, assault with a deadly weapon, manslaughter, murder.

I'm not a tough-sentencing judge. Pragmatically I'm opposed to jail time for most defendants most of the time, because I don't think it solves anything. I'm not attuned to the pound-of-flesh philosophy, since I don't think that in most cases that come before me, society is looking for a pound of flesh.

If I have a girl who is a prostitute, I can't see what good putting her in jail might do. It's not going to cure her, and society hasn't been injured too much by her actions.

If I have a narcotics addict before me and he's got a ten- or fifteen-year rap sheet for addiction, I'm not just going to put him out in the street. I'm going to dry him out a little bit. If I have a person who has been using just a little bit, then I don't think jail is going to solve the problem. I tend to feel that if he gets another chance, he may come out of it. So I order him into a viable narcotics rehabilitation program.

If there's a poor person standing before me who's clipped something from Sears, I might give him a minimum fine or sentence him to voluntary service in the community, working for the Red Cross or a church.

I just don't believe that a person who goes out and steals some apples for his kids is a big criminal. If he's a professional thief, that's another thing. But if he's a person with four kids and a wife and he's out stealing apples or a loaf of bread, he's not a crook. He's just trying to feed his family. The biggest crime most of the people who wind up in my court have committed is the crime of being poor.

In the next decade or so, things might change for the reservation Indian. A lot of land on the reservations might become valuable. There's some reason to believe there might be oil and minerals on some of the land. Much of it is scenic land, and that should bring in more tourists. With irrigation, much more of the land can be cultivated.

It's going to remain tough for the urban Indian. Many of them have sold their interest in tribal lands and spent the money. They are completely washed out. And the longer the Indian stays in the city, the more tendency he has to lose his Indianness. Unless job training opportunities and jobs are available to them, they are just going to stay poor.

It's going to take a long time for prosperity to reach America's last niggers.

GORDON TRESSEL

> *Stand up, stand up for Jesus,*
> *Ye soldiers of the cross;*
> *Lift high His royal banner,*
> *It must not suffer loss.*

Some three hundred men are lustily singing the venerable hymn as a visitor enters the Union Rescue Mission, located in the heart of the stark terrain of the Skid Row ghetto in Los Angeles.

The music echoes through the building, up a long flight of stairs to the second floor and down a freshly painted corridor to Tressel's wood-

paneled office. A big man, six feet one and 205 pounds, he's the Mission's business manager.

He appears not to be overly interested in money. "I don't know how much I make. Let's see—I guess it's $1,150 a month, plus housing."

Divorced and sixty-one years old, he says of his ex-wife: "I met her in a bar and left her in a bar." The six-year marriage was childless. "It was either fight all the time or drink all the time."

My father was a doctor, and he made very good money. We never wanted for anything. We lived in Wakefield, a small town in northern Michigan.

There was liquor around our house for parties, but there wasn't any drinking as such—maybe one or two before a party, and that was about it. I started drinking in high school, then drank my way through two or three colleges, which didn't prevent me from playing football and basketball.

I enlisted in the Army in the spring of 1941. I was sent to OCS and came out a second lieutenant and went up the ladder until I got discharged in 1945 as a major, despite the fact that I was drinking too much.

I was discharged in San Francisco, and I stayed there and got a very good job as office manager for a fellow who sold duplicating and addressographing equipment. But he was a drunk himself and was never there. So I was running the business and doing all the entertaining that he was supposed to be doing. Doing an awful lot of drinking, too. San Francisco is a hard-drinking town. You go out to lunch there and you expect to have, if you are in the drinking crowd, four or five martinis and take three or four hours for lunch. Stuff like that.

I was earning a tremendous salary for that time—$1,500 a month plus an unlimited expense account—but I lost the job in a year. The boss told me it was either quit drinking or quit working. I quit working. I'd guess, because of his own heavy drinking, he's probably long since destroyed the business. It's impossible to be a real alcoholic and run a business or hold a job for very long.

Next I went to work for a handbag manufacturer, at about the same salary. I was a traffic manager. I lost that job in three months, again because of drinking.

When I was let out, I drank up my last check. Then I didn't have a penny to my name, so I started taking odd jobs for whatever people would pay. Finally, after a year or so of that, I went home, thinking I could straighten myself out. While I was home, both my parents died, and I inherited $40,000.

I bought a combination bar and steak house at Chetek Lake in northern Wisconsin, which is beautiful fishing and resort country. With the bar, of course, I could get my drinks free. Not really free—I was drinking up much of the profits. It was a good business, but I was running it into the ground. So after three years of more or less getting by financially, I decided to sell. Luckily I got a good price, $47,000 cash.

I started on a long binge right there in Wisconsin. Then I drank my way through Chicago, Minneapolis, New Orleans and Las Vegas. Along the way, I got arrested as a drunk two or three times. I got kicked out of Las Vegas as a common drunk, a bum, and ended up here on the street, with no money. It had taken about a year and a half to drink my way through $47,000. That's a lot of booze and a lot of money.

I started panhandling, but I wasn't very good at it. A good panhandler can make $15 or $20 a day, and live off it.

On a cold, rainy day in 1967 I was sitting in the bus depot. I was broke, had no job, no home, no prospects. A cop walked over to me. I told him my story, and he suggested I come here. I walked in, listened to the hymns and the preaching. I didn't buy it at all. I went out into the street, panhandled a few dollars, and kept drinking.

A couple of nights later I came back and was listening to the service and feeling awfully sorry for myself. I had a real blue down-and-out feeling. This fellow who was about my age got up and said that Christ had helped him to stop drinking and helped him to quit cigarettes. He said that he'd never felt better in his life. Something clicked inside me. When the altar call came, I automatically went up and accepted Christ as my Savior. That was on April 26, 1967. I've been here ever since.

I started working here as a clean-up man in the dining room for $2 a month. Now I'm in charge of the entire business end of the Mission and an annual budget of between $1.2 million and $1.5 million. I take care of paying the bills, the buying of materials, the payroll, the processing of donations, the insurance, and all the government red tape, reports and forms, that we have to fill out.

We have over 200 employees altogether, in our two halfway houses, our ranch in Vista, California and here. When a man first comes to us and says he wants a job, he's usually assigned to the dining room, waiting on tables or busing dishes, things like that. He earns $3 a week. In a month he goes to $4; a month after that he makes $5 plus his room and board, clothing, haircuts, and first aid. Our payroll runs about $20,000 a month. We also provide quite a range of free services, including dormitory, counseling, and employment agency. Also, daily religious services.

We lodge six hundred men a night and feed eight hundred a day. That's an awful lot of traffic, but there are an awful lot of men who'd starve to death without us. It costs about fifteen cents per meal per man. But we get a lot of food donated. All our milk, bread, ice cream and pies are donated. We have to buy a certain amount of staples, fresh vegetables and meat. But even in these inflationary times, we can bed and board a man here for about $1 a day. However, our cost goes up in the winter, because then we handle more men and they need more food. We give them a hot instead of a cold breakfast. They drink more coffee, and the price of coffee right now is outlandish. Somehow I manage to find the extra money in our budget.

My personal philosophy of money is simple. It takes care of your basic needs. What I have left over I give to my church and to deserving people. I like to see money used to help people so they can get straightened out. I don't want any more money than I'm making right now. If I inherited $1 million tomorrow, I'd give it all away to the men who inhabit this Skid Row ghetto. The only regret I have about the money I went through while I was drinking, a couple of hundred thousand dollars, is that it was wasted. It did nobody any good.

Skid Row is a ghetto in the sense that a ghetto is composed of people who think alike, behave alike, and have about the same income, whether it's a lot of money or very little money.

Not everybody wants to get out of Skid Row. I think many men are satisfied with the kind of lives they lead down here; it's exactly what they want. But we realize that many do want to change, do want out of this ghetto, and those are the ones we aim for.

There are perhaps 15,000 to 20,000 men who live on Skid Row on a more or less permanent basis. Maybe another 100,000 are floaters who come into this part of Los Angeles, then move on to a Skid Row somewhere else.

In Skid Rows across the country there is rather a new trend. And that is that some of the men who used to be down-and-out have more money now. Some qualify for welfare. Some have pensions and Social Security checks. So missions across the country are developing resident programs, because the men do have a certain amount of money and they want to stay in a rescue mission atmosphere. They don't have enough money to make their way on the outside, but they are able to stay and survive in a mission because they pay relatively little for food and lodging.

Occasionally, the amount of money a few men have down here surprises you. We had a fellow, for example, who received a retroactive Social Security check for almost $2,000. Besides the sometimes large checks from the government, some men get quite a bit from forgiving or understanding relatives. Quite often they turn their checks over to us and ask us to keep the money for them. We put the checks in the safe and dole the money out to them on their request.

There was one man who died in the Mission here, and we discovered that he was hoarding money. He had more than $30,000. We thought of him as being down-and-out. Unfortunately, the state got hold of the money. We didn't see any of it.

Bequests from estates are what really see us through. A great many people die and leave us money. We get a little support from foundations. And then we get a lot of what I call the consecrated dollar. Little old ladies and little old men will send in $1 or $2, and with their donation a typical letter will say, "My husband and I have been interested in your work all our lives. He's gone now and I am alone in a nursing home. I have only a little pension, but here is my $1 contribution." To a large extent, we are dependent upon such consecrated dollars.

We also get some money from churches. They donate to us for this type of work. They don't want to do this type of work in their home churches, nor do they want any part of the type of man who walks through our door. They would never admit that, but that's the truth of it. They would rather give us money to take care of the poverty-stricken alcoholic than do it themselves. To be fair, I should say that these churches don't have the facilities to handle the alcoholic, and they don't understand the problems of the men who inhabit Skid Row.

No one chooses to be poor because of alcohol. The condition is a progressive one. A man forms certain habits, and those who develop a heavy drinking pattern may do so because of financial reverses. We see that in case after case. On the other hand, we see men down here from all walks of life who apparently didn't have money problems. Quite the reverse—at one time they may have had too much money. Men with professional backgrounds and a high level of education are fairly common around here— former society doctors, lawyers, engineers. The ultimate reason they end up on Skid Row is because they are absolutely destitute. They don't know where their next meal is coming from or where they are going to stay the night.

Only 3 percent of all the alcoholics in the country are on Skid Row. Those who come down here do so because they are broke, or nearly broke, and they don't have any place else to go. But the majority of the nation's alcoholics are being supported by indulgent or understanding families. The men we see are so forlorn that they don't even have a place to sit down in the daytime, because people will shoo them away from wherever they happen to be. And so they just have to move on. That's why we keep the Mission open twenty-four hours a day.

We see a lot of men who come out here from the East or the Middle West. They still think the streets here are paved with gold and that jobs are easy to find. They stop in a bar and end up inside our door. But a lot of them find they want no part of this life. So we get them home as soon as possible. We make telephone calls to their families and put them up for a few days until the financial arrangements for their fare can be made. In some instances, we use the Traveler's Aid Society.

A lot of new faces usually turn up after a weekend. They get rolled outside a bar on Saturday or Sunday night and they are looking for help on Monday. It goes without saying that it's a bad idea to flash your bankroll in a Skid Row bar, but it's amazing how many men do it, which leads to their getting robbed.

At the same time there's a good deal of camaraderie on Skid

Row. You've probably heard of the bottle gangs. Each fellow puts in a nickel or a dime and they buy one bottle and they all share it. So some of the men do have that kind of fellowship together.

The strangest thing I think we see in the Mission occurs at mealtimes. There are several hundred men eating in the dining room, and there isn't a sound. It's all dead silence, which is very unusual for such a large group. The person who becomes addicted to alcohol often becomes withdrawn, and he doesn't want to show his vulnerability; he doesn't want to talk; and he doesn't want to voice his opinion. What are they thinking about? Maybe that they've strayed from God. Maybe they are remembering a home, wives and children and the comfortable standard of living many of them once enjoyed.

We don't have a theft problem in the Mission. Very, very few things are stolen here. These men are not that far gone that they'd steal from a house of God. There's a lot of crime along Skid Row, but we don't see it inside our doors.

Most of the men on Skid Row are fundamentally decent, even though they are poor and friendless, even though they sometimes steal and panhandle. We owe it to ourselves and to God to help them out financially and spiritually. God tells us we must love our fellow man, that we must help our fellow man. Our love shouldn't be thrown out the window just because a man is a drunk. We should love that man whether he's a penniless alcoholic on Skid Row or the boss in the corner office earning $100,000 a year.

Hedging Against Inflation

*It's comforting to know that if bacon should
go to $100 a pound, you could use your gold
or silver to buy it.*

—TODD PARKER

BUD GOODE

Bud is one of America's 35 million stock market investors. A part-time publicity man, he was trained at USC in statistics and psychometry, the art of measuring and assessing group behavior. He's also a computer expert who writes a syndicated newspaper column in which he uses computer analysis to predict the outcome of sports events. "In my sports predictions, I'm right 75 percent of the time. But you can't use the computer to predict whether an individual stock will go up or down, because there are too many variables."

I was always interested in the market, even as a kid. I used to read the stock page before the sports page when I sold newspapers on the corner of Beverly and Vermont. The guy who had the corner drugstore was a speculator and he and I used to discuss the stocks he bought and sold.

I got into the market myself in the mid-50s. I put a few thousand dollars into Thiokol (principal businesses: chemicals, rocket motors and fuel) and Ampex (video-audio equipment and computers). At that time they were the fastest-moving stocks on the board.

I was unlucky. I made a little money on those deals—about $1,500—and I was really hooked. I became a market junkie, and I thought that anybody could make money in the market. I've since come to the conclusion that nobody can make money in the market, or I should say not many people can. The ruling reason has to do with the nature of gambling. The market is a crap shoot. You are just betting your money; that's what it amounts to. It's a very chancy thing.

If you are going to bet money on a football game, you have what's called in statistical-computer analysis a predictive variance of 75 percent. In other words, if you bet the favorite, you have a

75 percent chance of winning. If you are going to foretell how the Supreme Court is going to vote on a given issue, the predictive variance is 95 percent. I can hit that on the nose almost every time, assuming I program the computer correctly. But the predictive variance in the stock market is only 9 percent.

After making money in Thiokol and Ampex, I thought I had the magic touch. So I started to invest more, but the market fell. It went up and down, as it always does.

I've traded Thiokol and Ampex ten to fifteen times. The interesting thing is that if I'd just held on to my original Thiokol investment, made when I was a novice, I would now have a profit of 4,100 percent or $20,000 on a buy of 400 shares at 5. But I didn't reap that profit. I lost it by selling too soon.

I can't say that I've ever made a big killing in one stock, but I really haven't taken a bath in anything. I was close to taking a bath in Occidental Oil. I bought in at 18 and it went down to 8. But I simply bought more at 8, because they had coal by then, and that helped the stock. I've continued to buy the stock through the years at a range of 8 to 25. My average buy was 14. I sold some at 18 and 19 and came out three grand ahead. I still own 800 shares of Occidental.

A friend of mine, who is now unfortunately deceased, was a brilliant chemical engineer, and he damn near lost his house playing the market. He dropped $25,000 in one year.

The stock market in recent years has had a terrible press, and rightly so. Personally I don't know anybody who's made money in the market, except me. Why then do people continue to invest in the market if virtually all of them lose money?*

You have to remember that this is a capitalistic country and the stock market is a plank in the system. What happens to the system if everybody gets out of the market? What would happen is that you wouldn't have a capitalistic system anymore; you would have a totalitarian state, and the government would own the means of production.

Not that people go into the market with the noble motive of

---

*Financial commitment to the market is breathtaking. On the New York Stock Exchange alone, there are 1,555 companies listed. The value of their 22 billion shares is $660 billion.

preserving capitalism. Though the stock market was founded to help the development of industry in this country, people go into the market because they're greedy. They want to make money.

I consider myself a small investor, but a small investor really has no right in the market, because it is a gambling environment. In any gambling environment, you are betting your wallet into an infinite wallet and that's why you can't win in the market or in Las Vegas. Even a man who has $1 million to invest in the market hasn't got a prayer. What is that $1 million going to do in a situation where so many hundreds of billions of dollars change hands every year?

I stay in the market because I figure I can outsmart it, based on my knowledge of probabilities and mass psychology. Those are my crucial elements. Using them, I haven't made a great deal of money, but I haven't gone broke either.

I am sensitive to the moods of large numbers of people. I know when they are pessimistic and when they're optimistic. Emotion must always be taken into account in the market; it isn't all statistics. If you understand mass psychology, you *can* make out in the market pretty well. The ideal time to buy is when everybody else is selling, when there's the inevitable panic, with people wailing and moaning, saying the market is never coming back. Investors forget the market is a two-way street.

The market for the most part was up during the sixties. I had small profits during that period, a few thousand dollars each year. I sensed that the market was going to tumble in the early seventies. It did, and so when the bear market hit I bought a lot of stuff which I still own—Continental Oil, Exxon, Winn-Dixie (a supermarket chain), Bendix, World Air, Wells Fargo and Union Carbide.

I'm not the type of investor who calls his broker every day. When my broker calls me, I try to get rid of him. He calls twice a week, and I am very polite to him. I tell him that I fully expect to sell everything at a given point in time, and I thank him for the information he gives me. But his information and intuition aren't as good as mine.

It's strange, but most investors trust their brokers, though brokers seldom make money for them. People think brokers are insiders. But they are not insiders; they are merely salesmen.

The true insiders are the people who are running the business, the members of the board of directors who know the monthly profit and loss.

The people who make the most money in the market are the brokerage houses; they make it from commissions. If they weren't making an awful lot of money, they wouldn't be in business. It's true that a lot of brokerage houses went out of business in the down market of the early seventies, but that was because the number of shares traded fell off so rapidly and they were undercapitalized. They also had tremendous overhead and had to pay people to do their enormous paperwork. But those houses were really not in the brokerage business. They were in the accounting business; they just kept records. The business of a real brokerage house is not money or stocks, but research.

Right now, I own shares in about twenty stocks. It's not good to have shares in more stocks than that; you can spread yourself too thin. I have about $50,000 of my own money in the market. I owe $35,000 on my margin account—that's money I've borrowed from my broker. Overall, I'm showing a profit of $15,000 for all my efforts.

My stock market assets are $100,000. If the market should go way down, I'd just have fewer assets. It's all on paper anyway. If there was another 1929-type crash, I could absorb a one-third loss in my assets. If the market went down as much as 300 points, I would still be protected. But that's a remote possibility, in my opinion.

The market ultimately catches up with inflation, and this market sooner or later will go right through the roof. If it doesn't, then the capitalistic system will be doomed. We are heading toward socialism anyway, but it's not going to happen for a hundred years. At that point, there will be no stock market to speak of. But I can't be too concerned with what's going to happen a hundred years from now.

After the coming boom sometime in the next five years, I plan to get out of the market when I've doubled my present assets. I'll be home free with $200,000 cash, or even more. I'm then going to put that money into certificates of deposit, hopefully at 7, 8 or 9 percent, whatever the going interest is then. I can live very well on that. By the time I'm ready to retire, I'll be in a very good position.

Actually, I'm in a good position now. My wife works, we have no children, and I don't work very hard. I have plenty of time to devote to my fruit trees and my dogs. I have a Navy pension of $6,000 a year. My dividends bring me $3,300 a year. That's nearly $10,000 annually.

I keep a cash reserve of only $2,500. We have never lived it up and we don't spend much money. I owe very little on my house, only $3,700. The house was an excellent investment. We bought it for $20,000 in 1956 and I would say it's worth $75,000 now.

To tell the truth, I would like to have all the time I used to spend on the market. I don't spend that much time on it now. I should have devoted the time to something more productive.

Now I'm very objective about the market, unemotional. I used to get excited when Thiokol went up 5 points in a day. Or I'd get depressed if Ampex slid a couple of points. Of course, when you reach 50 you don't get excited about anything, except, I guess, preserving your money.

TODD PARKER

"I had no formal education beyond high school. And I certainly had no formal education in the business of trading gold and silver. That's what I am, a trader. To be successful, it takes a sixth sense."

Parker is a handsome unmarried thirty-seven-year-old, born in Peoria, Illinois. He, a partner and a small group of stockholders own the United States Gold Corporation and the United States Silver Corporation, whose home offices are in Van Nuys, California. They also own one of the largest precious-metals refineries in the nation. The total operation grosses between $70 million and $80 million a year.

We buy and sell gold and silver from people off the street. We buy and sell to industry, to jewel firms, to electronics companies—anyone that's in the market. We also refine all forms of scrap gold and silver after purchase. In addition, we act as gold and silver brokers. We buy and sell the metals at the going price established every day in London.

It became legal again for Americans to own gold on January 1, 1975. The price of gold actually went up substantially before legalization of bullion. One day it hit $204 an ounce. The price today happens to be $136.40. The drop has been caused because the supply has temporarily exceeded the demand.

There really is a scarcity of gold, but scarcity is a relative word. There is only one *Mona Lisa;* therefore it is scarce. But when you talk about gold, you are talking about more than scarcity. For thousands of years, gold has been used as a monetary metal, as a medium of exchange for one person to buy goods and services from another. Gold has considerable historical equity, and that's part of the reason it's considered valuable.

In the past fifty or sixty years, most countries found that it was impossible to increase the money supply while backing paper currency with gold. There simply wasn't enough gold to match the paper currency they were spreading around. So most countries, including the United States, abandoned the gold standard.

The implications of this in terms of the inflationary cycle, in terms of international monetary affairs, is yet to be fully realized. But the short-term impact has been that many nations, finding themselves with all this gold in their vaults, decided that since they no longer needed it to back paper currency, they might as well sell it. Which is precisely what they've been doing. Therefore, the market has been supplied with a great deal of gold.

Both gold and silver are excellent examples of how precious metals work as a hedge against inflation. If you chart the rate of inflation side by side with the price of gold and silver, you'll find that when inflation increases, so does the price of the metals. Often the metals outrun inflation.

The best example I can give in laymen's terms is silver coins. We don't use coins of precious metals in this country any longer, unfortunately. In 1964, when bread was selling for twenty cents a loaf, you could go out with a silver dollar or a paper dollar and buy five loaves. In 1976 bread was selling at fifty cents a loaf and your paper dollar bought two loaves. But a silver dollar was worth between $3.75 and $4.50 in paper money. So you actually could buy several more loaves of bread with your silver dollar in 1976 than you could in 1964. Somewhere along the line, silver has increased in value considerably in terms of purchasing power.

Silver will always be valuable. Its versatility is virtually infinite.

It's used in the manufacture of eyeglasses, batteries, rockets, mirrors, electronic parts, watches, tape recorders, ad infinitum. Actually the demand for silver is greater now for industrial use than for monetary use. Which gives silver a two-pronged thrust, and that isn't as true of gold.

If you ask what's happened to the investment of people who bought gold at $200, you also have to ask what's happened to the investment of those who bought at $40, $50 or $60 an ounce. Among people who've invested in gold, there are probably eight winners to every two losers. Now, there are many people like me who think that the demand for gold over the next four or five years is going to push the metal back up beyond the $200 mark and then to new highs. That, of course, is my opinion. But I think it's very possible that we'll see gold at $300 an ounce. By and large, it is very difficult to find anyone who has purchased gold and has not done very well with it in the long run.

Sometime in the future, in the next ten, twenty or thirty years, there will be such an overabundance of paper currency issued by governments throughout the world, and the inflation rate will be so great, that people will again turn to precious metals as a medium of exchange.

The great inflation in Germany in the 1920s is a beautiful example. People were actually cutting up silverware because they could use it to buy bacon, butter, bread, shoes, or whatever. I think that can happen again on a worldwide scale.

If it does happen, will there be enough gold to go around? Gold, because it is so much higher priced per ounce, is probably not the ideal metal for a worldwide medium of exchange. To get a piece of gold down to the denomination where you could use it to buy a candy bar would mean you would have to have a speck of gold so small that you couldn't even find it in your own pocket. But I suspect that a combination of gold and silver will be used for monetary purposes, and that will solve the problem.

It's very interesting to listen to people who come in here to buy gold and silver. We had a man in the other day who went through the German inflation after World War I. He'd lived in Frankfurt and had owned a tobacco shop. He had his two grown sons with him when he came in to buy some gold and silver.

The sons were doing their best to talk him out of it. Instead of gold and silver, they suggested he buy real estate or antiques or stocks, anything but precious metals. He finally looked at them and said, "I remember in Frankfurt when one of my customers wanted to buy an ounce of tobacco. He came into the shop and I agreed to give him an ounce for his wheelbarrow full of marks. When he went outside to bring the currency in, his marks were all over the street. Somebody had stolen his wheelbarrow because it had more value than the marks!"

This man knew the terrible things that could happen to paper currency. He wasn't going to be swayed by his bright, brilliantly educated sons. He had been through it, and he knew that in his portfolio, in his scheme of life, there was a place for a little gold and silver. I think more and more people are coming to realize this.

A middle-aged woman who had recently emigrated from France came in recently to buy some gold coins. In France, of course, you would be hard-pressed to find anyone who doesn't have some gold stashed away in a mattress or in a portfolio. The woman wanted a few gold coins to put under her mattress, as her parents had done all their lives. She said that the gold had always given her mother and father a feeling of security. "I want to recapture that comfort I felt with my family," she said as she made her purchase and went out the door smiling.

We were invited by the State Department to the relocation camps where the Vietnam refugees were being housed, to buy the gold they had taken out with them. Number one, they could have brought their wealth over in any number of forms. They could have had it in U.S. dollars. They could have brought it out in antiques. Or jewelry. Or paintings. But they brought their wealth to this country in gold. Why? Because they knew it was a universal medium of exchange, that it would be accepted anywhere.

Number two, they brought their gold to the United States in a very interesting form: not in coins or bullion, but in what they call taels. Each tael contained the metric equivalent of about 1.2 ounces of gold. These were very thin strips of gold foil, slightly heavier than the foil you find in supermarket aluminum foil.

The reason they brought it over in this form was that it was very easy to hide. It was very flat and thin, and they could hide the taels in their lapels or their belts or their shoes, which is very difficult to do, of course, if you have coins or a bar of bullion.

Even over here they weren't sure if their gold would be confiscated. That's why they kept it well hidden. When they were assured by the State Department that they could sell their gold, they revealed their taels.

We found some people who met us with tears in their eyes. We thought perhaps they were crying because they had to sell their wealth. In fact, we found out that they were crying because there was somebody ready, willing and able to buy their gold. They knew it was valuable, but they needed the reassurance nevertheless. So none of those refugees arrived here penniless; they arrived, in some cases, with a considerable amount of money. One man had about $15,000 worth of gold.

In my opinion, no one, no family, no breadwinner, no person who has any excess capital, ought to put all his eggs in one basket. He shouldn't invest entirely in gold, but neither should he keep all his money in a bank or savings and loan account, or real estate, or commodities.

Anyone who has studied history realizes that human crisis and human catastrophe come not only in the form of war or invasion; they also come in the form of the collapse of an economic system. Britain is in the infant stages of going through such a collapse at this point.

Americans are fortunate that they have never really gone through a total economic collapse, except perhaps during the Depression of the 1930s. Therefore, most people in this country aren't yet prepared to diversify their investment portfolios, however large or small, so that they can meet any contingency. Americans have had no experience, as have Europeans and South Americans and Asians, with the vagaries of paper currency.

Investment diversity, including gold and silver, makes good sense to me when you look at what's happening in this country. A couple of weeks ago I had a man in here whose property taxes had increased 33 percent. He cashed in some of his silver holdings in order to cover the bill.

That's another thing about gold and silver. It's liquid. If I had a choice between owning the *Mona Lisa* and its equivalent in gold, I would take the gold any day of the week. Where do you find a quick market for the *Mona Lisa* in case you need money fast? How many people or institutions in the world can afford to buy a priceless painting like the *Mona Lisa*? Gold and silver can be sold over the counter in a matter of minutes.

Real estate is also a very good investment and historically has done very well in relation to inflation. But it's not that liquid, either. It may take anywhere from thirty days to six months to three years to sell a piece of property.

I would be very afraid of tying up all my capital in assets that were not immediately liquid.

It's comforting to know that if bacon should go to $100 a pound, you could use your gold or silver to buy it.

MARVIN HIME

"Diamonds are still a girl's best friend. And sometimes they are a man's best friend. There are places called banks which are accepting diamonds as collateral today." So says Hime, an agreeable fifty-eight-year-old Beverly Hills diamond retailer. "I started this business thirty-one years ago with $300. Today we do between $1 million and $2 million a year."

Sitting in the living room of his $400,000 home, with a mountain view that extends beyond the brown felt pool table, Hime drinks a vintage Chablis and snacks on crackers spread with nut cheese.

There are also people called pawnbrokers who always accept diamonds. If you are in a jam as far as your business is concerned, you can always borrow against a diamond. You receive your money immediately. I have seen it come down to the point in some families where a precious stone made all the difference.

One of Beverly Hills' most famous doctors went through med school on his father's diamond ring. Whenever a new semester started, his father would hock the ring and pay his son's tuition. The father had a little grocery store in East Los Angeles, and every week he'd make a payment to the pawnbroker. It usually took him three months to redeem the ring. That went on year after year until the son graduated and started his practice. Today he's a leading ear man and teaches at UCLA.

Diamonds saved the lives of many Jews who came over the Pyrenees to Spain, running from the Nazis in World War II. They paid off the French and Spanish border guards with diamonds.

Diamonds are valuable because of their rarity, their beauty, their acceptance. A thing can be rare and beautiful, but if it's not accepted, forget it. Diamonds must be desired, someone must want to own a diamond, and that is a crucial factor in their value. Diamonds must be exciting. When you see a fine diamond, you should get excited, your stomach should rumble, you should have butterflies. Right now I happen to have a very, very fine sapphire in the office. It weighs sixteen carats and is worth a little under $70,000. Every time I look at it I get excited; my stomach gets butterflies.

Diamonds are a fine medium of international exchange. Everyone recognizes them as valuable—sophisticated people as well as uneducated people. People may not have an ounce of education but they know diamonds. They know sapphires, rubies and emeralds. I don't know how or why, but they know.

People are selling their stocks to buy diamonds. Diamonds are not a speculation. Diamonds have never gone down in price since the year 1900. What happened that year, I don't know. They leveled off for a couple of years during the Depression, but then they went up in value.

A fine carat was worth around $250 in 1900. Today it's worth more than $1,700. That is a great deal of appreciation, when you consider that through all those years the diamond has been worn, has been enjoyed and in addition has never been worth less than what was paid for it. If you bought XYZ stock in 1900 as a speculation, you threw money away in the street.

It's very important to buy a diamond right. If you go to certain places—I'm not going to mention any names—you can overpay. You come out with a nice package with a famous name on the box. But you don't wear the box. You don't have to go to the places with the big names. You'll do as well or better with an honest, truthful jeweler that isn't a chain operation, but like me has one nice store.

If you are buying diamonds for an investment, you first have to hop, skip and jump over the profit that I make. My profit on stones runs anywhere between 12 and 18 percent above cost.

You have to make up that difference. And you have to educate yourself about diamonds. You should go to three different jewelers and spend an hour talking to each of them. Ask them questions. Find out what you're putting your money into. That goes for anything. If I want to be a writer, I've got to learn construction, sentence structure; I've got to learn where to put the periods and how to spell. Education—that's terribly important.

It is possible to make quite a nice profit in stones if you know what you're doing. I have bought back stones I sold to people between 1950 and 1965. I've paid as much as $8,000 to $10,000 over what I charged for the stones originally. One was a beautiful round diamond that belonged to a lady who unfortunately passed away. The stone weighed seven carats. Her husband had paid $10,400 for it in 1961. I bought it back sixteen years later—and remember she had worn the diamond all that time—for $17,500. I sold it three days later for $19,000.

My business is doing fine. My business has always been good. You've got to understand that I succeeded in this business by working two shifts a day for a long time, sixteen hours instead of eight. So if someone says, "How long have you been in business, Marvin?" I tell him, "Sixty years"—not thirty years.

I always kept reinvesting the profits. I lived frugally and my wife Ann is a good manager. I wouldn't say we were tight. We always gave to charity and we never denied ourselves the right kind of food. But we didn't blow money on too many cars or too much Vegas or too much anything. Instead of blowing $500 on clothes or something, I bought another diamond, which I then resold at a profit. It's not difficult to make money when you do it that way. Luckily, we've been healthy. If you have an illness, it can drain the heck out of you and you have to give your money to doctors. We haven't had to do that. We've been very fortunate, thank God. The diamond business has been good to us. I have a fine clientele.

Bob Hope used to be a regular customer. After every trip overseas, he'd come in and have me make up souvenirs. One year after he came back from visiting our boys in Korea, he wanted to give everybody a memento. So I made him approximately a hundred money clips. On the clips I made him an entire map of the South Pacific in gold. I set little stones for all his different stops. There was a ruby for Hawaii, a little green emerald for the Philippines, another little stone for Bangkok, a little stone for Korea—the whole South Pacific was on those money clips. I put the same stones into pendants for the girls in Bob's troupe. Even to this day people talk about those particular items. Bob liked them so well he gave me one. He said, "This is for you," and I had already charged him for it. It had already been billed, so it was a real present. He's a fantastic guy.

I can go back to customers like Eddie Cantor, Al Jolson, Jack Benny, and Fanny Brice. Then a new crop came in and I started meeting people like Louis B. Mayer, Darryl Zanuck, Harry Cohn, Jimmy Stewart and Glenn Ford.

I was in Harry Cohn's office once when he was president of Columbia Pictures. Harry and I got along great. He wanted a cigarette case on that particular occasion, and I showed him one.

"How much?" he asked.

"For you, five hundred dollars."

"Is that the best price you can give me?" Not that he cared about money; it was just a game with him.

"Yes."

"Okay," Harry said, "I know I can't buy cheaper."

The current celebrities and those who've come up in the last twelve or fifteen years have gotten business managers, which is great because I think that people who are artists and don't have a head for numbers need someone who has a head for numbers. Just like I am not a doctor; if I don't feel good, I shouldn't try to take care of my own body. The same thing is true of people in the entertainment industry.

However, there are some business managers who are smart and some who aren't as smart. Say you are a celebrity and you have a choice of buying two real estate lots. They are both 50 feet wide and 150 feet deep. One lot is in Watts and the other is in Beverly Hills. The lot in Watts is $3,000 and the lot in Beverly Hills is $30,000, although, of course, you can't buy a lot in Beverly Hills for $30,000. But this is just an example. So you are in a position where you can buy the $3,000 lot or the $30,000 lot. Now, if you have a stupid business manager, he's going to advise you to buy the $3,000 lot because it's cheaper and you make less of an investment. But in ten years the $3,000 lot may be worth only $5,000 or $10,000. The $30,000 lot in ten years is going to be worth $80,000 or $100,000. The same is true of diamonds. A stone worth $3,000 will go up in price and a stone worth $30,000 will go up in price. But the $30,000 stone goes up faster and stronger. It appreciates in value much more. That's just the way things work. The rich do get richer, and the poor don't get rich as fast.

Another way to illustrate how stones keep their value is the story of the diamond and the Cadillac. Every day this fellow who wore a diamond ring on his finger walked by a beautiful new Cadillac. He found the owner and said, "I'll trade you my diamond for your Cadillac." The owner refused. But the fellow was persistent. He kept after the Cadillac owner for two weeks. Every day he made the same offer, his diamond for the Cadillac. Finally, the guy with the Cadillac made the trade. Three years later, the Cadillac was worth practically nothing and the diamond, of course, had increased in value.

Jewels are more than an investment. They are security. They are more than security. They are personal. In fact, they become a part of you. They become a heritage. They become what you can pass on and on and on. They become a theme through the generations of your family.

A lot of odd and funny things have happened to me in this business. I guess the funniest occurred last Christmas. A fellow who is a good customer of mine, a very sweet man, bought a pendant for his wife and a ring for his mistress.

"Wrap the pendant with blue ribbon and the ring with red ribbon, so I'll know the difference," he tells me.

Maybe four, five days later his wife walks in and says she wants to exchange the pendant for something else, because she already has a pendant. As I am talking to her, in walks the man's mistress, who says she wants to exchange the ring because she already has a similar ring.

The wife looks at her husband's mistress—they don't know each other—and says, "God, what a pretty ring."

The mistress looks at the wife and says, "I like your pendant."

So they end up exchanging, and they both walked out of the store very happy.

ROBERTA L. ALTOON

Educated at Bryn Mawr and the University of Miami, Roberta Altoon is the director of the art department for Sotheby Parke Bernet, the prestigious London–New York–Los Angeles firm which has been in the business of auctioneering and appraising fine art since 1744.

She is in the thick of a booming industry—the art market currently rings up sales of more than $1 billion a year. Sotheby alone sells $40 million worth of paintings annually, charging buyers an average 12 percent commission.

Ms. Altoon is ensconced in a cheerful, light-filled office off the huge antique-strewn reception room of Sotheby's, where she has worked for five years.

My responsibilities are putting together auctions of paintings, getting the art work in for sale, estimating the price of the paintings, researching them, putting them in the appropriate sale—and from there on out it's up to the public.

Sotheby's is the world's oldest and largest auctioneering firm. We have an art sale every month, a general sale; it encompasses a little bit of everything. Then, four times a year, we have special sales for the more important works.

I think art is an excellent hedge against inflation. If one buys wisely, one can say the painting probably will not depreciate. You aren't guaranteed that it will appreciate, but usually it doesn't depreciate. And you always have the work of art to sell, to enjoy, or whatever. Its price usually does not go down like a stock.

Buying a fine painting is like buying a very good diamond. You know it is always going to be a very good diamond, and there aren't that many good diamonds in the world. Nor are there that many really wonderful paintings in the world. If you own a picture that's really first-rate, you have a rare commodity, and there will always be a demand for it, in this country or internationally. And it's portable; you can always take it with you.

Contrary to what most people think, those who have paintings on their walls at home needn't be that concerned with security. I know people who've been robbed and they steal the television set, the stereo, the silver. I know one case where the thieves left $100,000 in art work on the walls.

Burglars don't bother with art, unless you have the rare case of an art heister, but usually the paintings aren't taken. It isn't very easy to sell a stolen painting; you can't cut it up like a piece of jewelry. Besides, the thieves in virtually every case wouldn't know what to do with the painting, how to dispose of it. If it came back on the market, it would be spotted. We get posters and notices all the time from the FBI and Interpol, telling us what paintings have been stolen, and we are always on the lookout for them. So, from a security point of view, a painting is a good investment.

Forgery is a problem. However, Sotheby guarantees everything it sells. If, by some happenstance, a forgery should be purchased here, the buyer's money is refunded in full.

We find a lot of people coming to our auctions who say they are interested in art because their dollars seem to be losing value. People are always looking for different ways to invest their money, and I think if one is visually oriented, art can be a prime investment.

It's amazing how some paintings have appreciated over the years. Take the Barbizon School, the French nineteenth-century painters who were the forerunners of the Impressionists. Five to six years ago a Barbizon painting by Rousseau, de la Pena, or Jacque was worth very little. You could have bought them under $2,000. But they've gone up quite a bit in the last couple of years. Some of them go for more than $15,000, depending on quality.

Investing in art usually isn't a short-term kind of thing. Generally there are peaks and valleys in the prices of paintings. In the case of the Barbizon School, the paintings during the twenties and thirties were extremely expensive. Then they dropped in value and didn't increase in price until a few years ago.

There's really no way of knowing why paintings fluctuate so much in value. Something becomes popular; it just happens. A trend develops; one school of painting suddenly begins to appeal to people.

The least fluctuation in the art market seems to be in Impressionist pictures. Paintings by Monet, Renoir and Pissarro have universal appeal. They are pretty, and people can identify with them quite readily. Many Impressionist paintings command a $1 million price tag.

Sometimes it's absolutely incredible what can happen to the value of a painting. In 1935 Rembrandt's *Juno* sold for about $214. In 1976 industrialist Armand Hammer paid $3.25 million for it. The picture had been incorrectly catalogued as being painted by a follower of Rembrandt. When it was authenticated, the value jumped. Even at $3.25 million, I think Mr. Hammer made a wise investment. If he chose to sell the painting in a few years, he would undoubtedly come out with a profit.

You often find people buying art who basically don't know anything about art, and who are in the art market only to invest their money. However, it's my feeling that before you start collecting, you should have some background. If you are very naïve and uninformed, the chance of your making a profit on a painting is slim.

You acquire the background through self-education. Basically, it's a matter of picking the brains of the right people. Who are the right people? It depends on the period in which you are interested—Old Masters, nineteenth-century European, Impressionist, American, Contemporary. You should go to knowledgeable people in those areas.

A Picasso can sell for $1 million. But not all Picassos sell for $1 million. A 1967 Picasso would not be as important as, say, a 1906 Picasso. Picasso's early works are important because they revolutionized the look of art. They had something new to communicate, something new to say.*

The person with an income of $10,000 to $25,000 isn't frozen out of the art market at all. Art isn't only for the super-rich and museums. There are very good nineteenth-century pictures which are not terribly, terribly expensive that anybody can collect with no hardship on the pocketbook. There are also fine prints available, if people want prints. You don't need hundreds of thousands or millions of dollars to begin collecting art. You can own something done in the sixteenth century for $600. That's not out of the realm of possibility for anybody, but people don't know that. They think that the age of a painting alone

---

*Picasso, a wily businessman as well as a gifted artist, undoubtedly died richer than any painter in history. He left an estate estimated at $1 billion.

makes it expensive, which is a fallacy. And there's still the undiscovered work of a lot of artists that can be purchased at relatively low cost.

By being judicious, I think a person could build up a very nice collection in a few years for $20,000. It would not, of course, be a great collection, but it would be acceptable; it would be small, nice and respectable. In ten years I couldn't tell you what those paintings would be worth, but I doubt that they would be worth less than your original $20,000 investment. I know a man who bought a contemporary painting, a Roy Lichtenstein, for $12,500, kept it for seven years, and sold it for $250,000. That sort of thing does happen, but it isn't an everyday occurrence. If one had a crystal ball, it would be wonderful.

Every month we have an heirloom day. People bring in their art and we give free appraisals. By and large, we don't make that many discoveries of neglected, valuable works. Unfortunately, we have to prick the bubbles of many people who think they have something valuable. Sometimes I just have to say, "Your painting is nice, it's decorative, but it isn't worth a great deal of money."

Some people have outrageous expectations of what their paintings are worth. They will bring in a picture that you know would not bring $500 on the market, yet they are convinced it's worth $20,000 or $30,000, or more. They've had it appraised by someone who doesn't know anything about paintings, who just collects a fee for the appraisal. He appeases people by telling them, Yes, your painting is worth an enormous amount of money. They are extremely happy when they take the appraiser's little piece of paper away—extremely happy—until they try to get the price the appraiser has given them.

People believe what they want to believe. A lot of paintings have Rembrandt's name at the bottom, and people think they have a missing Rembrandt, a needle in a haystack that the world doesn't know about. The odds in favor of that happening are incredible.

Conversely, you have instances where people come in and say, Well, I'm sure this painting isn't worth anything. And I find it's worth a good deal more than they thought. That happens mainly with nineteenth-century paintings, where the market was stifled for years but is very strong now. Maybe they bought it in a little antique store somewhere. And the painting is worth more than what they paid for it. I don't mean thousands of dollars more, but a lot more, where selling it would mean they would come out with a nice profit. That happens quite frequently, mainly because these people have a salable picture.

It's very important to have a painting that is salable, and the public decides what is salable. It's like the fashion world. One year it's long skirts, the next short skirts. With paintings, one year landscapes are in and figure paintings are out. It's that sort of thing.

Historically, works of art have always been a very good buffer against inflation. It certainly was for many Europeans who emigrated to America. Sometimes the only wealth they had were their works of art. And very often the value of the paintings outran the value of the currency in the country they left behind! To some extent, I think that's true in this country today.

"The Best
Is Yet To Be"

*"The cancer's racing to my brain, so why do I
need money?"*

—ANNA SCHWARTZ

HAZEL WALKER

Burbank, California (population: 88,871) is the home of Lockheed and a forest of small manufacturing firms whose blue-collar workers, by and large, are well paid, earning $6 to $9.50 an hour. The city, because of its entertainment complex, has become a solid tourist attraction. Within its 16.7 square miles are Warner Brothers and Columbia, which share the same lot, Disney Studios and NBC. Universal City is a silver-dollar throw away.

Hidden from tourist view is a docile, put-upon minority of some 10,000 poor senior citizens, their lives a grim counterpoint to the atmosphere of make-believe.

The seniors are the province of Mrs. Walker, gray-haired and blue-eyed, whose finely chiseled features retain a determined cheerfulness despite the dilemmas of her job. She is the Director of the Retired Seniors Volunteer and Outreach programs. She works out of a small, cluttered office in the city's Adult Center.

"Though I'm sixty-five, I don't consider myself a senior citizen," she declares. "You are a senior adult when you decide you are one. My mind is intact, I'm healthy, and I think I have a lot to give."

Mrs. Walker does indeed give a lot. "I work eight hours a day and, if need be, more than that. Many of these people call me in the middle of the night with their problems. They sort of think I belong to them."

In my job, I seldom meet a senior citizen who doesn't have money problems. The city is high income, but there's never enough money for the needs of the aged.

This is considered an affluent community, and yet we have thousands of impoverished seniors. Why are they poor? For a number of reasons. Most of the time it was just the men who worked. Too many of the women who are now in the 65-to-80-year bracket never held a job. And the men didn't make very good salaries, so there was no chance to save much, if anything. A lot of the men have died off; the women live longer, not only here but all over the United States. So the women have to go on with little of this world's riches. Few of the men left pensions. Most barely made enough to make ends meet during their lifetimes; they were happy just to have a job. All most of them did to plan for the future was to build a home and pay for it. But in our inflated economy, with real estate taxes, food and medical care out of sight, more of the seniors are losing their homes every month. They try to struggle by on minimum Social Security, usually about $300 for a couple, less if the woman is widowed.

Society has disenfranchised these senior adults. They are isolated by circumstances or they isolate themselves. Many do not have transportation and so they lack mobility. They have health problems so severe some can't get to the doctor. They all tell you if they had enough money they could take care of all their problems. But past sixty-five is the time in life when you have the least possible option of improving your money flow.

There are those who don't believe society, the taxpayer, should give financial aid to senior citizens. They say the seniors should have saved enough for retirement during their working lifetimes. But, given the economic situation in this country, that hasn't always been possible. Having lived through the Depression and seen a time when you did well to get a job and enough food for that day, the immediate present was all you could worry about. There are senior citizens who are still reaping the bitter harvest of the Depression; they got so far behind financially in the thirties that they never recovered. Few people realize that.

The difference between the senior citizen who has it made and the one who doesn't is money and health. Poor seniors who must rely on Medicare are disadvantaged if not cheated in our society. The way Medicare is set up doesn't give them the opportunity to practice preventive medicine. And everyone knows you can stay well, live longer, be in better health if you're capable of having your checkups and early detection before you are really a sick person. But Medicare doesn't allow funds for that.

I think the money the federal government allots to seniors is being skimmed. Washington dispenses the funds down to the state, and the state dispenses it to the county, the county to various agencies all the way down to me. Not enough of the money is actually going into the programs for seniors. The answer is to cut out a lot of the bureaucracy and increase Social Security payments.

To maintain a decent standard of living, a senior citizen needs at least $12,000 a year. Five percent of the seniors I see have that much income. Now, everybody's criteria of making it is different. There are people who are perfectly content to have three meals a day and a roof over their head, a television set, and that's it. But a lot of the elderly would like to have the opportunity to do some traveling and be involved in society and not feel they are put on the shelf.

Getting them off the shelf is my job. I've been able, in many cases, to locate isolated and disenfranchised Burbank seniors and make them aware of our programs. We have a mini-bus service for our seniors; we have a nutrition service under the federal government's Title Seven program which allows us to supply one hot meal a day to seniors here at the Center.

Where senior citizens are unable to leave their homes or apartments, we have a program, staffed by volunteers, who bring a hot meal to them. We deal with every type of need seniors have—food, health, housing, transportation, recreation, education. We do all we can. Sometimes it isn't easy. Sometimes I almost allow myself to get discouraged.

Many of the cases I see are so sad. I had a couple who implored me to try to get them to a doctor. They had no family and no way to get to their doctor. I took my car, a little Toyota, and it was hard for them to get in because it's so low. Both were in their early eighties. The man had had three strokes. And she was in serious need of eye surgery, cataracts. She couldn't see. He barely shuffled, but when they walked she put her arm in his, and he was the eyes and she was the feet.

They were determined above all else that nobody would put them in a home. The doctor and nurse immediately nailed me—they said I should get these people into a home. I felt that they could stay in their own home and function with a little supporting service from us. I felt they would be much happier that way, even if they lived ten years less.

So I did not put my voice to it. I did not acquiesce in taking them to a home. I took them back to their place. On the way, they asked me to stop at the market, because they hadn't any food. He led her to the lettuce stand and she felt all of them, so she could be sure what she was buying was fresh and crisp—because it had to last them a long time. They did very little shopping, just the lettuce, milk, bread and oatmeal.

As they shopped, he did the seeing and she supported him with his walking, because he couldn't walk alone. It was very pathetic yet brave.

The man soon had another stroke and died. She is still in the house, alone, determined that she's not going into a convalescent home. She has diabetes and her diet is difficult. She is one to whom we deliver a special hot meal each day. I wonder how much of her life is living, how much is existing.

Those stories you read about senior citizens eating cat and dog food—I doubt that they're true. The reason is that cat and dog food aren't that cheap. I have had cases where I was pretty certain that they were not eating much of anything, maybe just crackers or soup, particularly toward the end of the month when their money was gone. But I've never run into a case of seniors eating pet food.

I had a case where one of our judges called me and said a senior adult was going to be picked up again for shoplifting. The man would steal very small items like a package of gum but make it very obvious that he was stealing. He was, of course, trying to get himself put in jail so he could get a good meal. I investigated and met the man, but he would not accept our nutrition program; he would not accept any of our services. He would rather go to jail because he's so proud. He's not the only senior I've met who felt that there was a stigma about accepting what we had to offer. They feel it's a welfare thing. You must remember, this is a very proud generation. They don't feel that way about Social Security. They feel they've earned that—they call it their gold check.

Rent is a big factor for seniors who live in apartments. Their rent goes up but their income doesn't. The landlord has his legitimate reasons for raising the rent—his taxes and maintenance have increased, that sort of thing—but these people have no option. They have no way of increasing their money. We try to find part-time jobs for some who are healthy enough. Employers immediately downgrade them. In the opening interview they say, We will give you less than we would somebody else; that's the only reason we'll take you on.

I've had instances where elderly people have called me at four o'clock in the afternoon to say their apartments were cold. They haven't been able to pay for their electricity and gas. It's always a problem getting them turned back on. The problem is difficult because the city owns its own power company. I am a city employee and thus I have to act as an umpire; that's what I mainly do in these cases. It's a little precarious, but usually I'm able to get their electric and gas service back.

There are also landlords who take advantage of them. They rent them an apartment, promise them a stove or a refrigerator, but they don't get it. So they are cold and hungry. I have to call up the landlords and sort of bluff and bluster them into delivering on their promises.

Quite often there are relatives who won't or can't accept the responsibility for the aged in their families. They have their own families and their own financial problems. So there is no other choice but for us to take up the slack as well as we can.

I have pondered the question of why we don't venerate our elderly in this society. Our society has just moved in a different direction, toward youth—youth worship. I don't think that's bad, because I have great rapport with young people. I've been married forty-five years, have two children and four grandchildren. But there has been such a tremendous change in our world in the last forty or fifty years, from the horse and buggy to flying through the air and landing on the moon and all the other technology that has come about. I think this has made the normal generation gap wider. Unless a person has been able to move along with progress and move along with all the innovations, the younger generation gets upset. Many people who are aged can't realize that the young are not going to do what we did; they are not going to behave as we did. They do not have the same values, because the whole system has changed.

My job pays me a salary of $1,165 a month, and that will soon be lost when I retire. My husband and I have tried hard to plan financially for the future. But I find that each year when we think we have it made, inflation has taken up what we were able to accumulate and put away the year before. So we haven't reached the point yet where I think we can live comfortably without my salary. I am talking about having some of the luxuries of life. I don't think that you should have to give up everything because you have reached a certain age. What society doesn't understand is that you have all the same desires; when you get older you don't just turn off a faucet as to the way you feel about doing things other than just eating and sleeping.

I have found that there's a great difference between living and breathing. Most senior citizens are merely breathing, and the lack of money is the number-one reason for that deplorable condition.

HARRY LENNON, ZOLA PRIMM, LAVERNE WALKER

"They're the cream of the crop," according to Reverend Richard C. Hall, who directs the Los Angeles Episcopal City Mission Society, a haven for the aged located in a neglected office building at the lower, unfashionable end of Wilshire Boulevard. "You should come with me to visit some of the elderly who won't or can't leave their apartments or homes. Harry, Zola and LaVerne are the best I have to offer you."

Harry, originally from Boston, is a small, wiry man, a Navy veteran of World War I. "I'll be eighty-one years old on my next birthday . . . if I live."

Seventy-nine-year-old Zola is a petite brunette, born in Johnstown, Pennsylvania. "I had relatives killed in the flood of '89 when the Conemaugh Dam burst. They were among the 2,200 who drowned."

The youngster of the panel is LaVerne, 59, a handsome, ailing black from Chicago. "I was in the hospital for a little surgery, and the nurse inserted a piece of twine in my vein and it went into my right lung. I'm having it removed sometime in the next couple of months. I am a victim of malpractice, and if I can find a lawyer to take my case, I'm going to sue."

The total monthly income of the trio is $822.23.

Harry: I get $235 a month in Social Security, and my Navy pension is $62.23 a month.

Zola: Social Security pays me $205 a month. It isn't much, but it's a good bit, too.

LaVerne: My Social Security check is for $320 a month. I live at Stan's boardinghouse, where I pay $300 a month for meals and a room.

Harry: Out of my total income of $297.23 a month, they take out $7.20 for Medicare. So as far as saving is concerned, there is very little chance for that. There are clothes to get and other things, and I have to eat. I pay $104 a month rent. You can't live on that little money and have any luxuries. I get a senior citizen's ticket every month, which costs $4, to pay for the bus. In real hot weather I go out to buy food, because it is just as cheap to eat out as it is to take the food home and cook it.

Zola: I keep a budget. But I'm not saving anything. In fact, I go over a little bit every now and then, especially this month. I'm spending a lot of money for groceries because my sisters from Arizona are coming to see me. I am buying food in packages so that we can have our meals at home. If they want to eat out, I will have the packages left for me to eat. I used to go out for coffee every morning and drink four, five or six cups. Then at noon I would have coffee, and I always talked with people at the cafeteria. I had good conversations, and it made a pleasant day. I met very nice people that way. But I quit the coffee breaks because the doctor told me that I have high blood pressure. That gives me $10 a month more to spend on food. That's a very good thing to do, quit the coffee and buy food. I consider everything in life a luxury, from the time I get up through the whole day. One thing that I do is spend money to join things which are only $1 or $1.25. I go to many churches and to several senior citizens clubs like this one. So I think I have a good life that way.

LaVerne: My only luxury is going to a movie every two or three months. I go to the beach occasionally on a Sunday. I wear out a lot of shoes, and it costs me $3 or $4 to get them repaired every two months. Other than that, luxuries can be forgotten. I can't even afford steak once a month.

Harry: I don't want to have a great deal of money, just enough to be comfortable, to get the things I need. That's all I ask out of life. If there's a nice concert going or something, and it costs three or four dollars, well, I would rather take that money and put it toward food. I eat two good meals a day, a good breakfast and a good dinner. In between, if I get a little hungry, I stay a little hungry, or I come here and have a donut or two and coffee. I would rather eat as well as I can and go without something else.

Zola: I try to live within my means. When I think something is beyond my means, it worries me. I'm kind of worried now, because they are raising the rent on my apartment. When I first moved in, the rent was $90 a month. Then they raised it to $100. A short time after that, the building was sold and I got a knock at my door. There were three or four people standing there, and one of them said, "We are the new owners. The rent now will be $135." I said, "You mean, including lights and gas." He said, "Not including anything. That's just the rent for the place." I said, "Oh, my goodness, $135 a month. What am I going to do?" Well, I've lived through it this far. But $135 a month is an awful lot of money. That takes everything but $54 of the $189 I get from the government. I do have a little savings account, so I won't have to go hungry. That's where the extra money for the rent is coming from. When that savings account runs out, I'm going to be in trouble. What am I going to do? I don't know.

LaVerne: My philosophy of money is the same as Joseph Medill Patterson's, of the Chicago *Tribune*. He wrote in a book that money possesses everyone, the poor in different ways than the rich. I just feel that everyone should have a little savings as a buffer against absolute poverty.

Harry: The reason I'm not rich is that at my age I am not working. I was a clerk at the Statler-Hilton for eleven years. We opened the hotel, and of course in those days you didn't make money like you do today. We didn't work any eight hours, we worked ten and eleven hours; and the money you made wasn't heavy money. What you made just got you by. Thirty-five years ago you could live all right with what you made. But today you've got to make good money to get by. I think I am rich in one way . . . the Lord has been good to me in my health. Let's face it, when you hit my age, there are very few people as healthy as I am. My doctor said, "Harry, if I didn't know you and I saw you on the street, I would never believe your years." I feel good, I am active, and I don't have to worry about my health. What's money compared to that?

Zola: I could have been rich. I had plenty of ideas. I had one idea after another, and why I never tried them out, I don't know. I know I could have opened a dress shop. I always loved beautiful clothes. I've had so many ideas about doing things, and I guess I was stupid not to take advantage of all my opportunities. I was too backward, too shy to just go out and do all those things that would have made me a success. My husband passed away in 1973. He was the best husband anybody could have. He gave me everything. He brought his checks home and he gave them to me. He never even asked what I did with the money. When he began having trouble breathing, I gave him $100 and I told him, "You go to a doctor and find out what's wrong." So what do you think happened? He came back and told me the doctor said he could drop dead at any moment. He never said another word about his illness. He was never sick in bed one day. He got up every day and dressed; he never sat around in a bathrobe. The last couple of nights before he died he kept saying, "Zola, you know, I'm restless." I'd taken him to another doctor who said, "Mrs. Primm, your husband has a heart condition." The doctor said he should take nitroglycerine or he wouldn't be here very long. And what do you think? My husband and I thought nitroglycerine was an explosive liquid and we were afraid of it, so he never took the stuff.

LaVerne: On the one hand, I never had the opportunity to become rich. On the other hand, my grandparents were wealthy. They died when I was away from home, and I was robbed of my inheritance by relatives. It was $1 million worth of artifacts, antiques, jade, china, silverware and what not. The lawyer made an excessive amount of claims against the estate of my grandparents, and I came out with only $1,800. Also, I was robbed of designs, automobile designs and designs for boats and other mechanical devices by people with whom I was associated. The FBI can verify the fact that I was robbed of what was rightfully mine. No, I don't think I've fared poorly because I'm black. The reason was my lack of knowledge of how to go about making money.

Harry: The most money I ever had at one time in my life was

what I made weekly. That's about the truth of things. But I saved money by never marrying. I stayed a single, selfish old bachelor. I had plenty of chances to get married, but I just didn't get around to it. I don't know if it was because I was afraid to take on the responsibility of supporting a wife. Most of my life, before I retired, I made around $50 or $55 a week. But in those days that went a long way. Maybe I should have gotten married, but it's too late to think about that now.

Zola: In my whole life, I never had more than $1,000 in one bundle. Everything else went for necessities, you can believe that.

LaVerne: I never had a pile larger than the $1,800 I received from the estate of my grandparents.

Harry: I consider myself lucky. I was never unemployed, not even during the Depression. Besides my job as a clerk at the Statler-Hilton, I also held jobs as a nurse and a cashier. I retired in 1961 or 1962. The most money I ever earned was about $125 to $150 a week.

Zola: I love to work. I've had to work all my life, even when I was married. My husband and I managed a motel for years. I don't know why I'm not working now. I really should. I worked as a stockroom girl when I was younger. I worked in an ice cream parlor and I sold candy in the five and dime, and those jobs were swell. I love candy and ice cream, but nowadays I can't afford them.

LaVerne: I've been a barber, worked in a warehouse; I've been a writer. As a kid I sold newspapers and worked in grocery stores as a clerk and poultry man. When I was a barber, I bought all my own tools. I've supported myself all my life. I always bought secondhand cars and clothes. Never could buy anything better.

Harry: I've never been broke. I always managed to hang onto a job. But as far as going down and putting anything in the bank, that was out. I was never in a bank in my life to make a deposit, only to cash my checks.

Zola: I've never been completely broke, either. I just don't remember being without enough money to pay for food and rent, though I've been pretty low many, many times toward the last of the month. But I got through because I budget. I try to think what I'm going to need, and I try to have that much all the time. I've always been that way, even when I was young.

LaVerne: I've been dead-rock broke many times, without a

cent and without any source of income whatsoever and no way to get money. I went hungry until someone happened along who would give me a dollar for a meal. I saw all that poverty around me, and I was part of the poverty, but somehow I managed to survive.

Harry: In all honesty, I have never envied rich people. I haven't envied anybody because he or she had more than I did. But I have said lots of times to myself, I wish I could be comfortable. To me, being comfortable means having the necessities in life. I have no animosity or mean feelings toward people who have more money than I do. They had to work as hard as I did, and, I don't know, maybe they were luckier. You can't envy luck.

Zola: I love the rich but I don't envy them—my goodness, no. I even had the opportunity to marry a millionaire one time. Do you know that I was too shy to go through with it? I simply don't understand it to this day. But, anyway, I sure didn't marry that millionaire.

LaVerne: I learned early in life the philosophy that has tided me over all these years. When I was a child and I asked my father for a bicycle and he told me no, I told him the kid next door has a bicycle. He told me that as long as I lived I would always see somebody who had more than I did. So that's always been my belief—never worry about what the next man has, but to try to get something for myself.

Harry: I really have no financial fears about the future. My pension used to be $72.50 a month, which wasn't much. As soon as I got my Social Security, they cut it down to $62.23, which I thought was unnecessary. But there's nothing I can do about it. Don't misunderstand me, I am not ungrateful, because my government, God bless it, and my Uncle Sam owe me nothing. I am living in the best country in the world.

Zola: What am I afraid of? I'm afraid they're going to raise my rent again. I'm afraid I will lose all my possessions, and I'm afraid I won't be able to pay the rent.

LaVerne: My fear is of losing the basics in life. At my age, I don't expect to become a millionaire, unless I win my malpractice suit. I'm just content to live from day to ‑day, week to week, month to month, and not to have to live in missions or depend on the largesse of charities, other than my government.

Harry: Financially, I look forward to the government raising my pension. There's a bill in Congress that would increase the pensions of veterans who've passed their eightieth birthday. My increase, according to what they told me at my American Legion post, would be $7.25 a month. That would be a livable condition; then I wouldn't have to worry so much if I got a $10 a month rent increase.

Zola: I hope in the future I can quit thinking about finances, because I want to do other things. I want to study music, I want to join more clubs. I want to do something other than think about the rent and about money. That's what I look forward to.

LaVerne: I look forward to living in decent quarters and getting out of where I live now, in a borderline skid-row neighborhood.

ANNA SCHWARTZ

Born on New York's Lower East Side, Anna is seventy-four years old. Her weight, after a ten-year battle with lung cancer (she has never smoked a cigarette in her life), is down to eighty-three pounds.

She lies, frail and resigned, in the bed of a clean, well-run convalescent hospital, the $550 monthly bill paid by her son. "I know I'm going to die," she says. "I'm not afraid. It will be a relief, sort of. I won't have to struggle for money anymore. The doctor says the cancer's racing to my brain, so why do I need money?"

Her facial features are taut, the timbre of her voice firm. Except for the weight loss, she doesn't give the impression of being ill.

Until I was fourteen years old, my allowance was a penny every night from my mother. In those days you could get a lot for a penny—a stick of gum, a Hershey bar, the same Hershey bar you get today for a quarter.

We were two brothers and five sisters. Both brothers and four of my sisters are dead—they all had to work very hard throughout their lives. We were one Jewish family that didn't produce a doctor, a lawyer, or a millionaire.

When I was six, we moved to the Bronx. My father was a skilled tailor who always managed to work. I would say at that time he made $50 a week. With $150 today, you couldn't do what you could do then with $50. We always had food on the table. I never knew what it was to go hungry until the Depression.

I began working when I was sixteen years old. I wasn't allowed to go to high school. My father wanted me to work. I got through junior high, and then he sent me to a business school for six months, where I learned shorthand and typing. I remember my first job, working for a photographer in downtown New York City. I was making $30 a week, which was a lot of money. I worked for the photographer for two years, and was earning $45 a week when I left to get married.

In 1925, my husband was making around $6 a day as a plumber, which also was good money. Then he took a permanent plumber's job for $60 a week, and that seemed like a fortune, especially in that day and age when nobody paid taxes.

My husband lost his job in the Depression. He went to work one day and the boss said, "Things are slow. We can't use you anymore."

Life became very, very hard. There were times when we ate potatoes three times a day. And there were times when we didn't eat, we just went hungry. What saved us from starving was that we used to go to my mother's house for dinner. I appreciated her feeding us, but it was very aggravating to know that you had to depend on your own mother.

My son was born in 1927, and, no matter what, I managed to feed him. I would steal before I would allow him to go hungry. Every morning my son had cereal, and at night I'd open a can of soup for him. It helped when he started going to P.S. 66—they gave him a free lunch there.

My husband was driving a cab. In a good week, he made $15. People didn't ride in cabs much during the thirties. Then my husband got sick and was hardly able to work. I had married him, knowing he had a heart condition.

We were constantly moving from one apartment to another, because we didn't have the money to pay the rent. We owed rent on every apartment we moved from. In those days you could get away with it. Today you can't even get away with a day. We would just pack up and leave in the middle of the night. I don't know how many apartments we had in the Grand Concourse area of the Bronx—fifteen, twenty, twenty-five. I remember one place where we stayed the longest, almost a year. It was two and a half rooms for $38 a month, and we never paid a dollar in rent. The landlord carried us until we sneaked out on him in shame. Years later I went back to pay the landlord the rent I owed. But he was dead.

I went to work again when my son was twelve years old. I didn't want to, but it was necessary when I was forced to divorce my husband. He started drinking and playing around with other women, I think out of frustration, so he could forget that he couldn't support his family.

I was a cashier in a very exclusive restaurant in the East Seventies. For a dollar you could get a very good meal there. I started at $25 a week and was raised up to $50. But the thing was this: I had to quit the steady job and become a part-time mail order clerk so I could be home when my son got out of school. We were living in this beat-up neighborhood and he had terrible friends, all Italians. One of them killed a man in a robbery and got the electric chair when he was nineteen years old.

I worked in the mail-order department of a lot of publishing companies, including Putnam and McGraw-Hill. I used to put these circulars into envelopes and then put labels on the envelopes. They all liked me and they thought I ought to go along to better things if I could work full hours. But I only worked from nine to one p.m., with a thirty-five-minute subway ride both ways. I was paid $1.50 an hour.

The work would run out and I would just go from place to place in the mail-order world. I was never out of a job very long. Then I started to work as a clerk in a cigar store, selling lighters and cigarettes and newspapers and stuff. I was with them for years. One day I just took off and lost a good job. The reason I took off was that my son, who was twenty-one years old by now, had gotten a job in Munich, Germany, as a writer for Radio Free Europe, and I went to the boat to see him off. I just excused myself and I walked out and said I had to leave. The man who owned the store got very angry and told me not to come back. But it was worth it. My son sailed on the *Queen Mary,* and he had champagne in the cabin and I was thrilled. Anyway, there was always more mail-order work.

The most money I ever earned in one year was—let's see, in 1958 or 1959—I made $4,500. I always paid cheap rent and I was able to save money. When a person pays cheap rent, no matter how little you make, you can always put a dollar away. I moved to a railroad flat on West 16th Street in Manhattan and was there for fifteen years, paying $35 a month.

At first, it was an elegant neighborhood. There were nice people, different nationalities and religions. I was the only Jew. But little by little it started to change. The first five years were very good; people didn't move away. But then it got pretty rough when the Puerto Ricans and the colored invaded the block. They used to hold block parties and have rock groups. I was on the third floor, and with closed windows I could hear that terrible music. They littered the street with beer cans and broke windows, and I was robbed three times. I had to start thinking about finding another place to live.

In 1957 one of my sisters died. When she was dying in the hospital, she gave me one of her bankbooks, which was for $14,000. After she died I got that money. I just went to the bank and showed them the death certificate and they gave me the money.

My sister wanted me to have that $14,000, but a lot of greed came up in the family. Another sister of mine and a sister-in-law hired lawyers to try and get the $14,000 away from me. It was very bitter. I had to hire two lawyers. The first one was my cousin, but he didn't do much for me except charge me $4,000. The second lawyer cost me $3,000. It ended up that I had to pay my sister and sister-in-law $1,000 apiece. So with that $2,000 plus the $7,000 in lawyer's charges, I only had $5,000 of the original $14,000.

Then there was another bitter fight for the additional $65,000 in cash my dead sister also left. Finally, it was divided among several members of the family. I got $12,000 and came out with $17,000 altogether.

If only my sister had left a will. She knew what a hard life I'd had, how I'd struggled, and she wanted me to have her money. She said so on her deathbed. All the others in the family had more money than I did. I still don't speak to any of them. Money makes enemies. I'll never forgive them, not even in the grave. At one point while we were fighting over the money, one of my sisters called me a fink and a thief. You don't forgive those things.

I got sick in 1967. The Big C. That changed everything. My New York doctors gave me three to six months to live. But here I am. Too tough and mean to die. I moved to Los Angeles, where my son was working for a television station. The trip I'd planned to take around the world was out—I spent all the money from my sister's estate on doctors.

I live on $2,400 a year I get from Social Security. Until I came into the hospital, my son paid the rent for my apartment. When they raised Social Security 4 percent a couple of years ago, I didn't get the increase. I went to the Social Security office downtown to find out about it. There wasn't a seat in the place, it was so crowded. We were like cattle. I wanted to walk out but then I figured I had already given the girl my name. She told me it would be an hour wait, but then it turned out to be four hours. Finally, she said that I didn't qualify for the raise because I had worked part-time for so many years.

As I look back, I have a lot of regrets. My life is a very sad story. I made a lot of mistakes. I shouldn't have married the husband I married. If my father hadn't made me work, I could have gone on with my education. I wanted to be a teacher or maybe do something in radio. But it never worked out. The only thing that worked out was my son. He's got a good job, thank God, and a lovely family.

Now I just lie in this place day after day, with the cancer eating at me. I've learned one thing in this bed—I don't envy millionaires, I envy people who have their health.

M. ANDREUS VARGO

Vargo is eighty-eight years old and a millionaire. "I feel sound as a dollar," he says. "On second thought, I may be in better shape than the dollar."

Vigorous and healthy, he's up at six o'clock and in his office by eight to attend to personal business affairs and the duties, mostly fund-raising, of the more than a dozen charities in which he's involved.

He's at a gym twice a week for mild exercise. His major recreation—a Wednesday night ten-cent-limit poker game—has recently been deactivated by the death of several regular players. "One of the troubles with living as long as I have is that so many of your friends are dying around you."

My father walked from eastern Czechoslovakia to Bremen, Germany to get a boat for America. He settled in Trenton, New Jersey, where he became a steel worker. He helped to make the steel that built the Brooklyn Bridge.

When I was five my parents moved to a prairie farm seven miles south of Lakefield, Minnesota. My father had a hankering to be a pioneer. I went to a country school through the eighth grade and to a business college for five or six months. That was the extent of my formal education.

Back home in Lakefield, the farmers co-op asked me to keep its books, which I did for $40 a month. That was a very good, very respectable wage at the time. A couple of months later I took a job with the Jackson County state bank in Lakefield as a bookkeeper at the same pay.

I left a year and a half later to seek my fortune. I went to Thurston, a small town in northeastern Nebraska on the Winnebago reservation. I met my wife there. She lived in Bancroft, which was a couple of towns down on the railroad. What brought me to Thurston was an increase in salary to $65 a month. I was always alert to an opportunity that offered more money.

After I was in Thurston for a while, I heard that there was a need for a bank in Salem, which was a town in the southern part of the state with a population of about three hundred. I decided, at the age of twenty-three, to open my own bank. I managed to raise $15,000, which was our total capital. Imagine trying to open a bank these days with $15,000.

I'd married my wife Mae by now and she put in $1,000 that she'd earned giving music lessons. My father invested $1,000. I borrowed $1,000 from my father for my share of ownership. The other $12,000 I raised from the sale of stock in the bank.

I took an empty store building and converted it by having a vault and safety deposit boxes put in. In those days, it was a showy thing for a small-town bank to have the big steel safe standing in the front window, so that's what I did.

It cost about $3,000 to open the door in November 1913. I was very disappointed when we didn't prosper. I hadn't researched the area for potentialities until after the bank opened. Then I discovered that most of the tenant farmers around Salem were on land owned by a bank in the next town, Fall City, which was a sizable town and the county seat. Naturally, the farmers were doing business with the Fall City bank.

We sold out in a year at par. I didn't make any profit, but I didn't lose any money. I considered myself fortunate. I came out of the deal about even—maybe a little better than even, since I'd been giving myself a salary of $75 a month.

Next, I was offered a job with a life insurance company, which I accepted. It was a very difficult job, like trying to revive a dead horse. People had bought insurance and were unhappy with it for some reason or other; maybe the agent had oversold them, and they didn't want to renew. It was my task to get them to renew. But it wasn't a paying thing, and I didn't like it. And the company didn't like my production, so we parted.

I heard that a man on the Omaha *World-Herald* needed a bookkeeper, so I went there. It turned out to be the Audit Bureau of Circulations, better known in the trade as the ABC. It was formed to audit the circulations of newspapers, so that they could justify their advertising rates. The ABC was a new concern then, and they needed young men. I got the job, and pretty soon they sent me out on the road to audit the circulation of papers in Lincoln and a lot of farm papers in small towns. I was paid $63 a week plus $28 for expenses. It was fascinating work, a constant challenge. The ABC was new to publishers, and frequently their records were incomplete. The job challenged your ingenuity.

I quit the Bureau after seven years because I was tired of traveling. By this time I'd saved $10,000. Mae and I were very thrifty; we always saved a minimum of $10 a week. People forget how even that seemingly small amount of money adds up.

I considered myself a fairly successful young man. I took a look around to see what else I could do. Through an old friend of my wife's, I got a job selling lots on what had once been an oil field. Then I sold lots on a subdivision that's now the Los Angeles International Airport.

I did that for a number of years and then landed in Toluca Lake, which a lot of people call the Beverly Hills of the San

Fernando Valley. Practically all the movie stars you can name have lived here at one time, or still live here, because it's so close to the studios. Warner Brothers, Universal and Disney are just a stone's throw away.

In the early thirties I sold Bing Crosby three lots for $5,000, and he built a house. That property today is easily worth $300,000. I rented a house on the lake in September 1931 to W. C. Fields. Fields had come from New York, where he was a star in the *Ziegfeld Follies*. He was trying to break into motion pictures and was having a difficult time. He was very prompt about paying the rent—it was due on the first and he would come over to my office and pay his $250 a month on the twenty-eighth.

Fields had a devilish sense of humor, or maybe he was bored. Anyway, he passed some of his afternoons drenching pieces of bread in whiskey and feeding them to the ducks, who'd walk up to his lawn from the lake, then wobble back into the lake dead drunk.

William Randolph Hearst's son George rented a house from me for $85 a month during the Depression. George was working on the *Examiner,* and he told me that Harry Chandler, the publisher of the *Times,* had loaned his father money because he didn't want the competing paper to fail. So the *Times* actually rescued the *Examiner* in the thirties.

Mae and I got by during the Depression because I had saved a little more money. By now we had about $25,000. We were still living frugally and we had no children. We wanted children, but my wife miscarried three times.

At the lowest point in the Depression, '32 or '33, I only grossed $1,200. I could hardly sell any property, and most of that income came from renting houses. By the same token, things were cheaper. We had a four-room apartment in Los Angeles at that time for which we'd been paying $65 a month. But gradually I managed to persuade the landlord to reduce the rent to $35. So you can see that money in those times was all relative.

Up to 1940, I'd been trying to make money any way I could, primarily by selling and buying real estate and by buying stocks. I opened a margin account with a broker, but all I was doing was sending money down the chute. Every time I bought a stock it went down. So finally I said the heck with it.

So I decided to lend money. I went into the mortgage banking business. If a person came into the office and bought a lot, say, for $1,500 and had only $500 as a down payment, I said I'd loan him the other $1,000 at a competitive interest rate, rarely over 6 percent. I charged no points and no penalties. Over a period of thirty years that multiplied itself to where at one time I had more than $500,000 out in loans.

As the payments came in on one loan, I would use that money to make another loan. To show you how money multiplies itself in an amortized loan, I made one deal in which I loaned a man and his wife $70,000 at 6½ percent interest, repayable at $525 per month. That was in September 1965, and at the end of eleven years they had paid $44,445 in interest and still owed $39,806 on the principal.

In another case, I loaned a man $10,000 at 6½ percent, payable at $75 a month. At the end of twelve years, he had paid $6,558 in interest and still owed $6,000 on the principal.

The mortgage business made me a millionaire, and I've been in semiretirement since 1946. Mae passed away in October 1975, and they assessed the estate as community property. They cut into you pretty heavily, and what happens is you pay an inheritance tax on half your holdings. You pay a federal tax and you also pay a California tax. The federal tax was something like $172,000 and the California tax a little less than $50,000.

Someone once said that you should pay yourself first, that a portion of what you make is yours to keep. My wife and I were thrifty and economical. We didn't spend a lot on living expenses. About my only luxury is a Cadillac that's several years old. My house is comparatively modest for the Toluca Lake area.

I was helped by the fact that in the early days there wasn't the income tax that there is today. And then when it did come in, it wasn't as high as it is today.

I still have a good deal of money out in loans. Also, I have an apartment building that pays $500 a month and a parking lot that pays $300, so there is $800 a month coming in that's clear, because they pay the taxes.

They say the wise thing to do nowadays is to give your money away while you are living. To reduce my estate, that's what I should be doing, giving my money away to some favorite nephews in Chicago. But no one can guess what the future will bring. And with inflation, I'm puzzled as to how much money I'll need for the rest of my life.

One of the things that brought me a lot of comfort and relaxed me in the Depression was not worrying about money even though I wasn't making a great deal of it then. But everybody was scared of shadows. So I took stock of myself and I said, Well, if I have to I can live on $100 a month. And then I figured that I had maybe fifty years to live. So at $1,200 a year for fifty years, I'd need $60,000. And I had $60,000 at the time in cash and assets. So I suddenly woke up and said, What am I worrying about? If I don't make a nickel, if things go on just the way they are now, I have ample to live on. And you'd be surprised how much relaxation and peace of mind that gave me, because from then on I wasn't fretting about business or having enough money. I had satisfied myself that I had enough to live on for the rest of my days.

That's not a bad way to inventory yourself. Figure out how much it is costing you to live, and have your life insurance agent tell you how many years you have left. Then multiply the years by the amount of money you have or can save, and you are in.

Naturally, from my initial estimate I went on and earned more money. I earned it to keep pace with the rising cost of living over the years and because I have to be active. But I never worried about money again.

I can't tell you exactly why I made money and so many others who are my age are living in poverty. We have had the poor with us since the beginning of time. Some of us are either more fortunate or more adept at making money. I'm no wizard with money. I don't know what it takes to make it or why some people make it and others don't. I'm afraid that some people just never learn how to manage their money or themselves.

I feel very secure about money for the rest of my life. Fortunately, I played my cards right. I come from a long-lived family. My father died at ninety-four, my mother at ninety-two. I have a sister who's eighty-two and a brother who is eighty-four. I plan to outlive them all, with as much financial comfort as this world affords us.

"Give Me . . . Your Huddled Masses"

I'm down to my last four Rolls-Royces.

—ROCKY AOKI

ANTHONY ANDREOLA

Occasionally he gets a call from one of the nearby movie or television studios. Thus, he has cut the hair of Frank Sinatra, Bob Hope, Jonathan Winters and Rossano Brazzi. Their autographed pictures adorn a wall of his shop.

Andreola is a small, blond, balding man in his fiftieth year, the father of six. He was born in the southern Italian province of Potenza, in the town of Ripacanolida.

It's a mighty small town, not even on most maps. It is the poorest place in Italy. There is no industry, only agriculture. Almost everybody owns a little piece of land. The people work hard, long hours on their land. They get up before the sun, carry their tools to the fields, and work until after the sun goes down. They grow wheat, chestnuts, a few vegetables like beans and potatoes. Mostly, they produce wine. They make the wine without machinery, all by hand. For the winter, they store food. Whatever is left over, they sell.

The average family's income is between $300 and $400 a year. From that money, they pay their bills and buy their tools and seed. Nobody goes hungry, but the meals are usually bread and wine. When they can eat hot chili, it's a rare luxury.

I started as a barber when I was nine years old. I never made any money, because people used to pay with wheat. At harvest time, in July or August, each of my customers would bring me a little bushel of wheat for my services throughout the year. From that, my mother made our own bread. We never had money to buy clothes. What clothes we had were sent by relatives in America. In order to live, we had to sell or trade the wheat. That was how we paid our rent, paid the doctor, paid for the food to feed the family. At Easter and Christmas, customers would also give me a little wine. The wine and the wheat were all I ever received for giving haircuts and shaves.

We had a big house, and all the members of the family lived together—my father, my mother, my grandfather, two aunts, cousins, grandchildren and children, thirteen of us.

The only money we had was what my father made. He served the church. When somebody died, he used to ring the bell—dong, dong, dong—you know, to let all the people on the farms know somebody is dead and tomorrow there will be a funeral. For that, he received a few lire.

There were about fifteen barbers in town, and I tried to revolutionize things, form them into a union. I said, "Let's get together to make some money." But they didn't like my idea. They said it went against the tradition of hundreds of years. So I realized I could not change this thing, and I thought if the opportunity ever came I would leave Ripacanolida.

About that time, my father received an invitation from a cousin in Argentina, inviting him there. My father said he didn't have the money for the journey. The cousin said he would pay for the trip and my father could pay him back little by little.

So my father went first, in 1950. Then one of my brothers. In 1952, my mother left with two of my sisters and my other brother. I had to wait. During this time, I was married. My wife and I were the last to leave. Not until 1956, when my father had made enough money working in a clothing factory in Buenos Aires, could he send me the money to join the family in Argentina.

At first, I worked for somebody else as a barber. Then I opened my own shop, with $400 in savings. A year later, I bought another shop that was for sale. I was making good money and life was not bad. My father and brothers were also working. We put all our money together, and we were doing all right.

Then something happened, something very sad to remember. All the money we made was taken by somebody smarter than us.

One day a friend told me that there was a man who ran a private bank, and he paid much more interest on money than the regular banks. I was skeptical and cautious, but I thought I would go over to see the man just to find out what it was all about. When I got there, there was a long line of people, all waiting to put their savings with that man in his bank. The man was about ninety years old; he looked like a big king sitting in the center of his little storefront bank with four or five assistants around him.

When I saw so many people waiting to deposit money with him, I thought it must be a respectable company. I said to my father, "Let's put our money in this bank." So we took the $10,000 that our whole family had saved by sacrificing. In our whole lives, we'd never had so much money before.

A year and a half after we gave him our money, I received a phone call from my friend. He said, "The banker is dead, and all the money is gone. The man's assistants have disappeared with it." I ran to the bank, and there were hundreds of others like me there. The bank was empty. We'd all been cheated. We complained to the government, but the government didn't do anything.

Many people who invested in the bank shot themselves. I didn't shoot myself because I was young and thought I could still make a future for myself and my family. But I decided to leave Argentina. I said to my wife, "This is no country for me. Argentina is not a serious country, not an honest country."

I sold my shops and came to New York and saw the Statue of Liberty, which impressed me very much. I knew that the Statue of Liberty represented freedom, represented a serious country.

I visited relatives in New York and Chicago. They all said I should come to Los Angeles; there was opportunity in this city. So I took the advice and arrived in Los Angeles on November 7, 1964. We celebrated our first American Thanksgiving here. For what was I thankful? I was thankful for my job as a dishwasher in a restaurant, which allowed us to survive on the $115 I earned every two weeks.

By day, I went to school to study English and to get my barber's license. After school, I went to the restaurant to work from midnight until eight in the morning. In a year I had learned sufficient English to obtain my license. I went to work in the daytime as a barber, making $17 to $20 a day, and kept my job in the restaurant.

In May 1966 I bought this shop for $3,000. How much is it worth now? It is worth nothing. Who would want to buy a barber shop? All over Los Angeles, all over America, barber shops have closed for lack of work, for lack of customers. Two years ago, somebody came around and said he wanted to buy my shop. I said, "How much do you want to pay?" He said, "A thousand dollars." I said, "I couldn't take a $2,000 loss." Now I don't think I could get even the $1,000 for the shop.

The change in hair styles has hurt my business. Men don't take haircuts as often as before. They never take shaves. Who wants a shave in a barber shop? Before, customers used to come in every two weeks or three weeks. Now it's a couple of months. Some come only every Christmas. They say when they leave, "See you next Christmas."

I charge $4.50 for a haircut. Some weeks I make only $100, $110. In a good week, I earn $150, including tips. In other words, I am lucky if I can keep the shop open.

I have a house for which I paid $27,000. The mortgage payment is $147 a month for thirty years. How do we manage? For one thing, we never go to a restaurant. My wife and I have never eaten in a restaurant in our whole lives—not in Italy, not in Argentina, not here. My wife makes her own bread, she makes her own pasta. We grow tomatoes in the backyard and she makes our tomato sauce.

I don't have insurance. See, I am not a 100 percent American. It's the American way to have life insurance, car insurance, health insurance. We have none of that. We can't afford it.

I have a 1967 Datsun. I bought a secondhand television set for the kids. We never go out anyplace. Since I arrived in America, we have never been out even to a movie.

I go to night school, where I'm studying automobile and television mechanics. Now I can tune up my own car and fix the television set. So we don't have to spend money on those things.

I have about $2,000 in savings—for emergencies. In 1975 I took four hundred and some dollars to go back and visit Ripacanolida, to see relatives and friends. It scared me, talking with the people there. They are all Communists. They have bad feelings against America; I don't know why. Maybe they feel America has neglected them. They think they are punishing America by voting Communist.

I brought shirts and cigarettes to Ripacanolida. They think

everybody in America is rich. I told them it's not true, but they don't believe it. I told them I had to work very hard. They don't believe that either; nobody can change their minds.

Ripacanolida is almost a ghost city. The younger generation doesn't like to work so hard and so long, so they leave, as I did. When I left there were 6,000 people in Ripacanolida. Today there are only 2,000. There were five churches. Now there is only one church that is open. Only four barbers are left.

I am worried about the future. I worry about my country. I am an American citizen now, and I am very concerned about the expansion of communism and our economy. The economy is not healthy if small businessmen like me can't make a living.

In Italy I wanted to be a professional, not just a barber. I wanted to go to school, but my family had no money. This country offers my children opportunity. They can be something, not a barber like me. I teach my children to love school. One of them says he wants to be a doctor, but unless he earns a scholarship I can't afford a medical school education. Maybe his son can be a doctor.

But don't misunderstand what I am saying. I am grateful to America. As long as your family is healthy and there is food on the table, things can't be too bad. I lead a better life here than I ever had before. America is a serious country.

ROCKY AOKI

The Japanese Horatio Alger, Rocky has more than $1 million for each year he's lived. Hiroaki (he insists everyone call him Rocky) Aoki is a thirty-eight-year-old tycoon with a $45 million fortune.

He lives on a three-and-a-half-acre estate in Englewood, New Jersey, sports a $12,000 diamond ring, favors T shirts and inexpensive cords, and commutes to his Manhattan office by chauffeured Rolls-Royce, usually watching television in the back seat.

He first set foot on American soil in 1959 as a member of the Japanese Olympic wrestling team. "Right away, I knew America was the land of comfort and opportunity. Turn the faucet and you get hot water when you want hot water. I didn't exactly believe the streets of America were paved

*with gold, but in the airport terminal in Hawaii I saw a dollar bill lying
on the ground. I didn't pick it up, because I didn't want to be greedy and I
knew there were a lot more from where that one came. The incident was
an omen. It reinforced my idea that there was money, plenty of it, to be
made in the U.S.A."*

*After deciding to remain in New York, he spent his $400 grubstake.
Penniless, he took a job as an eighty-cent-an-hour parking lot attendant.*

They cheated me. At that time, the minimum wage was $1 an
hour. I couldn't make a decent living just parking cars, so I went
next door and got a job at the bakery shop of Horn and Hardart.
They paid me $1 an hour. I kept both jobs, working sixteen hours
a day until I'd saved a few hundred dollars.

I decided the way to make money was to become my own boss.
I subleased an ice cream truck and got a route in Harlem. There
were two reasons for choosing Harlem: number one, nobody
wanted to go there; and number two, there were a lot of kids and
adults running around the streets, especially in the summertime.
With all that traffic and without competition, I figured I could
make out pretty good.

The first day on the route I almost got killed. Three guys held
me up. They took me to an empty building and stole about $200.
One of them knifed me in the neck and on the thigh.

I wasn't scared off. I kept up the route. I got up at seven
o'clock in the morning. I was living on the west side of Manhattan in a $40-a-month apartment and rode the subway for almost
an hour to the Bronx, where the man who owned the truck kept
it parked. By eight-thirty I was on the Harlem streets, and I
worked until three or four o'clock in the morning. You'd be
amazed how many people are on the streets there at that hour.
Everybody bought ice cream. I had lots of good customers in
Harlem; I was very popular. At least no one held me up again.

I was making so much money I didn't even count it. The bag in
which I carried the change was so heavy I could hardly lift it.
Besides, after working so many hours, I was too tired to count
my money. I just dragged the bag to the bank and let them count
it.

In five months I had saved $10,000, and I decided to open a
restaurant. But first, I enrolled at the restaurant management

school at Cornell University. They kicked me out right away, because I couldn't pass the English test they gave me. I still remember the dean who kicked me out. A couple of years later he wrote me a letter and said he was sorry I didn't get into the school. He wanted me to be a guest lecturer. I would have done it—I had no hard feelings—but I didn't have the time.

I needed another $10,000 to open the restaurant. I went to the Bank of Tokyo, and they turned me down for a loan. They thought I was crazy; they said New York already had too many restaurants. I called my father in Japan. He had a chain of nine small restaurants in Tokyo and had a friend who worked at the Bank of Tokyo in New York. I didn't want any money from my father; I just wanted him to use his influence to get me a loan.

It worked. I named my new enterprise Benihana, for a red flower that grows in Japan.

It was hard getting started. I had to pay $500 a month for a tiny location at 60 West 56th Street. I had only four tables. For dinner sometimes there was only one customer. The big trouble was that I couldn't get a liquor license. The lack of booze, rather than the quality of my food and the unique way in which it was cooked and served, was keeping customers away. Then, little by little, through word of mouth we began getting more people. And finally, after a year, I got my liquor license and put in a cocktail lounge which produced 22 percent of my volume.

I knew I had a good thing going. When it caught on, America would like it. The first year and a half I averaged $20 a night. My wife, brothers, and mother worked for me, which meant my only important overhead was rent. I wasn't taking any salary. Since I had to do everything at the place, I just stayed there. I slept in the men's room where the heat was, so I'd be warm and so I wouldn't waste time going back and forth to my apartment.

Then one night Clementine Paddleford walked in. She gave Benihana a rave review in the *Herald Tribune* the next day, and, wham, the place was packed. The waiting line outside kept growing. I added a couple of tables to the original four and a year later I opened my second restaurant. Then pretty soon I had the third one. I was a millionaire before I knew it. Now I have twenty-six Benihanas from New York to Hawaii. Eight more are under construction.

The reason for the success of Benihana was that I introduced something new. I wasn't just selling food. A lot of people say it's a gimmick, but I call it a dining experience. I introduced Teppanyaki, or steel grill cooking, to America. Some people call it hibachi cooking. I set up communal tables and had the chefs cook the meals while the guests watched. It seemed to me that Americans were lonely people and wanted to talk with strangers but didn't know how. Besides, you go out to dinner with your wife, and how much fun is that? You see her every day, at every meal. One of the biggest reasons people come to Benihana is because they meet other people easily and they enjoy the skill and showmanship of the chefs at the tables who chop vegetables and slice meat like they are performing on a stage. In a sense, they are.

I knew Americans wouldn't go for Japanese food in a big way, so I didn't serve raw fish or any of the traditional slimy delectables from Japan. My entrées were and are steak, filet mignon, chicken and shrimp. The only things that are Japanese are the salad seasonings, the sauces, the help, and the kimonos the waitresses wear.

I never could have made it in Japan. The seniority system and the economic structure there would have made it impossible. Young people in Japan are under a lot of pressure because of skepticism and lack of trust by the older generation. It's changing, but not fast enough. A guy with my temperament and aggressiveness would have been killed in Japan. Young Japanese still fall into certain slots, depending on their family, background and education. They join the big companies, live in a company house, and live a company life. They move up according to how long they've been with the company. The American system, which rewards initiative and enterprise, is superior by far.

Each Benihana grosses more than $1 million a year. But it's not the gross that counts. The bottom line is the net. Each unit nets annually between $500,000 and $700,000.

I've found a new way to build eight or nine Benihanas a year, using someone else's money, while I retain 100 percent ownership. It works like this. First, I find a location. Then I make a deal with the owner to lease his site. I tell him I need $600,000 to build a new unit. I offer him a twenty-five-year lease at $100,000 a year for his location. In exchange, he borrows $600,000 from the bank—I even find the bank for him—and he gives me that money. It's a good deal for him and a good deal for me. I net approximately half a million dollars even after paying him the $100,000 a year and all the other expenses. So I make a tremendous amount of profit without spending any of my own money. Using this system to develop the chain, I hope to have a Benihana in every American state within a few years. I plan to expand to Europe, too, but the money is really here, in America.

How does it feel to be worth $45 million? I can't tell you, because I don't feel anything. I'm just a regular guy. I never get to touch the $45 million. I don't see the money. The cash that flows in every day goes to the bank. I just see a balance sheet at the end of the month. So I don't really feel like I'm a multimillionaire.

I'm stingier now than I used to be. When I saw good stuff, I didn't care how much I spent. I used to have eight Rolls-Royces. They cost $45,000 to $90,000 apiece. When I liked something I just bought it. But then the stories got back to me. People were saying, "This kid doesn't know what the hell he's doing." So I sold half my fleet of cars. I'm down to my last four Rolls-Royces.

I went through a period when I became bored by just running the restaurants. So I got into other things. I promoted the Muhammad Ali–Mac Foster fight in Japan. I just about broke even, but I had a good time. The kids in Japan thought I was some kind of a hero. I'd walk down the street and they'd ask for my autograph.

I backed two Broadway shows, both of which failed. I bought a string of racehorses, with my eye on the Kentucky Derby, but the horses turned out to be losers. I saw that *Playboy* was successful, and I figured if Hugh Hefner could have a big magazine, why couldn't I? So I started *Genesis,* a skin magazine. It didn't turn out too well. The magazine business is more competitive than the restaurant business. I've sold most of my interest in *Genesis.* I also opened a nightclub in New York, but that was a failure and I lost a bundle.

I have only two luxuries left: flying my Cessna and racing my powerboat.

I've changed my philosophy, my way of spending money. I

feel that people are watching me, so I try not to do anything foolish with my money. I once thought money was for spending. Now I realize money is for keeping.

If I lost every penny, what would I do? I'd go back to the ice cream truck in Harlem. I have a lot more ideas, and I'd sell a hell of a lot more ice cream than I did before.

When I was a kid I read in books and magazines and newspapers that there was a lot of opportunity in America. It's true. Of course I was very lucky. But anyone can get lucky. You just have to know how to use the luck.

I don't sleep much. It isn't money worries that keep me awake. I don't know what it is. I am not a happy person. I am a very unhappy person. Because of business. Because of my job. I get a lot of pressure. I go crazy thinking about the business. It's too much. I can't ever take a vacation.

What good is having all this money if I'm not happy?

That's my question.

PHAN THI KIEU NGA

On April 22, 1975, Mrs. Nga, with her husband and two children, fled Saigon aboard an American plane at virtually the last minute. South Vietnam surrendered unconditionally to the North Vietnamese only a week after the Nga family got out.

"We kept hoping we wouldn't have to leave," she says. "Now we are here, and we are caught between the past and the future."

She weighs ninety pounds and has enormous liquid brown eyes. At 37, she looks like an attractive teen-ager.

The family lives in a modest two-bedroom home, in the flight pattern of a nearby airport which interrupts conversation every few moments. Each time a plane comes over, Mrs. Nga tenses, working her hands into a knot. The memories of Communist and American bombs have not been forgotten.

Our first stop in the United States was El Paso, Texas. It was very difficult finding jobs. My husband worked as a janitor and a messenger before he went to college and studied to be an accountant. Now he works for NBC and earns $850 a month. I work as a teacher's aide in the Los Angeles school system. My pay is $3.58 an hour and I work fifteen hours a week. I wish I could work more hours.

Had we stayed in Saigon, our lives would have been in danger. My husband was a civil servant in the Ministry of Foreign Affairs. Everyone at the Ministry dealt with Americans, and that would have made him unacceptable to the Communists.

In Vietnam, my husband earned $40 a month. I was a French teacher and also earned $40 a month. Our combined income doesn't sound like much to an American, but we enjoyed a higher standard of living in Vietnam than we do here.

When we arrived we didn't know anything about America. We had relatives in both El Paso and California, and we were told that there was more opportunity in California than in El Paso, which is really a small town.

We were one of the few refugee families from Vietnam that did not have a sponsor. My sister sponsored us at first, but then she decided to leave America for Hong Kong. So we were on our own. We didn't want to rely on anybody; we wanted to be independent.

Our adjustment to America has been difficult. In order to find his present job, my husband had to learn to speak English well. Before he joined the Foreign Ministry in Saigon, he worked as an accountant. But he really had no skill at that profession. He didn't know how to use an adding machine. He had several accountants and secretaries under him. He was more a manager of the firm than an accountant.

When we first got here, I tried to get a job as a waitress. Maybe it was because I looked so skinny that I was turned down. They were afraid I didn't weigh enough to carry the food, perhaps. Also, I had no experience as a waitress, and they asked for experience.

I enrolled at the University of El Paso, to learn English and American history. What I would really like to do is teach French, but I don't think I'll have the opportunity. Teaching is very competitive in America.

The price of everything here is terrible. Our rent is very high, $325 a month. In America, everyone dreams of buying a home.

We will never own a home; we can never make it. My husband earns just enough to cover our expenses. I am earning only enough to make the payments on my car. I don't foresee either of us finding jobs that will pay enough so that we can afford a home.

Financially, we were better off in Vietnam, even though we earned less money. The cost of living was lower and there were other compensations. We had an easy life in Saigon. We owned a house. I had two maids. We had everything we wanted. I never had to sew my own clothes in my country. I had my own dressmaker. And then we had so many friends that could not come here. They had too many children and they did not speak English, and they were not too sure what they would find in the States.

I think we were happier in Vietnam, because we had our house and more luxuries. During our first year here, we intended to go back. There were always worries about money because we couldn't find good jobs. And then we got news from Vietnam that life wasn't so terrible over there. Things had changed, but not so much that you had to worry for your life like I imagined. But I'm glad we didn't go back. Things have changed again. We receive letters which say people are hungry. Many of our friends who've been sent to reeducation camps haven't returned yet.

Many things impress me about America. First, it is so peaceful. When we came here, I understood for the first time why the American people did not want to stay involved in the Vietnam War. You never hear a bomb explode here; you never hear shots fired. That was my first impression.

America is such a big country, so beautiful, and so rich. When we came to El Paso, my cousin took us for a ride around the town at night, and when we saw all the lights, in so many colors, we thought that Americans waste a lot of electricity. We thought that just the money spent on electricity each night would be enough to feed the Vietnamese people for one whole day, or maybe a week. In my country, electricity costs a fortune, so nobody can afford to use much of it.

You have so much food here. So much meat and cereals and pet chow. We don't have pet chow in Vietnam. Our dogs eat the remains from our tables.

All the paper you use, the bags and newspapers, it's amazing. Paper is very expensive in Vietnam. When you go to the market in Vietnam, your food is wrapped in a newspaper. We do not have bags like here. We used to sell used paper. You know, after you read the newspapers you saved them and then sold them to a factory. The bottles here are something that you just throw away. You can sell them in Vietnam. They would be used to make other bottles. In my country, no one throws anything away. But now I'm beginning to throw things away too. What else can I do with all these empty bottles of beer that my husband is drinking? What can you do with the bags from the supermarket?

When I was in high school I studied American geography. My teacher said, "God has given the American people the best land in the world. But God has given the USSR the same rich land, and the Soviets are only now beginning to use their resources wisely. The American people have used up almost all their resources, and in the future the Soviet Union will be richer than the United States." I always remember that.

We spend money the way other Americans do. We've been to Disneyland, which was very expensive—$7.50 for each ticket. We've gone to Knott's Berry Farm, Universal Studios, Magic Mountain. We go where everybody goes. Now that we are in the States, it would be un-American if we didn't visit the places Americans visit.

In Vietnam, everybody has a bicycle or a Honda. There are very few cars. Here everybody has a car. We also have two cars. My husband has a 1966 Mustang, which we bought in El Paso. My husband had to have a car to go to work. When I got my job, I bought a Pinto, because my husband had to go in one direction and I had to go the other way.

The Pinto costs $143 each month. We have to make payments for three years. The price of the car was $5,800. We had no experience in buying a car. We went to a dealer, and when I left I just had a car. I don't know how, I don't know why. The dealer just made me buy the car.

There are luxuries that I miss. I don't have a washing machine. Our furniture is not as good as what we had in Vietnam. All the furniture you see here I bought at garage sales, except my sewing machine, which I purchased at a pawn shop for $125.

I would like my daughter to study medicine and my son to study science. When I was young, we moved from Hanoi to Saigon and lost all our money when the north came under the control of the Communists. So there wasn't enough money for me to become a doctor, which was my dream. My father, who was a pharmacist, died when I was very young, and my mother had to go to work. It was not yet the tradition for women in Vietnam to work. Women were expected to stay home and take care of the children. But because my mother was a widow she had to work, in spite of the tradition.

Even though we've not had an easy time, we are happy here. I will tell you the biggest difference between Vietnam and America. Here you don't feel scared. And that's worth more than money, not feeling scared.

Money really means nothing to us, not when you've had an experience like we had. When you have to run for your life and abandon everything, then you don't care about money. You care only about survival.

In my country, we used to save, because we thought we had a future. But here we do not save. All you have to do is just earn enough to eat and for your basic expenses.

In America, even if you don't have enough money, you get help from everywhere. You have free medical care. You get food stamps. There is welfare. So what is there to worry about?

Money, of course, has a place in life; it has its importance. But if you measure money against your life, against friendship, against honor, against freedom, you would have to say that money is really nothing.

Since leaving Vietnam I try not to care about money anymore. We know that America will not let us starve.

JOSEPH SURECK

The statistic comes as a shock. According to Sureck, a $40,000-a-year district director of the U.S. Justice Department's Immigration and Naturalization Service, there are a whopping 8,200,000 illegal aliens in the United States. The figure represents a total body count larger than the

*number of people (7,895,000) who live in New York, the world's third
most populous city. More than 5 million of the illegals, adds Sureck, are
natives of Mexico, which means that almost 12 percent of Mexico's total
population (58 million) is surreptitiously in residence in the U.S.A.*

*Sureck, sixty-three, a conservative dresser, is a distinguished, thought-
ful, busy public official, gray-haired, with a salt and pepper mustache.
A University of Oklahoma law school graduate, he's ensconced
in an eighth-floor aerie of the Federal Building in Los Angeles.*

Immigrants no longer come to the United States because
they're looking for adventure, or in behalf of a king or queen to
acquire riches for their country.

Today legal and illegal immigration has a direct relationship to
the economies of the mother countries. If a country is underprivileged or developing, we are going to have more people
from that country coming to the United States, because the
financial opportunities are here in the United States or in countries like the United States. Canada, to a lesser degree, is one of
the latter. So is Australia, except that immigrants don't seem to
adjust there very well.

They come to America, in short, because of money, or, less
crudely, because of economics. Let's say the primary reason for
which they come is to look for work.

In the Midwest and the East, in the Chicago area, in the New
York area, in Philadelphia and New England, many illegal immigrants, contrary to what most people think, earn handsome
incomes, far, far more than what they can earn at home. I am
talking about $4 to $10 an hour for those who work in the trades
as carpenters, mechanics, plumbers and painters.

In Los Angeles, the illegal alien, primarily the Mexican,
doesn't usually do that well, but he still does better than he would
at home, where the standard of living is quite a cut below ours.
He takes jobs that American citizens will not take, because the
American citizen doesn't want that kind of work at the salary
being paid. A Mexican illegal is willing to accept a minimum or
under-minimum wage. We've even had instances where a foreman gets a kickback from what is being paid. We have gotten
statements from Mexicans that they have been paid as little as
$1.80 or $1.90 an hour. In most jobs in the electronics, shoe,

leather and furniture industries, they make about $2.50 an hour.* About the same wage is paid in restaurants where they are busboys or in hotels where they do the custodial or house-keeping work.

Our enforcement officers visit police stations every day. The police call us and say they've rounded up a group of Mexican illegals that we may want to question. Sixty or 70 percent of the apprehensions that are made each day are people who are found on the job. Of that number about 70 percent stated that they were receiving $2 or less an hour. However, the illegals don't say this in a complaining way. They are very matter-of-fact about it.

The economic merry-go-round vis-à-vis the alien never ends. We'll pick up a group of illegals working in a plant at nine in the morning, have them processed by noon, and back across the border in Tijuana by three or four P.M. Some of them will be back in the United States that evening. And a large number will be back within the next thirty days and will be reemployed at the same plant.

We can't keep up with the traffic, because we have a shortage of enforcement personnel and because of the sheer number of people we have to deal with. If we had more officers, we would make more apprehensions, but that isn't the answer. What's the point in sending them back if they can get in again so readily?

The only way we will have any control over the problem is to make it unlawful for an employer to hire illegal aliens from Mexico or any other country and to impose sanctions or penalties on employers who break the law. Though such a law has frequently been introduced in Congress, it has failed to pass. I don't know when or if it's ever going to pass.

Such a sanctions policy wouldn't be in conflict with our Statue of Liberty tradition. As early as 1870 we had quality conditions governing immigrants. By law, we kept criminals out, prostitutes out; we kept out people with certain diseases as well as those who would become public charges. This started because some European countries began dumping their criminals and prostitutes and people from their poorhouses in the United States. So when Congress saw that other countries were shipping their undesir-

*The average daily minimum wage in Mexico is $2. Per capita income is $600 a year.

ables here, putting them on boats and sending them to the New World, they began to realize that something had to be done.

Even in the time of the Statue of Liberty,* when we said we would take the ragged and the poor, this was on the assumption that there was something for these people to do here, that there was work for them. At the high tide of immigration into the U.S., from 1890 to about 1917, we were receiving approximately 1 million immigrants a year. This continued up to the beginning of World War I. Then we had large segments of Americans who began to complain about unrestricted immigration, because it was having an effect on our economy. The aliens were creating an unemployment problem for American citizens, because aliens then were also working for cheaper wages.

The group that took the lead in trying to get Congress to do something to control the number of immigrants coming into the United States was the unions. Even today the unions are committed to a policy of controlling the number of people who are allowed on our shores.

In 1924 Congress passed the first law that placed quotas on the number of immigrants, setting the legal total at 160,000 a year.

Thus we've had restrictions for a good part of our history. The new sanctions proposal, should it become law, obviously would hit Mexicans hardest, since their nationals constitute the largest group of illegals in the United States.

In my opinion, there would be nothing objectionable in such a law, but there are certain groups who speak very loudly and very effectively against it. Church groups. Many Mexican-American groups. Politicians who have a large number of Mexican-Americans in their districts.

Some of these people want a total open-door policy. In effect, they are saying that since this land once belonged to Mexico, Mexicans should have free access back and forth. But the principal objection to sanctions, really, is that if you had a law saying the employer would be penalized if he hired an illegal alien, the employer would take the easy way out and say, "I'm not going to

---

*A gift from the people of France, the Statue was dedicated by President Grover Cleveland on October 28, 1886.

hire any aliens, period, because I don't want to be caught violating the law." That argument is raised primarily by Latin groups who say they won't be hired because of the color of their skin.

I don't agree. It's a simple matter, even now, for the employer to distinguish between the legal and the illegal alien. Permanent and some temporary aliens are issued what is known as a green card. That document entitles them to work.* An employer who is obeying the law will ask for a green card as he would a Social Security or union card. With a sanctions law, it's likely we'll still have green-card workers. So the Mexican who is here with permission won't suffer; neither will the native-born Mexican-American.

This country has to come to the point where we must make a distinction between those who are admitted on a legal basis—to visit relatives, say, or go to school—and the totally illegal immigrant.

Actually, many Mexican-Americans are in favor of sanctions, because the lack of sanctions is affecting them economically. Illegal aliens take jobs away from them. But Mexican-Americans are afraid to speak out, in contrast to those who are against sanctions. In some cases, there have been threats against those in the Mexican-American community who favor sanctions.

Some time ago I participated in a panel discussion sponsored by the AFL-CIO, which on a national level supports sanctions. During that meeting, no one in the audience of 250 spoke out to agree with me that there should be sanctions. But when I got through, a dozen or more people, union members and Mexican-Americans, came up and whispered in my ear that they agreed with me. Later on, I got a number of letters from Mexican-Americans who also said they agreed with me. However, it's reached the point where not one Mexican-American who shares my position will speak out publicly because this is such a volatile issue. I don't want to say those who are against sanctions are rabble-rousers, but they are very, very emotional about the issue and aren't afraid to let their opinions be known.

The problem with Mexico is the 2,000-mile border which we cannot guard. It's simply impossible to guard that much ground, although we make a large number of apprehensions on the

---

*In California alone, there are 1.2 million Mexicans who hold green cards.

border. This year we will apprehend 700,000 illegals, but for each one we locate, there must be at least two or three who get by. So you see, if we make 700,000 apprehensions, we're talking about some 2 million who aren't caught.

It used to be, some ten years ago, that the illegals from Mexico would come in alone. Only the breadwinner of the family came over. His family remained at home. If he worked in agriculture he would follow the crops around, and if he escaped Immigration he would stay here eight or nine months through the harvest season and take his money home.

Now we have whole families coming in—father, mother, and children—and they aren't going home. One reason they come to the States is because of our compulsory education laws. California and Arizona alone are paying out millions upon millions of dollars to educate the children of illegals, giving them an education that isn't available to them in Mexico.

The attitude of the Mexican government is interesting and frightening. I think the Mexican government looks upon the illegal immigration of its nationals to the United States as a safety valve. I would hesitate to guess what would happen inside Mexico if those 5 million Mexicans couldn't gain entrance to the United States and remained at home without jobs. There simply isn't work for them in Mexico, where the unemployment rate is 40 to 50 percent. Incidentally, the amount of money that illegal Mexican aliens earn here is considerable—some $3 billion a year.

If sanctions are put in force in this country, it could affect our relations with Mexico. This is another argument that's used against sanctions. Conceivably, a sanctions law could overturn the Mexican government.

Nevertheless, we must face up to the problem and either do something to legalize the status of illegals or get some immigration tools to keep illegals out. It has to be one way or the other.

What is happening now is a breakdown in law and order. What is happening now is apathy, a kind of acceptance of the status quo. Nobody seems to object very much if people buy fraudulent documents to come in illegally, if they hire smugglers to bring them in, if they lie to Immigration inspectors, if they go through sham marriages with American citizens so that they can remain here.

All of that is apparently acceptable because of the promise on the Statue of Liberty: that we are here to help the oppressed and the underprivileged. Mind you, I don't think the promise on the Statue of Liberty is completely dead. When there's been a catastrophic situation we have opened our doors generously. The Hungarians who fled the Communists in 1956 are an example. The Cubans fleeing Castro and the Vietnamese are other examples. Let us hope that we will be a land of refuge and opportunity for many years to come.

But we must have law; we must be able to control our own development. After all, we build schools and hospitals and other facilities based on our estimated needs. I can tell you that the illegal-alien population in some areas has thrown all that out of kilter, and cities have had to make financial adjustments to meet the influx.

I think Americans are entitled to expect that people of other nations respect our laws and traditions. That doesn't mean that within the framework of our laws we shouldn't continue to let new seed and new blood come in, and even to some extent forgive those who've violated our laws.

However, there has to be a balance; there must be controls. I think it's time we began enforcing our laws. We have to use judgment in determining how many of the more than 8 million illegal aliens we can permit to remain on our soil. You see, we can't do, in my opinion, what some congressman has said: Let everybody who has been here for three years stay here. That's why I don't think President Carter's amnesty proposal for illegals who've been here seven years or longer is fair or equitable. That would be an insult to the tens of thousands of people who've been waiting abroad for many years trying to come in legally.

We have to begin considering our own self-interest. How much selfishness are we allowed? We have to look at the number of immigrants as against our own economy. How many can we take in and still preserve jobs for the people of the United States? Our own population is increasing slowly but surely every year. How much do we owe to our own citizens?

If we could maintain our legal quota of immigrants, which now is 400,000 a year, we would be in pretty good shape. We can absorb 400,000, but the fallout from absorbing more than 8 million, with more coming every day, is that a lot of Americans are being forced onto welfare rolls and unemployment compensation.

I don't know if it's fair to say that the situation is a national disaster. But it's very critical. Illegal immigration is one of the most serious domestic problems we have today. It requires, in the last analysis, a firm policy toward aliens. It requires asking ourselves: Can the flood of illegals continue to increase at the expense of our own people and institutions? Unfortunately, the Statue of Liberty doesn't offer us an answer.

"The Hippocratic Oath Doesn't Say Anything About Money"

The bill for my wife's illness so far is more than $150,000, and the end isn't in sight.

—RICHARD EASTMAN

MALCOLM C. TODD

*Dr. Todd was the 1974–75 president of the American Medical
Association. A general surgeon who performs fifty to fifty-five major
operations a month, he practices in a modern, spic-and-span medical
building in Long Beach, California (population: 359,000).*

*Though he is as sophisticated and influential a spokesman as there is in
America for organized medicine, he conveys the impression of a cherubic,
guileless country doctor. He is extremely popular with his patients, and
his bedside manner, as well as his interview manner, is friendly and
down to earth. A short, 180-pound green-eyed man, he was wearing a
white smock and brown slacks.*

Being president of the AMA was a big financial sacrifice. It is a
three-year term. You serve as president-elect one year, then
president, then immediate past president. I was quite busy with
AMA affairs and quit my practice during those three years. I
would say I lost between $250,000 and $275,000. It would be
more today, because the fees we are getting are so much higher.

During my term as AMA president, I tried to steer doctors
away from an economic focus to a human focus. I think the
AMA's goals and objectives have been misunderstood. The
media and the public tend to think that the AMA is an organization that only has the interests of its own members at heart, that
it is only concerned with the politics and economics of medicine,
that we don't care about people.

I tried to direct the AMA away from that image and get it to
reflect its concern for the human needs of people. I suppose that
is one of the things I will be remembered for—that I was
concerned. I was vitally concerned about people. I visited the
ghetto in Chicago, I visited Harlem, and I visited ghettos in
Atlanta and San Francisco. I wanted to see these places first-

hand so I could respond to people's questions about the quality or lack of quality of medical care in our ghetto areas.

To tell the truth, I didn't get to do all I wanted to do in steering the AMA toward its human responsibilities, because I didn't have enough time. I had to deal with other problems, such as the politics in which the Association was involved, and our membership loss, which resulted in financial reverses.

There are 400,000 physicians in this country, but only 300,000 are engaged in patient care. The others are in administrative jobs of one type or another. The membership of the AMA is 160,000. In recent years we've lost 15,000 members. I think one reason for the membership loss is the increase in dues, which rose from $115 to $250 a year. That may not seem like very much measured against a doctor's income, but it gives those doctors who are dissatisfied with what the AMA has done or didn't want to do a reason for quitting or not joining.

How much does the average doctor earn? That's a good question. Now let's put it in the proper context. Let's not mix apples and oranges. Let's talk about gross income and net income. After all expenses are deducted from the gross, the net income of American doctors averages $53,000 a year. Yes, I believe that is the highest average income of any profession in the country.

No, I don't think doctors earn too much money. If their income is accrued by providing service to patients, providing the best possible medical care to patients, and they work seventeen or eighteen hours a day, they are entitled to that income.

It's perfectly true that the fees of physicians have escalated 76.1 percent since 1967. But let's get back to apples and oranges again. I personally checked out a black doctor who works in the Oakland (California) ghetto and earned $128,000 last year. He was working seventy to seventy-five hours a week. He was the only doctor in that part of Oakland. And I submit to you that by the time he got $128, 000, his overhead took 50 percent. Now you are talking about $64,000, and of the $64,000, he paid $31,000 in federal income tax. That leaves him about $33,000, and I also submit to you that that is not very much for a man who is working that hard and has not had a vacation in six years. So you have to look at these things in their proper context.

The Hippocratic oath doesn't say anything about money.

Money, of course, should be a secondary consideration for doctors. Healing the sick is first and foremost. I think the majority of doctors feel that way. Medicine is still the noblest of all professions. It really is. And I'm proud to say that. But it's a business, too. It has become a business because government and our society have made it become a business and a political football.

The AMA didn't want to get into the political arena in Washington. We were forced into it. We were forced into it to protect our own interests. Labor and other vested-interest groups were represented in Washington. So professional people such as doctors had to be represented too.

The AMA had to form a political action committee, which contributes money to various candidates for Congress who we feel will best represent medicine's interests and the patient's interest.

I just happen to have a newspaper article here which lists the top ten contributors to politicians in the last election. It is a discredit to publish a thing like this. Here at the top is the AMA, with a contribution of $904,000, supposedly more than any other group. But that includes all doctors, all specialists. Why don't they put all labor together? The teachers unions, the Teamsters, the machinists, the CIO and AFL, the steelworkers all made political contributions, but their contributions are not lumped together. Put them all together and it would far exceed the AMA's contribution. Labor probably gave at least $2 million to $3 million to political candidates.

In the AMA's Washington office, we have six paid lobbyists. They lobby for good health legislation. The 95th Congress had 2,000 bills introduced that pertained to health and medicine. It would be an impossible task for any congressman to even read all of them. So one of our jobs is to read all those bills and decide which ones we are going to support, oppose, or be neutral on. Once policy has been set by the board of trustees of the AMA, we put our lobbyists out to meet these congressmen in order to sell our position.

Legislation we have supported includes federal funding for medical schools. Also, more government scholarships and grants for medical students.

The most notable piece of legislation that we opposed in recent years was the Medicare law. We fought it for many years, and I was an activist in this regard. We said it was bad legislation, and it *was* bad legislation. We didn't oppose it because we were against people over sixty-five getting medical care; that wasn't the point at all. We said that when this piece of legislation was passed, it was going to cost the taxpayers more money than its proponents said it would, that there wouldn't be enough funding for it, that we would become enmeshed in red tape, and that we would be bogged down with bureaucracy. Every one of those predictions has come true.

Nevertheless, America still has the best health care system in the world. And if you don't believe it, all you have to do is go to any other country and see what the medical care is. But we also have the most expensive health system in the world. And one of the gaps in our system is that there are millions of people who can't afford medical care and insurance protection against catastrophic illness.

We estimate that between 22 million and 24 million people do not have access to medical care in America. But that's not the fault of doctors. You see, big labor should be supplying the means to provide transportation for the pregnant mother to get fifteen blocks or fifteen miles for her prenatal care. They don't do this. These are social problems, not medical problems as such.

There are hundreds of small American towns, perhaps thousands, that do not have a doctor. But all these places don't need a resident physician. The people in North and South Dakota are used to traveling fifty miles to buy five pounds of sugar or to visit a doctor. Really, they are. The people of North and South Dakota are quite happy and content with their medical care. The Dakotas have a pretty good system, despite the distances. The people there get excellent care.

However, more accessibility to doctors is desirable—we need to send doctors into smaller communities. But we need to send them in pairs. Maybe one would practice in a community of 5,000, and the other would be six miles away in a community of 3,500 or 7,500. You see, the two doctors would then have something in common. They wouldn't be lonely. They could talk. One could cover for the other if one goes on vacation or takes a postgraduate course.

Most doctors want to be in places like New York and Los Angeles, with the amenities big cities afford. You can't blame them for that. That's human; that's what happens. But that isn't corrected under a socialistic system of medicine either. So the AMA is trying to develop incentives for doctors to practice in small communities, such as sending two men out together.

There must also be financial incentives. There has to be a tax forgiveness. The communities have to provide the facilities for the doctors to practice. There must be both financial and environmental incentives if you are going to get doctors to work out there.

Another thing this country needs is a program that will provide financial assistance for the catastrophic bills that add up in cancer cases, strokes, heart failure cases, and the like. I can cite you case after case right here in Long Beach of people going to the financial wall because of astronomical medical costs. I have one patient who ended up with a $57,000 bill for heart surgery. Even though he's well off, that's quite a bite.

Let's come to the crux of the matter. In 1976, the United States spent $130 billion on health care, which was 9 percent of the gross national product. In 1977 the figure was $150 billion. Each year the amount increases. But let's put it in the proper context. Where do the greatest part of these costs come from? It's the hospitalization. It isn't the doctor's bill. The doctor's share of each dollar spent on medical care is about 17 or 18 cents.

Even though hospitalization is expensive, I must defend the hospitals, which take about 55 or 60 cents of the medical dollar. I have to defend them because labor's wages and salaries are so high. The hospitals have had to raise nurses' salaries, technicians' salaries, and the salaries of all their other employees.

The Memorial Hospital in Long Beach has 800 patients. But it has 2,400 employees, three employees per patient. That's where the cost comes in. That's why you can't have a hospital room that's going to cost the same as a hotel room. The average cost per day in hospitals on the West Coast is about $275. In the nation as a whole the figure is $200 per day.

Besides salaries, costs for medical care have gone up because of general inflation, welfare payments, and federal health care programs, including Medicare, Medicaid, maternal welfare payments, health care for military dependents. All these programs cost the government 38 percent of the country's total health care bill.

Why is the government spending so much money on medicine? It's because people nowadays are demanding these services. I operated the other day on a woman whose uterus was hanging out of her vagina. Before Medicare, she probably would not have had the condition corrected. I operated just this morning on a man with a large hernia. This man is eighty years old. The hernia could have caused his death. The operation was very, very successful, and the man is going to live a longer, happier life. Before Medicare, he could not have had that done.

So Medicare, despite its costs and red tape, has done a lot of good. Now what we need is a program to provide protection against catastrophic illness. That's the big gap—that's what Congress should be taking care of now. How do you know that you or I are not going to have a coronary thrombosis, and have to end up with a couple of bypass operations and intensive care for thirty days, plus a couple of months' rest with medical attention? We need a federal program, paid for out of taxes, to provide protection against this kind of malady. The program, however, should be administered by the private sector, with private insurance companies being responsible to the secretary of HEW, who must put control measures into the system.

I hope funding for protection against catastrophic illness won't result in a tax increase or an increase in Social Security taxes. I think the Social Security system is already in trouble. Catastrophic protection should be paid for by general tax revenues and employer participation. If you work for an employer who protects you against serious illness and he pays part of your bill, he is going to get a tax-deductible item out of it. It's not as big an item as it sounds. This kind of approach is progressive thinking; this is a positive program. I think we'll get it from Congress.

We must differentiate between national health insurance and a national compulsory health insurance program such as England has. We don't need a system like that. That will bankrupt this nation, just exactly as it is bankrupting England today. The same thing is happening in Germany and Sweden. These countries can't pay the cost of the health care they are providing their people.

I don't think Congress is going to blanket the nation with a full compulsive national health insurance system, because I don't think the nation can afford it. I don't think we have enough money. Even our most liberal congressmen are coming to believe that compulsory health insurance is a dangerous thing and can bankrupt this nation.

My malpractice insurance currently is $27,850 a year. When I started to practice in 1941, I paid $57 a year, and that was for $20,000 worth of coverage. Now the awards have escalated, so we are talking about $3 million to $5 million worth of coverage. What's more, we have just been notified that our malpractice insurance is going up another 25 percent. Now, who pays for that? There is no place else in the world the money can come from except our fees. Blue Cross estimates that malpractice costs add 26 percent to the health care bill of the nation.

Even if a patient dies during an operation, or he is bedridden for the rest of his life because of medical negligence, I still don't think these million-dollar and multimillion-dollar settlements are justified.

If an injury has occurred by some act of the physician, the patient should be equitably and justly compensated for that injury. But there is no way at the present time that we can provide the costs for lifetime medical care and make up for the loss of that patient's earning power until we reach the point where we make a distinction between what is an error by the surgeon and what is malpractice negligence.

Medicine isn't an exact science. You can't guarantee results. Every bad result isn't malpractice. Until the distinction is made between unanticipated injury and negligence, we are going to continue to have a problem. And we are going to have to pass on to our patients these ever higher costs for malpractice insurance.

That will be the case until society says we can't tolerate this system of huge awards any longer; something else has to be done. Then our juries and judges, who know nothing about medical practice, will separate what is injury from what is negligence. Ultimately we will come up with a workmen's compensation type of program, which should also be administered by the private sector in conjunction with the commissioner of insurance in each state. Contributions for the malpractice fund would be made by doctors, hospitals, state funds, and patients.

What we really need is legislation that measures the damage. If a doctor takes off the wrong finger, that should be worth X number of dollars. If the doctor removes the wrong kidney, it has done harm to the patient, and he should be awarded compensation of X number of dollars. I want a program of uniform measurement of damages, rather than this type of thing where awards can go through the ceiling.

The awards in malpractice cases are now too high. They are based on emotion. There was a case recently of a twenty-three-year-old girl who went blind, supposedly as a result of her doctor's improper care. The jury was ready to award her $950,000. Now, a pair of eyes might be worth $950,000, but there has to be a predetermined amount set. In this case, the award that was finally made was $165,000. I think that was satisfactory.

I'm convinced that money is secondary to the vast majority of doctors. One of the reasons a man becomes a doctor is that there is this thing inside him that wants to help people. Doctors by and large practice for the good of their fellow man.

For me, the most rewarding thing in the world is to heal people. Recently I walked into the hospital room of a nine-year-old girl who was crying and screaming. She had a ruptured appendix, and she knew I was there to help her. "Dr. Todd, I'm so glad you're here," she said. This is the type of thing that is most satisfying to me. I wouldn't care if I didn't get a penny from that child's parents.

I have removed galbladders and stomachs, I've done all types of surgery at the county hospital. I never got a penny for those operations. I never expected a penny. It was part of what I contribute to society.

VICTOR R. NELSON

"I think there's always been medical malpractice," Nelson says, "but nobody until the last decade or two has been trying to prove it by looking over the shoulders of doctors with a critical eye."

At fifty-two, with merry blue eyes, he is easygoing and pipe-smoking. In court, however, he's a lion, and thus one of the leading malpractice attorneys in Los Angeles. Married, with two sons, he lives in suburban Hidden Hills, where he entertains frequently. His guests, as often as not, are doctors. "Some of my best friends are doctors. And some of my worst enemies are doctors."

There was no particular reason why I came to specialize in malpractice. It was largely a process of elimination. The law firm I was with, before I opened my own practice, handled a number of personal-injury cases. Then we began getting into heavier, more complicated medical cases. It became a natural step to concentrate on malpractice.

In the post-World War II era, there were very few attorneys in the nation who dealt with malpractice. There were only one or two in Los Angeles, and they were rather unsuccessful in that they rarely won a case, and when they did, the judgments weren't too large. But occasionally there would be cases in which a wrong kidney or some other organ would be removed and the doctors' insurance companies would have to pay a substantial sum. The word got out to patients that they could make recovery against doctors for injuries.

The problem in the 1950s was that the plaintiff seldom won because you couldn't get experts. In malpractice adjudication, you have to get one doctor to testify against another. If it's a specialist being sued, you have to get someone in the same specialty. Otherwise your case is dismissed.

The medical profession traditionally has been very close, very clubby. It still is. It only became easier to get doctor-experts in the sixties, largely because Los Angeles became more metropolitan and the medical community wasn't so incestuous. It's still very difficult to get doctors to testify against each other in small towns like Santa Barbara and Bakersfield. You can all but forget it there. You have to bring in experts from Los Angeles, which has its problems because the defense can get a local doctor, and local juries are more prone to believe the hometown doctor than an "outsider." It makes things more difficult.

What also helped malpractice plaintiffs was the fact that a few doctors began to step forward when it became apparent that there was a lot of malpractice going on and the medical associations weren't doing anything about it. They said they would review a particular case, and if the plaintiff had a legitimate grievance, the doctors agreed to testify.

We also began drawing expert witnesses from doctor-professors in many of the universities in the area. They were highly qualified, and they weren't involved in the day-to-day economics of the medical profession, so no retribution could be brought against them.

One of the breakthrough cases leading to substantial damages occurred about fifteen years ago. A Los Angeles attorney won $1,400,000 for a woman who'd been paralyzed after surgery on her spine was botched. But such high awards, even today, are comparatively rare. Malpractice awards can vary from $10,000 to $2 million, but the average is in the $75,000-to-$400,000 range, depending on the nature of the injury and on the age and income of the plaintiff. It's also little realized that the doctors win most malpractice suits.*

Nobody really knows how much malpractice there is. The only cases that surface are those where there is significant injury. An attorney can't afford to take the smaller cases.

Usually patients and their relatives don't realize that malpractice has taken place. Frequently the patients die and the doctors cover up. An autopsy surgeon at a major hospital once told me, "I could send you three or four malpractices a week." Obviously he was in a position to know. But of course I never get those cases, and the survivors aren't informed that there was something terribly amiss in the doctors' treatment. The atmosphere is one of cover-up and a conspiracy of silence. So what we see in malpractice work is probably only 5 to 10 percent of the cases that actually occur.

I agree with doctors who say that medicine is an art and not a precise science. That makes it very difficult to prove malpractice. When a doctor chooses one drug rather than another, and that drug leads to tragedy; or a doctor follows one surgical procedure instead of another, and it fails—that isn't malpractice, although in hindsight we know those were terribly bad choices. Before it is

---

*Correct. According to statistics released by the Los Angeles Superior Court, 75 percent of all plaintiffs suing for malpractice lose their cases when they come to trial.

malpractice, the bad choice has to be below the standard of care. It must be established that no competent doctor would have made that choice. Therein lies the difference between poor judgment and malpractice.

A successful malpractice attorney earns about $100,000 a year. Some years I've earned that, but my income fluctuates. There are bad years as well as good. The overhead in these cases is fantastic. If you go to trial and lose, you are out a lot of money. I tried a case last year and lost it, and it cost me $25,000 out of pocket. Most of the money went for expert witnesses, who are very expensive. It costs from $750 to $1,000 a day for an expert's testimony. In that particular case we had five experts testify.

All my cases are taken on a contingency basis. I would be happy to take any case on a straight-fee basis, but I've never met anybody who wanted to gamble. My average fee is a third to 40 percent of the judgment, if we win. It's cheaper for the client if we settle out of court. If we go to trial, the costs are higher for everyone.

To be a malpractice attorney, you have to have confidence in yourself and be willing to shell out a lot of money. It's like a gambling table in Las Vegas when you go to trial. It's worse, actually, because you don't know what the odds are in a courtroom. I always go to trial convinced that my client should win, but of course not all cases are won.

There is no recovery in malpractice cases for grief at the loss of a loved one. Emotion, no matter how deep and sincere, is not an issue in a lawsuit. Insofar as awarding damages is concerned, it is essentially a black-and-white situation. The law says the plaintiff can recover only for his pecuniary loss. If you have a disabled man who is forty years old, earning $25,000 a year, with a wife and three small children, you can project what he would have earned through the rest of his working life. His award will be greater, all things considered, than if he were, say, a 70-year-old unmarried man who had been severely injured.

Doctors all over the country are screaming at the high cost of malpractice insurance. But they bitched even in the days when their insurance payments for malpractice were nominal.

One reason doctors are so outspoken on the malpractice issue is that the medical profession has always been on a pedestal. A lot of doctors want to keep it that way. A lot of doctors mutter mumbo jumbo to patients, in effect telling them nothing. Such doctors prefer to keep everything secret from patients. They don't even want to tell a patient his temperature because they feel that the patient is too stupid to understand anything about his own condition. Moreover, a lot of doctors consider themselves above the law. If you criticize such doctors, they get very uptight, very vicious.

It is also true that the good doctors are paying for the bad. I find a number of doctors who are malpractice repeaters. But it's next to impossible to get even the bad ones drummed out of the profession. They are permitted to keep butchering their patients, and their incompetence and greed continue to earn them $200,000 to $300,000 a year. In a metropolitan community, a doctor's practice doesn't suffer even when he's lost two or three malpractice cases.

There was a famous case in Sacramento in which a doctor on the staff of one of the major hospitals had been performing unnecessary surgery for fifteen years. He was a poor surgeon who maimed an awful lot of people. Every doctor in town knew it. But everyone let him go on practicing. Finally the lid was blown off the thing when one attorney worked very hard to develop a case against him. At his trial, a dozen of his colleagues testified against him. The doctor himself admitted to the judge—there was no jury in this case—that he had performed unnecessary surgery. He admitted malpractice. The judge awarded the plaintiff $1,500,000. That doctor wasn't forced out of practice, however, and the last I heard he was still butchering people.

Let me tell you what happened not long ago in Phoenix, Arizona. A hospital there wanted to get rid of a very poor doctor, but the medical community got behind the offending doctor and told the hospital he would have to stay. The hospital held its ground at first. So the doctors boycotted the hospital. For six weeks they refused to send any patients there. In that period of time, the hospital went $2 million in the red. The hospital was forced to its knees. The doctors won and their lousy colleague stayed on.

By and large, I think American medicine does a good job. There is nothing vindictive in my attitude. I just feel that those who do a bad job should be made to pay. I can cite you case after case from my own experience of medical abuse.

A young Mexican who was a swimming champion was training at the Los Angeles Health Club. When he complained of spinal pain, his doctor operated on him, and his aorta was punctured fatally. We collected $300,000 in damages.

A doctor, while performing a routine circumcision known as a cautery with an electric knife, burned the hell out of a kid's penis. They had to chop part of it off. The award was $1 million.

I got a $300,000 settlement for a client of mine, the wife of a man in his early fifties who walked into the office of his doctor with a nasty gash in his forehead. The man had been in a minor car accident. The doctor checked him into a hospital for suturing and observation. Forgetting that his patient had a history of heart trouble and needed daily doses of oxygen, the doctor neglected to order the inhalation therapy. As a result, the patient died.

An eye specialist performed a retinal detachment operation on a woman in her seventies. The operation was successful. For the postoperative period, the ophthalmologist wrote a prescription for a drug that was supposed to keep her eye dilated. However, I proved in court that the prescription was the opposite of what my client required, that it contracted rather than dilated the eye, and that it was responsible for the loss of one eye. The damages came to $175,000.

A twenty-five-year-old woman, the wife of an airline pilot, had had a lump on her breast for about a year. The damn thing kept growing, even after she visited her doctor. The doctor wouldn't see the husband and sent word through his secretary, "Let him fly the planes, and I'll take care of the medicine." Mastitis developed during the next year and inflammation spread to her lungs. They lost her when she could so easily have been saved. There was no excuse for not doing a biopsy on her breast. We settled for $170,000.

The most fantastic case I've ever had involved a plastic surgeon. A forty-six-year-old woman, accompanied by her niece, went to him for a face-lift, for which he charged $5,000. The doctor began the operation in his office at nine A.M. By three P.M. the procedure was finished, but the patient hadn't snapped out of the anesthetic.

The doctor told the niece, "I'll get the janitor to help you get her into your car." And he left.

With the aid of the doctor's nurse and the building's janitor, the unconscious woman was strapped into a wheelchair, taken down the elevator and out the back door, and lifted bodily into the front seat of the car.

"What am I going to do if my aunt hasn't revived by the time I get her home?" the niece asked the nurse. "I'm not strong enough to carry her upstairs by myself."

"Leave the window down as you drive, and maybe she'll wake up before you reach home. If she doesn't, stop at a fire station. Firemen are nice people, and they'll probably help you carry her into the house."

Since her aunt hadn't awakened as they neared home, the niece did stop at a fire station. The accommodating firemen followed them home and carried the still-unconscious woman to her bed.

The niece went downstairs to prepare dinner. When she returned a short time later to check her aunt, she found her dead.

The violent thing about it was just dumping the woman out into the street without waiting for her to revive, without further examination, without taking her to a hospital, without calling a consultant, without considering the possibility of emergency or follow-through care.

During the trial, the plastic surgeon testified, "This was perfectly normal and natural; nothing unusual here."

"You mean to tell me," I said, "that you have the janitor in your building help carry out all your patients through the back door?"

"Well," the doctor admitted, "*that* hasn't happened before."

I hate to tell you what we settled for. There was no insurance, no children. The niece was the only heir, and wrongful death damages are based primarily on how much support the heirs should receive. We got $25,000.

RICHARD EASTMAN

Chain-smoking long, slim brown cigarettes, Eastman is on the verge of tears as he sits on a stained yellow sofa in a bleak San Fernando Valley apartment. Now fifty-five years old, he attended James Monroe High School in the Bronx and dropped out of New York University after a year.

"I went into the supermarket business with two friends, first in Bedford-Stuyvesant in Brooklyn; then, when that became an impossible neighborhood twenty years ago, we moved the business out here.

"It's ironic. I spent all my life chasing dollars—I never liked the grocery business—and now there are very few dollars left to chase."

His wife's illness, he says, and her progressive deterioration caught him woefully unprepared, emotionally and financially.

My wife fell off a bicycle when she was nineteen years old. The result was two spinal surgeries in two years, which were successful. That was in 1947, when major medical insurance coverage for catastrophic bills was a rarity, practically unheard of. The two surgeries on my wife cost about $10,000. We'd been married just six months, and I didn't have the money, so my father-in-law paid it. At the time, all I had was a one-third piece of a small independent market, and it wasn't generating much income beyond providing for our necessities.

My wife wouldn't hear of me spending money on medical insurance. She said we could put the money to better use elsewhere. I should have bought the insurance anyway. It was the greatest mistake of my life.

We discovered my wife was a diabetic eleven years ago. Nothing dramatic. The doctor prescribed insulin, and she was able to function quite well.

Then in January 1974 she had a severe stroke, and she was legally blind for nine months. But suddenly her sight returned—just like that! So did her health. She recovered completely. The doctor called it a miracle. He had no other explanation. The bill for that illness was relatively inexpensive, a little less than $5,000. By now the business was prospering fairly well—we had acquired two other small markets, and I could afford the expense.

In August 1975 my wife developed an excruciating pain in her lower left leg while we were on vacation in Palm Springs. We went to an emergency hospital, and a local doctor said there was nothing that could be done, other than for her to take pain pills.

We came right back to Los Angeles, to our regular doctor, who, unfortunately, was out of town. There was a younger doctor covering for him, and he elected to run certain diagnostic tests, a venagram and an angiogram. You have to sign a release in order for these tests to be done; they are very dangerous. As I understand it now, the doctor in the course of the tests knocked some junk loose in her veins or arteries which caused a thrombosis or block in her left foot. And she developed ischemia or lack of blood flow to the toes in her left foot. I think what that doctor did was malpractice, just gross negligence, but I've never pursued it with a lawyer.

A vascular surgeon was called in, and he said that if an arterial bypass operation wasn't performed, sooner or later they would have to cut off her left leg. Also, without the operation, ultimately her heart would fail.

The operation was not a success. As a result of the operation, my wife suffered liver failure, kidney failure, and brain damage. She was in intensive care for five weeks, and nobody yet understands how she lived through it at the age of fifty-one.

The complications from that surgery led to what is happening now. All sorts of sophisticated tests were run with fancy machines. One test was on an X-ray machine so rare that there are only two of them in all of southern California. On that machine they discovered the brain damage.

One other result was that the toes in her left leg weren't getting any blood flow at all. They were allowed to fall off. The doctor explained to me that if they were amputated surgically, they would have to remove a lot more skin and bone than if they allowed them to fall off. The doctor said that in this case it was preferable to let nature take its course. Nevertheless, the loss of the toes caused her terrible pain for months.

With the toes gone, with her diabetes, with her liver and

kidney malfunctioning, with the brain damage, she has, of course, gotten progressively worse. She's been in and out of the hospital I don't know how many times. I'd say she's been in the hospital 75 percent of the time in about the last year and a half. She's there now.

Her brain damage is at the point where I think she knows me when I visit her or talk to her on the phone, but you can't have a rational conversation with her, and I'm sure the moment I stop talking to her, she doesn't remember me. Not only me, but everybody else, too.

I talked to the doctor just today, and he said he's run all the tests he can run. He is out of ideas of what to do about her. He said he really can't do anything. They are going to have to discharge her from the hospital, and she is going to have to be in a convalescent hospital, probably for as long as she lives. The doctor says she may live a year, or she could live for ten years.

Even if I had the fantastic amount of money it costs for round-the-clock nurses, I couldn't keep her at home. She'd be better off in a convalescent hospital, because she has to be kept under restraint. Despite the restraints, last night they found her wandering around in some other patient's room at the hospital.

I even need a special kind of convalescent hospital, one that could take care of and keep her in restraints at the same time. I haven't yet investigated this type of hospital, and even her doctor doesn't know of one. He said he'd look into it, and guessed that it would cost me a minimum of $1,000 a month.

The bill for my wife's illness so far is more than $150,000, and the end isn't in sight. There have been so many doctors, so many specialists. The hospital bill is about $110,000. The doctors have cost almost $40,000. The bill includes all the extras, the operating room, physical therapy service, inhalation therapy, occupational therapy. They charged $250 a day for intensive care. The hospital gives you a computer run on your bill, and that computer never stops.

So far I've managed to pay $100,000 of the $150,000 by selling everything—the house, my wife's car, her jewelry, and some antique furniture pieces we had. I also sold my share of the markets to my partners for $52,000. I am now employed as the manager of the markets, at $12,000 a year before deductions.

For some strange reason which I haven't figured out, the

hospital and the doctors haven't been bugging me for the money I owe them. They got me to sign a promissory note, agreeing to pay $700 a month. But I haven't been paying it, and they haven't started asking me for it . . . yet.

I don't know what's going to happen. I have $3,000 left in my savings account, and that should go to the convalescent hospital. I am in the position where I make too much money for federal or state aid, but I don't make enough money to afford my wife's bills.

So my only alternative, at my lawyer's suggestion, is to divorce my wife. We're beginning the legal work on that next week. Once we are divorced, Medi-Cal will step in and take over all the bills. I don't know what else to do.

I'm pretty close to the breaking point. It's been kind of hard on me, too, running to the hospital every day and contending with the bills. I stay home a lot of nights doing nothing, and I just have got to get out and start doing things. I am tired of looking at the four goddamn walls in this place. I have been alone so much for such a long period of time. I have one married daughter whom I never see. She lives in Boston.

Also, you must realize that my wife in her mind is not really a person. She's a vegetable. It doesn't hurt me to talk about it. I'm a pretty realistic guy. I call a spade a spade. There is no hope for my wife, and things aren't going to change, so that's the way it is. I don't expect a miracle to occur this time—because it can't. She's suffering a complete degeneration of her nervous system and the brain. It's not a reversible process. It isn't about to get better. I am at the point where I am numb. I don't even think about the bills anymore. Money doesn't worry me at all. Maybe that's because I am slowly losing my mind. I feel as if I'm on the verge of hysteria.

The hell with money. Maybe I'll go out and buy a $500 suit. Maybe I'll buy a new car. I might just as well go out and spend what little I have left, because the hospital and the doctors are going to take it away from me sooner or later.

ESTELLE ANTELL

"I've been in health services for a good part of my life." Trained as a social psychologist, Estelle has worked for HEW; county health departments in New York, Texas and Los Angeles; Planned Parenthood; and the Institute for Social Research at the University of Michigan. Born in New York's Greenwich Village, she exudes vitality, a diminutive blonde who is a tough observer of the medical profession.

"I make $20,000 a year. That's enough. I'm a widow and it's all I need." She quit a higher paying job, $24,000 a year with a management consultant firm in New York, to assume her present post as director of what she calls "a loose consortium of thirty-five free clinics in Los Angeles, Orange, Ventura and Riverside counties."

My first experience with a free clinic was in Tulsa, Oklahoma in the middle to late sixties. Those were the days of heavy drug use by youngsters who were trying to find a new life-style. They were street people, and though they had severe health problems, they would not or could not go to establishment doctors. A lot of them didn't have any money, and they mistrusted the average physician who they thought would turn them in to the cops.

I wanted a facility that would be attractive to street people. I recruited a doctor and a lab technician who were concerned about these young people. I got hold of everything we needed, across the board. I found a store that had been abandoned because the city was going to put a freeway through there, and we built the clinic. We opened for business, at first one night a week, then five. We were open from ten P.M. to two A.M. because that's when the kids hung around the streets.

They started coming in, but they were suspicious of us at first. It took a while to convince them that we weren't there to turn them over to the cops, or do other bad things to them. We had to develop a whole new technique of treating people. We rewrote the usual form that asked for their medical histories. They could give us whatever information they chose. If they chose not to give us so much as their names, we didn't turn them away.

243

The Tulsa Free Clinic began as a drug treatment center, a VD screening facility, and a place to get birth control information. But pretty soon kids were coming in with all sorts of other health problems. They were beginning to trust us. And they were bringing their friends. And we didn't charge. I specifically remember one young woman who had cut her leg very badly while walking barefoot. She'd gone to the emergency room of a Tulsa hospital and got stitches put in it. But she'd been hassled so badly for payment, which she didn't have, that she never went back. She came to us for the removal of the stitches.

The Tulsa clinic wasn't the first one in the country. Similar free clinics grew up simultaneously all over the country in the sixties to aid street people, a lot but not all of them on drugs, but all exhibiting what we would consider antisocial behavior. Kids who wake up in the morning and hope they'll make it through the day—that was their philosophy. They weren't interested in money, except to get enough to scrape along.

With the Tulsa facility on its feet, I got a federal grant to open a free clinic in Austin, Texas and got into all kinds of trouble there trying to explain why I was giving away medical treatment without charge.

A short time later I landed here, and I have been running the southern California free clinics for two and a half years. They are flourishing because they offer an alternative to establishment medicine for people who have little or no money. We now offer quite a list of expanded services, virtually anything except surgery and complex, expensive diagnostic equipment. You can walk in off the street and receive general medical care, prescriptions, treatment for VD and tuberculosis, X rays, family planning advice, prenatal care, pap smears, gynecological exams, pregnancy testing, pediatric care, psych services, premarital blood tests, abortion referral, dermatology, immunizations, and welfare information, plus referral for other governmental monetary aid.

The thing that's different about free clinics, though, is that we don't have a vested interest in anybody's poor health. We have a vested interest in preventive medicine, teaching people how to care for themselves so they don't get sick. We are interested in nutrition as well as VD treatment. We are interested in treating people who are on drugs, but it's just as important for us to tell

them why they shouldn't be on drugs. We are interested in
providing abortions, but it's equally important to provide a birth
control device to women so they don't have to get pregnant
unless that's their choice.

Nobody pays for anything at any time. There is no charge
whatever. We do ask people for voluntary donations. I just came
from the Hollywood-Sunset clinic, and they have a big sign over
the pharmacy department saying what the equivalent service
would cost if you went to a drugstore. At each clinic, we have a
jar with a narrow neck for donations. But nobody is forced to
make a contribution. Nobody is embarrassed into making a donation. Nobody even watches to see if you put anything in or not.
People give what they can afford, usually $1 or $2. On rare
occasions we'll get a $10 bill.

The bulk of the money to keep the clinics open comes from
HEW and fund-raising activities in the community. Our greatest
asset is the services of physicians, nurses, lab technicians, social
workers, psychiatrists and pharmacists—medical personnel with
a conscience who donate their time.

Doctors work in our clinics for the best and worst of motives.
There are physicians who take the free clinic seriously, who feel
that they have a skill and they should practice that skill for the
betterment of people. It gives them personal satisfaction to help
others. They will freely give their time to aid those in our society
who have the fewest advantages—the poor; people who have no
power, no authority, and no access to authority. Maybe the illegal
immigrant—who would care about him save the free clinic? At
the other end of the spectrum is the physician who volunteers to
work in one of our clinics because he wants referrals, patients
who might be eligible for Medicare or Medi-Cal or welfare. We
get that kind of physician, too.

But I don't care what their motives are. I'm very pragmatic. If
a physician is trained, respectful to the patients, comes on time,
treats the patient the best he can, that's all I ask.

In our clinics there is never a judgmental attitude. When a
patient walks in, no matter how different he may be from you
and me, no matter how bizarre he might appear, he is treated
with courtesy and respect.

We're seeing about 500,000 patients a year in our clinics.
Figure low, and say each one of those patients would have been

charged $20 for an office visit by an establishment doctor. We are thus providing $10 million worth of medical services gratis or at little cost. There are free clinics of our type in every major city. Add up the dollar figure of the services they're providing and you can see what's happening. The free clinics are filling a need for the impoverished and those struggling along on low incomes.

We are still growing here, but not so much among the counterculture. Interestingly enough, we are seeing more older people whose Medicare is too expensive. Medicare is quite expensive now for a lot of the aged. We are also seeing many middle-aged people who are out of work. When they lose their jobs, they also lose their health insurance. And if they have some chronic illness like diabetes, where they need to go to a doctor regularly, that's expensive at $20, $30 or $40 a clip.

Obviously one of the reasons for the popularity of free clinics is that establishment medicine is too expensive. Medicine has always been too expensive in the United States. It's always been for the middle class and the rich, who traditionally have been the only ones able to afford good health care.

We've had people in here who've told me they've paid as much as forty bucks for an office visit to a doctor, and that doesn't include lab work or X rays. A fee that size is appalling. That's a big chunk of dough out of anybody's income. And if you have a family, it's a terrible burden to try to pay for medical care at those prices.

I get angry every time I think about how much money doctors make. Most physicians are more interested in profits than in care. They're busier looking for ways to invest their money than in looking for better ways to care for their patients.

Doctors resist every bit of progress that will improve the care of patients. When the federal government attempted to start a peer review program in which physicians would look at one another's procedures, the AMA fought it like hell and is still fighting it.

When I get on a plane, my life is in the pilot's hands. Pilots are required to take regular tests to make certain their reflexes are correct, that their hearts are good, and that they understand the latest technology. Why shouldn't physicians be subjected to the same standards? Physicians have resisted any kind of relicensing procedure. They fail to respond when the public says, In order to keep your license you must take X number of courses every two, three or five years so you can keep up to date.

When new med schools want to open, the AMA resists that too. They don't want more doctors, they want fewer doctors. This guarantees the income of doctors who are already in practice.

A young physician just out of med school can expect to earn $75,000 to $100,000 within two years. That is a great deal of money and one of the major reasons that the cost of medical care has gone up faster than inflation.

I just don't know what happens to the young men and women in med school. When they enter they are really idealistic, but they go through some kind of machinery, and when they crank them out at the other end, they are money-hungry and their ideals have been forgotten.

I've had physicians tell me, I am going to give my patients the best possible care, but, by God, I want a lot of money. I want a yacht, a fine car; I want to be able to travel; I want to be able to buy whatever I want to buy, and my patients are going to pay for it.

Physicians have priced themselves out of the reach of too many people in our society. In our culture, value is set by whatever number of bucks you have. So I guess a physician is very valuable. But in the last generation they have set their life-style too high. This wasn't true two generations ago. My grandfather was a doctor, and he wasn't a rich man. I don't know a physician today who isn't rich. They may not be rich by the standards of Rockefeller, but by normal standards they are very rich.

Malpractice problems have also driven up the cost of medical care. You have to look at malpractice in two ways. One, I think people are suing doctors because they get mad when they receive lousy treatment, and you can't blame them. Two, doctors have never done anything about policing themselves.

There are physicians who drink too much and go into surgery the next morning hung over. There are physicians who operate who've taken too many tranquilizers. There are physicians who are busy in motels with their mistresses and don't leave a number where their patients in hospitals can reach them.

I used to have a professor who said you could judge the morality of a civilization by how it treats its pregnant women. In America, if pregnant women are rich or middle class, they are treated well. If they're poor, their treatment is terrible. I don't have the statistics at hand to prove it, but I'll bet anything that the infant mortality rate is two or three times higher in Watts or in the East Los Angeles barrio than it is in West Lost Angeles. So you see, money makes a crucial difference to all of us, from the day we're born, from the day we're conceived, actually.

I think we have reached that level of sophistication in our civilization where food, shelter and clothing aren't the only necessities in life. Health services are also a necessity. And a physician is as necessary for health care as a carpenter is for shelter, as a farmer for food. The skills of physicians should be available to everyone, whatever you need or whoever you are.

I have a handicapped child, so I can tell you from personal experience what it's like to be in medical debt all your life. Our debt was never very severe—we were just a few grand behind—but it was enough so that I was really aware of it. I was always skimping and doing without something because I had another doctor bill to pay. My son is a hemophiliac, which is a continuing illness. He's twenty-five years old now and is a bright young man who works for the government as an ecologist. He can function very well, and he is making a contribution to society. Over the years, I would estimate that his medical costs have been between $200,000 and $300,000. Part of it came from my late husband's insurance. He always worked for a place that had health insurance. That consideration was always more important than the salary. I shudder to think what would have happened to my son if we hadn't managed to come up with the means and the money for his care.

We need a system of medical care in the United States that is available to everyone, rich or poor. Americans have a right to it. They are entitled.

The purpose of medicine shouldn't be to make doctors rich. The purpose of medicine is still embodied in the ideals of the Hippocratic oath. And I think it's time the doctors began living up to that oath.

Brother, Can You Spare a Job?

Why couldn't I wear a sandwich sign, too,
advertising myself instead of a place to eat?

—LEE GOODMAN-MALAMUTH

DAVID FORBES

*Born in 1919, he's a lean, neat man in a red and white striped shirt,
white tie and blue slacks who sits behind a plain gray steel desk in the
unostentatious headquarters of the Los Angeles branch of Forty Plus, a
remarkable, little-known, privately funded job-finding organization for
seasoned middle- and upper-management executives.*

*Forbes, the international president of Forty Plus, was an aerospace
purchasing agent and contracts administrator for Lockheed, Northrop
and Douglas. Throughout most of his professional life, he earned from
$20,000 to $35,000 a year. He hasn't worked since 1968, preferring to
devote his time to helping others who are unemployed.*

When a man first comes in here he usually is in trauma. He
thinks he's the only person in the world who is unemployed. He
thinks the whole world is conspiring against him. His morale is
practically zero.

The biggest shock he suffers is having his dignity destroyed.
Money is right there in second place, but most of them have put
aside sufficient money to live on for quite a period of time. It is
the attack on his ego, on his confidence in himself that we have to
deal with. These highly paid, suddenly unemployed executives
have lost their self-image, their manhood. To their families,
they're no longer the heroic providers.

You have a man who has worked twenty-five to thirty years for
the same company and suddenly finds himself out of a job. What
does he do? He's never faced the unemployment problem before
in his working career. He doesn't know how to solve his problem.
The longer that goes on, the worse his morale gets. He finally
comes here, in most cases in a sort of desperate condition. We
start him on our training course, and within a week or so the
change is phenomenal.

We put him through a very detailed program which teaches him how to write a résumé, how to conduct himself in a job interview—we do that with the use of videotape so that he sees and hears what he looks like to a prospective employer. It may surprise you to learn that almost every man who's held a high-level job needs this kind of fundamental instruction in looking for work, because, as I've indicated, he's never been in this position before.

We also teach him that there is a right way and a wrong way to look for a job. He learns how to list his twenty-five major accomplishments, how to plan a job-search campaign, how to write a letter to a corporation asking for a job interview. He learns what type of companies he should be looking at. And don't forget that his dignity and confidence are restored by associating with others here who are in the same fix and who understand his problem. His self-image is fully restored, of course, when he lands a job.

We are not particularly interested in the personnel departments of corporations. We want to get to the person who will say, "Yes, I am going to hire you," or "No, I won't hire you." The decision-maker, in other words. That may or may not be the president of the firm; usually it isn't. Generally it will be the department or division head.

The guiding light of Forty Plus was a man by the name of Henry Simmler. He worked in New York for Remington Rand and lost his job in 1939. He took a look around and saw a great many other technical and executive types who were older, who were out of work, and whose talents were being wasted. Simmler had an inspiration, and Forty Plus was founded.

The goal was and still is to try to package these people and their qualifications in such a way that they can be quickly put back to work. The whole thing has been eminently, enormously successful for two reasons: our people have experience, and employers know that if we say a man has certain qualifications, he has those qualifications. The employer knows that if we send, say, three men for an interview, any one of them can do his job, and all he has to do is choose among personalities.

We have chapters in Canada, Australia and every major American city. The Los Angeles branch was started in 1964. We seldom miss placing any of our members in a job. Right now we

252 / MONEY TALKS

have 145 members, and I'm certain virtually all of them will find
work at an average salary of between $22,000 and $25,000 a
year.

We find them jobs, for example, in advertising, in sales, as
controllers, accountants, managers, corporation presidents,
project engineers and research chemists. The firms who've hired
Forty Plus people include General Motors, Bendix, Burroughs,
Kaiser Industries, the Times-Mirror Corporation, Occidental
Life and Walt Disney Productions.

Forty Plus doesn't discriminate on the basis of sex, religion or
race. We accept anyone who meets three qualifications: he or she
must be over forty years of age, must be unemployed, and must
have earned an average of $12,000 to $18,000 a year for the last
five years. The $18,000 figure is for men. The $12,000 requirement is for women, since we recognize that employers haven't
paid women the same salaries as men.

Because of their age and their salary requirements, our people
are the most difficult of the unemployed to place. We have to be
selective, and each year we accept only 2,000 people.

This is a membership organization. We resent being called an
employment agency, because we are nonprofit. We do not
charge employers a dime for supplying them with talented professionals. For the employers, that represents a saving of over $1
million a year in advertising costs, search fees and other executive recruiting expenses.

We are run by and for our members. Everybody you see here
is unpaid, including myself. What we are really is an educational
or training institution. An employment agency is a concern in
business to make a profit, and employment agencies will invariably handle only the most easily placed people, not people of our
age and in our salary bracket. It's the factory worker, the production worker, the blue-collar people who are most easily
placed and whom the employment agencies work with. Nor are
we an executive research firm. We refer to executive research
firms by the somewhat uncomplimentary title of headhunters.

There are eight people on our staff: a president, a vice-
president and six department managers. The staff support
themselves. Most of us have outside incomes, investments or a
pension. I am particularly fortunate. I am also unique. I have an

income of $2,000 a month, mostly from stocks, with which I support myself. Most of the people here do not have that much backing.

The oldest man we ever placed was eighty-two—an accountant at a salary of $32,000. He was placed six years ago and is still working, and as far as his employer is concerned he can have any amount of money he wants and work until he sees fit to stop working.

His case and many others we have here proves that mandatory retirement is an abomination. Mandatory retirement is an idea that was dreamed up years ago on the premise that going by the calendar, when you arrive at sixty-five you immediately lose all your faculties or the ability to be productive or creative. We don't hold with that, and I think we've proved it to be untrue.

In most cases I've seen, when you turn a sixty-five-year-old man out to pasture it's a mistake, because you can't replace all that experience, all that talent very easily. I grant that not everybody is able to work beyond sixty-five, but in my estimation the vast majority of people in that age bracket can continue working—and they should be allowed to continue working.

What isn't sufficiently realized is that mandatory retirement is a killer. My father practiced law for fifty-one years. Then he decided he didn't want to work anymore. It was the worst mistake he ever made. When he retired, he was dead within a year. The day he retired he was as sharp as he'd ever been. Voluntary or forced retirement kills men and women because they have no reason to live, no reason to get up in the morning.

I recall the president of a large moving van company who came here a year or so ago. He had been forced to retire. We placed him as company president of another van company, at a salary of $95,000 annually, and he's managed to make large inroads into the business of his ex-employer.

Five years ago the hiring trend in business was to take the young tiger in the Brooks Brothers suit, with the spanking new attaché case and the just-minted Master of Business Administration degree. The thought then was, Well, we'll get this young chap to work for less money, and because he's young and ambitious and anxious, he'll do a tremendous job for us. Or they thought, Why pay one man $40,000 when we can pay two young hotshots $20,000 apiece? We'll double production and efficiency. But it didn't work. Employers found out that although those youngsters were well educated, they didn't have the experience, and they made some absolutely horrendous errors. So now the trend is back to the older man with the experience.

The business world is a jungle, at least in many companies I know about. It is very tough. It is highly competitive. There are always people coming up from underneath who are looking to take your job. I think in the medium-size and small companies that's not particularly true; in such firms performance and merit count for more.

I must add that I don't think that just because a corporation is big it's bad. It didn't necessarily get to be big by being bad. There are large companies that are run in a vicious, immoral manner, but a large percentage of corporations are run reasonably well.

Despite the excesses of business, despite the immorality you find, there isn't a damn thing I would do to change our political system or the way in which business is regulated. Our system is still the one that enables more people to live better here than anywhere else in the world.

I've traveled halfway around the world. I've seen the welfare state where everybody is taken care of, where there's a guaranteed income, where your medical needs are taken care of automatically. Well, look at what's happened in those countries that have tried that. Look at Sweden and England, where incentive has been killed. The people there say, Why should I go out and exert myself to make more money when I know that no matter what I do, the government is going to take care of me? Our country, even with all its faults, didn't get to where it is with a system like that. It got to where it is with the free enterprise system, where a man can, in most cases, go as far as he's able to go.

One of the continuing dilemmas of our system is that there is always at least a 4 to 6 percent unemployment rate, including the type of executive who comes to Forty Plus. Do you know that Forty Plus was formed to go out of business? We have been trying to go out of business for as long as the organization has been in existence. But it would take one hell of an economic boom to make us disappear. We haven't made it yet.

LEE GOODMAN-MALAMUTH

Lee is a strapping, handsome 190-pounder, twenty-seven years old, six feet four, married, with no children.

When he began looking for a job early in 1976, he was one of America's best and brightest young men. At the time his job search began, the national unemployment rate was 7.9 percent, and in California it was 9.8 percent. Even so, he didn't anticipate difficulty. He'd been educated at a prep school in Switzerland and spoke French fluently. He had taken several courses at Oxford; he had served three years with the U.S. Army, including a stint at the Army War College; and he had a college degree. Both his parents were doctors who were successful, influential and well connected.

I went to college on the GI Bill, which provided me $220 a month. I had to live on that because I didn't have a job while I was in school.

I went to San Diego State. I chose a state university because the tuition was cheaper there than at a major private school like the University of Southern California or Stanford. My parents would have put me through a private school, but I wanted to do college on my own. They'd already done enough.

Originally, I was premed. But I got out of that because I did not fare well in chemistry and I had a run-in with the professor. That turned me off, and it ended all my hope of becoming a doctor. I switched to international economics, thinking that degree would prepare me for the business world or the diplomatic corps.

I was taking courses during the Watergate affair, and I could see the impact that Watergate was having on economic systems all over the world. Government after government was asking, If we have an economic crisis, can we count on the United States to support us? Watergate turned all our attention inward, and foreign countries were worried. And at that time the world trade market was going through tremendous turmoil because of double-digit and in some cases triple-digit inflation. The dollar was devalued on the European money market, which had a high inflationary impact. The British pound had also dipped severely. All this upheaval almost exactly paralleled the Watergate affair.

In college, from day one, we were conditioned to believe that if you had a college education, you were guaranteed a good job and that your lifetime income would be greater than that of someone with only a high school education. When I graduated, I walked smack into a very tightly closed job market. Many of my friends stayed in graduate school because they couldn't find jobs. Some of them were teachers. Educators keep screaming, We need more teachers, and in the next breath they say, We can't have more teachers because there is no funding for them.

I thought that as soon as I graduated I was going to have a job with an important man who was connected with the U.S. diplomatic corps. I was going to travel to Europe with him and be his interpreter. It would have been a fantastic opportunity, but it fell through. It turned out that the man wasn't what he said he was. Then I applied to the diplomatic corps on my own, but nothing came of it.

I used all the personal and family contacts I had to get a job. There were people my father recommended, people my mother recommended, people my uncle recommended. The response I received in interviews was that we are cutting back, we aren't taking anybody now. So I accepted that as a fact. I didn't think I was deficient in my capabilities. There was something wrong with the nation's economy, not me.

It got to the point where I was looking for just about anything other than sales, any kind of entry-level position. I didn't want to start as an executive vice-president but at the bottom, like everybody else. But every major corporation I tried said they weren't taking on entry-level personnel, and what's more, they were reducing or doing away with their training programs.

I found that there was such an abundance of college graduates that corporations could sit back and say, Well, we are only going to take 4.0-average students from USC, Stanford and Ivy League universities. They were in a position to do exactly that. And on that basis I didn't precisely qualify, because I had gone to a school that wasn't prestigious and my grade average was 3.1.

The more time passed, the more depressed I became when I

couldn't find a job. I had to borrow money, $1,500, to keep going. I spent most of that—down to a couple hundred—and that was it.

I was very close to the point where I felt the system was cheating me. I was pretty frustrated with what was going on. Here I was, one of those who'd had the golden opportunity of going to college and graduating, and yet I was not able to find a job. Maybe the worst part of it was knowing that so many others were in precisely the same fix; the job market was absolutely flooded with college-educated people.

I was stymied. It seemed hopeless. I had tried San Diego State's counseling center and everything else. I had tried employment agencies. I had knocked on doors. Nothing.

I finally decided, when every single door seemed closed and when there appeared to be no more doors through which I could walk, that I couldn't be like everybody else. I had to do something special, something that would draw the attention of people to me. Even though I wasn't a straight-A student, I knew I had a lot to offer. A lot of productivity was wrapped up inside me, yearning to get out.

So I thought, What can I do and where can I go to do it? Where can I find people in a position to hire me, and how can I get their attention? What turns employers on? What can I do that is subtle and blatant at the same time?

I'd heard conversations in my parents' house about *the* restaurant in Beverly Hills, the Bistro. Supposedly it was the most elegant and expensive restaurant in town. That must be where all the presidents of corporations go for lunch. I figured, Okay, Beverly Hills, that's a pretty nice place to start. I'd learned by now that if I had any hope of getting a job I had to get in contact with the president or a top-echelon executive of a firm, not a middle man like a personnel director. So I thought, All right, I'll hit up the presidents and the executives of companies at the Bistro.

Since it was a rich atmosphere around the Bistro, and since I wanted to make a good impression, I decided I'd deck myself out to the hilt. I'd wear my three-piece Yves Saint Laurent suit, a light blue shirt, a nice dark tie, and patent leather shoes. I'd get all shipshape.

But I had a nagging feeling that something was missing. I needed something more. I'd seen a movie on television that had a street scene showing a hobo with a sandwich sign. Why couldn't I wear a sandwich sign, too, advertising myself instead of a place to eat?

I went to an art store in Hollywood and got one of those big pieces of white display cardboard material and some block letters that were already cut and very professional looking. Then I went home and started to make the sign. I thought, What am I going to put on the sign that can be subtle and blatant at the same time? I could put on it, I Need A Job. But that wasn't very original. What I wanted wasn't really a job; I wanted a career, someplace where I could start and work my way through a company or a business. I figured that asking for a career meant you wanted to stay with it and you were willing to put 110 percent into it.

So I put on the sign, "I Need A Career." Then I added, "College Graduate." And I gave the name of my college, the year of my graduation and my degree. Then I added an extra little touch at the bottom of the sign which said *Résumé ici* (Here is my résumé). I figured that was appropriate because it was a French restaurant.

At last I was ready. I went down to the Bistro and stood in front of it, sandwich sign and all, careful not to block people going inside. It was a very hot day, and for the first twenty minutes people weren't paying too much attention.

After a while the maître d' of the Bistro came out and said, "You can't stand here. You'll have to move down the street. What you're doing is not becoming for an establishment of this type."

So I smiled and said, "Okay, I'll move."

Before he went inside, the maître d' turned back to me and said, "Oh, by the way, you are dressed very nicely."

I went next door to an expensive lamp shop and introduced myself to the owner. I got to talking with him and he showed me around. He was very proud of his lamps. I told him what I was doing, and he rather enjoyed the whole idea, so I said, "Do you mind if I stand outside your store?" He said, "Of course not; go right ahead."

That was an excellent location. There was only a small alley, just wide enough for a car, between the lamp shop and the Bistro. Nobody coming into the Bistro could miss me; everyone had to walk past me to get in. So it was an ideal place to stand, even better than where I'd been before.

I got a lot of mixed comment, some strange, some good. One man came up to me and said, "The way you're dressed, you don't have to work. Why are you doing this? You should be a male prostitute." That shocked me a little.

A lot of people asked me why I was doing what I was doing. They said I shouldn't be on the street this way looking for a job. One man said, "They did this kind of thing in the Depression, not in 1976."

Many people gave me looks of disbelief. Some would kind of look at me in an odd way—you know, they'd look at you and they wouldn't look at you.

Some people stopped and said they thought what I was doing was great; it showed initiative.

A man who said he was a movie producer stopped and took one of my résumés. "I want to look this over, and then I'll get in touch with you," he said.

I got a similar response from another man. I have no idea what kind of company he was with, but he was a smartly dressed man, elderly, in a chauffeur-driven car. He came up and asked for one of my résumés, smiled, and said, "Thank you." Then he walked into the Bistro.

Another man, a young fellow about thirty-eight, walked by me at first. Then when he got about five feet past me he stopped and turned around, and something seemed to click in his head. He told me he was the president of a paint company. He handed me his card and said, "Call me tomorrow. I'd like to talk to you."

I spent about five hours in front of the Bistro and I had three leads.

I never heard from the producer or the elderly man. I called the fellow from the paint company the next day, but I couldn't get through to him. So I just kept calling every day for about a week. Finally I reached one of his assistants, who told me the president was in Europe and I would hear from him when he returned in two weeks. Not too long after that I heard from the assistant, who said they wanted to hire me in a marketing position at a starting salary of $16,000 a year.

But I turned it down. I turned it down because the job I really wanted had come through, an administrative internship at the

Long Beach Community Hospital. It only paid $750 a month, considerably less than what I was offered at the paint company, but I still harbored the idea of working in medicine. If I couldn't be a doctor, hospital administration was the next best thing. In my job-hunting rounds, I'd had an interview with the executive director of the hospital, and he finally decided he would take me on.

So my stunt in front of the Bistro worked, I guess, because I went to a place where I could possibly meet people who were in a position to get me in or direct me to people who would hire me. If I hadn't landed the hospital job, I think I'd be working for the paint company today. The stunt also worked because it was different. It was a gimmick, something a little out of the ordinary. It proved that somebody with a little bit of imagination and a little bit of enthusiasm and a little bit of gumption could go out and do something different from the average Joe who just goes to a personnel office and fills out an application, then goes home and waits for a call that never comes.

I would say to other young people in my position that in order to find a job, you've got to have a gimmick that will bring attention to yourself. I know one guy who took a box in to a personnel manager. Inside the box was a telephone with a note attached that said, "Please call me." He did something that stuck out in the man's mind; it separated him from everyone else.

What does it say about our system that a fellow with my background has to resort to this kind of thing in order to get a job? It says that there's something terribly wrong with the system at the present time. It says that the all-American Dream is not the all-American Dream anymore. Having a college education doesn't mean that in fact you will make more money or even get a job. A guy with a high school diploma can go out and work as a common laborer and make twice the money that a kid with a college education can make.

The educated individual is not needed as much in our society now. Universities have become factories. They're just grinding out thousands and thousands of college-educated individuals every year. There's already talk that maybe we're sending too many young people to college. I think a lot of kids and parents are realizing that perhaps college isn't necessary.

Ten years from now I expect to be a full-fledged hospital

administrator, earning $15,000, $18,000 or $20,000 a year, a good basic income that will allow me a few luxuries.

I have no regrets about the stunt with the sandwich sign. It was an enjoyable experience, even though it was symptomatic of my desperation. If I lost my present job, I'd take my own advice. Maybe I'd wear the sandwich sign again. Or find another gimmick.

WELDON AND CONNIE GREENLEE

The Greenlees have been married twelve years and have two sons, nine and six years old.

Born in Boswell, Oklahoma, Weldon, thirty-eight, left school after the eleventh grade. He started driving a truck in the sixties for $50 a week. "I don't own my own rig. I work for a big outfit. I earn anywhere from $5,000 to $20,000 a year, depending on how much work there is."

Connie is twenty-nine, a native of Los Angeles and a high school graduate. They live in a three-bedroom, two-bath home in suburban Canoga Park, California.

Weldon: I work six days a week, midnight to ten or eleven in the morning. I drive an 18-wheeler and I haul appliances, tennis stuff, TV sets, anything you can find in a department store. Sometimes my trip is just within California, sometimes nearby to a place like Phoenix, Arizona, sometimes coast-to-coast. My hours are controlled by the federal government. I can drive for a maximum of ten hours and then I have to have eight off. When I can't make it home at night, I rent a motel room for $10.50.

Connie: Until 1972, things were going pretty well for us.

Weldon: That was the year the recession started and the bottom fell out of everything. I got laid off on Thanksgiving Day. I didn't go back that time for nine months. Layoff has happened every year since. No work for three months, six months, or more.

Connie: While Weldon's working and bringing home a check, we save as much as we can. We have $3,000 in the bank. No, make that $2,000. We just had to spend $1,000 to repair a big leak in the roof. Water was leaking into six rooms.

Weldon: Every time I'm on layoff, I go on unemployment, and we also get food stamps. Otherwise we couldn't make it. I get $104 a week from unemployment and $156 worth of food stamps for two weeks.

Connie: We have a $359-a-month payment on the house and a $135-a-month payment on our '72 Thunderbird.

Weldon: We bought the house and car just before I was laid off the first time. I never thought I'd be standing on an unemployment line or getting food stamps.

Connie: I always feel bad when I have to use the stamps. It's a downer. I can't help it. In the store, the clerk looks at you when you say you have food stamps. I mean, they are very nice. They don't say anything. But you can't help feeling bad about it. I'd never look down on anyone else who has to use food stamps. The justification I give myself is that it's not a permanent thing. We'll be off the stamps as soon as Weldon's work picks up.

Weldon: The first few times I went to the store with Connie, I felt pretty lousy about the stamps. But then I said, "The hell with it." We had to do it, and there's no sense feeling rotten. It's a federal program and it's coming out of my taxes. So it's something I'm entitled to. Why not take advantage of it when you need it? But I did feel kind of funny about going down and applying for the stamps, because there's always a whole bunch of people there, and I don't like crowds anyway. But when it's a question of feeding your kids, you adjust to the shame and the stigma.

Connie: There's been a lot we've had to adjust to. While Weldon was on layoff in 1976, our oldest son came down with encephalitis. The doctor told us he would never survive the night, that he had no chance. But his brain hadn't been damaged and he rallied and he made it. He was in the hospital five months. It cost at least $15,000, but the Teamsters medical plan picked up 80 percent of it.

Weldon: Even with the insurance, we came close to having to sell the house. At one point, we didn't know how long our boy would be in the hospital. The illness wiped out our savings.

Connie: The scary part was the nurses. Our boy had to have round-the-clock nursing care for a couple of weeks. You have to pay the nurses right then. They don't wait for their money.

Every eight-hour shift I had to give a nurse a check for $52. I didn't care about the money, but many times I wondered, What if we didn't have the money? How would we pay for the special care he needed? I thought to myself, How many people don't have money when someone in the family gets terribly ill? What do they do?

Weldon: I almost went to the bank to see if I could get a second mortgage on our house.

Connie: I don't know if that would have worked. I was really scared.

Weldon: We've also found out we can't afford our house. The taxes just went up to $1,700. So we're selling. We'll move to a place that will be more within our means, where the taxes aren't more than $400 a year. In the summertime, our utility bill here, with the air-conditioner, is 150 bucks every two months. That's just the electric. Then you have water and gas. On a year-round basis, it costs us almost $600 a month to live in this house.

I managed to make $16,000 last year, and that should be enough for us to live as we want to live. But we had the medical expenses, expenses for the house, and it costs me money for food and lodging when I'm on the road. Last year I did ninety-eight trips out-of-state, and so you are talking about $2,000 for expenses.

Connie: We should have been able to make it. But with Weldon getting laid off so much, we have found ourselves just getting pushed further and further back financially. It's sad, it's really sad.

Weldon: Well, it's not all that sad. I mean—

Connie: It is to me. You work so hard, and to have really nothing to show for it is sad. We had a dream that we would own the house someday and our children would be well taken care of. You know, we could give them the things they needed. And it has been very hard to do that. I remember when I was a child I never worried about money. I mean, we never had a lot, but my dad never said to me, We can't afford to do that. I can't count the times I've told our kids, Gee, we can't afford to do this or that. Ordinary things like going to the movies or to Disneyland. Weldon and I like to bowl, but we don't. There have been so many times when we wanted to do things as a family—just take the kids to a movie and a restaurant. But we said, Gee, we'd better not spend the money.

Weldon: Just living every day is expensive. Feeding our kids. Clothing our kids. We have our oldest son in boxing lessons, and even that's gone up from $10 to $15 a month. And it's $25 apiece for the boys to play baseball. It's just those kinds of things that seem to eat up all our money.

Connie: One of these days I would love to say to Weldon, "I don't want you to go to work today." He's always so exhausted when he comes home. It would be wonderful to have that feeling of security, knowing he doesn't have to go to work when he's tired. Just being able to relax a little bit and slow down the pressure of making a living and worrying about money. It's that fast pace all the time—you have to work to pay this, and then you have to work some more to pay that. It's really ridiculous. I had to go to work when Weldon got laid off and the money ran out. I've had to take a temporary job as a bookkeeper.

Weldon: But you're not going to work anymore.

Connie: When Weldon is on layoff, it strains our relationship. I mean, when you're together for twenty-four hours a day, just little things begin to annoy you. You think, Oh, why doesn't he just go out and take a walk? If I could just get away from the kids for a little while. I'm sure Weldon feels the same way. But we do get on each other's nerves. That's funny, because here I am wishing he could take a day off from work, and when he is off from work, we're at each other's throats. We don't enjoy each other as much as we should.

Weldon: The reason is that there's always the money pressure in the background. But I don't know how I can work harder or make more money.

Connie: I really wonder if the American Dream is out there anymore. I don't know; as a child we used to be able to dream. But now the money isn't there for my children. I think, What will the dreams of my children be when they grow up? Are they going to be comfortable or poor?

Weldon: I'm more optimistic. I think if you did away with your American Dream, you would have a totalitarian country here. The American Dream to me is initiative. You have to have drive and stamina to become what you want to be. This is still a free country. You can do what you want to do and be what you want to be. I doubt if people in Communist countries own their own homes. I'm just an American; that's all I am. I believe in the American way of life, and if you don't have the American Dream, then you just don't have anything. We are the wealthiest nation in the world. True, we have people on welfare, other people who are hungry. But that doesn't mean the Dream is dead. Connie and I and the kids live pretty good, despite everything. I mean, we eat; we don't have to eat beans and cornbread like my parents did during the Depression. We have never gone hungry.

Connie: We've come so close to financial disaster these past few years. Even so, it hasn't been as bad for us as for some of the other drivers Weldon knows. They had a lot less preparation than we did. At least we had a couple of thousand in the bank most of the time so we could cope a little bit when the layoffs came. We've had to lend money to some of the guys who make more than Weldon does. They were in worse shape than we were, even though they were earning more. To tell the truth, I don't know how they make it. To tell the truth, I don't know how we make it.

Weldon: Selling the house is going to give us a fresh start. Our experiences with money have taught us that we have to cut expenses. Sure, we've made mistakes, but from now on I don't think we should have any problems with money. This is still the greatest country in the world.

NICHOLAS PANZA

Panza, fifty-eight, Rutgers-educated, is president of Goodwill Industries of Southern California, one of the largest branches of Goodwill, which is a sizable American industry—167 outlets nationwide, with total operating revenues of $175 million. A wounded army of 57,869 is employed by the organization.

Panza oversees an annual budget of $5 million and 782 workers. "Most people still don't really know much about us and the work we do with the handicapped. But they should. After all, 10 percent of our *population, about 21 million Americans, are handicapped physically or emotionally.*

"I have to be honest with you. Like so many people, I knew nothing at all about Goodwill Industries when I moved to California from New Jersey in 1961. I put my name down at the employment office, and one job interview they sent me on was to Goodwill. I accepted the job. In my mind I was only going to stay here a few months, until I found something else. But I've been hooked on Goodwill ever since. I've never looked elsewhere. I have enjoyed every minute of it, and I don't intend to leave."

Goodwill was founded by a Methodist minister, Dr. Edgar Helms, back in 1902 in Boston. At that time America was different than it is today. Dr. Helms had people in his church who had come from Europe because they'd heard this was a land of opportunity, a place to get ahead, a place to make a life for themselves. There was a depression in 1902. Dr. Helms's church was in a poor section of Boston and a lot of people in his congregation were unemployed immigrants. And of course the winters were cold there. He wanted to do something to help his people, so he decided to go over to the other side of town and ask wealthier people to fill a gunnysack with clothing that he could bring back to his parishioners so they would be warm. Most of his people couldn't afford bread, much less clothing.

Well, he got a lot of clothing given to him, and he came back to his church to give it away. But no one would take any of the clothing, because these were people who were proud. They didn't come to America for handouts; they didn't come here to be on the dole. If they had wanted that, they would have stayed in their own countries. They came to America, the land of riches and promises, to participate in those riches and promises. It just wasn't acceptable to them to take anything free.

Dr. Helms wondered what he was going to do with all the clothing. Finally he hit on the idea of asking the women to come to the church basement to repair the clothing in lieu of wages. The women and their husbands could accept that, because their dignity was preserved. And that was the beginning of Goodwill's helping the needy and the poor.

Soon other ministers heard about Dr. Helms's program, and they began doing the same thing. The program spread to large churches in New York, Chicago, San Francisco, Los Angeles, all the big cities.

In the late twenties Dr. Helms came across a place in Brooklyn, New York that was aiding the handicapped. He discovered a whole new population that needed help. So he expanded the clothing program and started working with the handicapped. He began developing factories to repair clothing and other discards.

Goodwill's growth surged as a result of World War II. What happened was that we had a big population that came back from the war who were handicapped. Then we had Korea and Vietnam. In the late sixties and early seventies we found that our life-style had changed—television, shooting people to the moon, and rolling rockets around the earth. We started finding a greater number of emotionally disturbed people and began working with them. Also with the mentally retarded, especially children born to people who were or are drug addicts. Now 40 percent of the people we serve are mentally retarded.

Today the total mission of Goodwill is to provide jobs for the mentally retarded, people with physical handicaps, those who are emotionally disturbed, and what we call the socially disadvantaged—people who have parole records, are on dope or drink, or possibly do not have an education. Particularly here in southern California we have a lot of people who come across the border from Mexico and can't even speak English. We're able to give them a place where they can make a beginning.

We are about 95 percent self-supporting. The rest of our money comes from wills, private donations, corporations and foundations. We use the repairable discards we collect to create a job, a work station for a handicapped person. Once the item goes to this work station and is repaired or renovated, it has some value. We sell the item in our own stores, and we also use our stores for training clerks and other retail personnel. I might mention, by the way, that the new popularity of garage sales and our lackluster economy have resulted in about a 20 percent drop in the amount of merchandise we are able to collect.

We have a staff of approximately thirty people, a board of directors, job placement specialists, a part-time doctor, two nurses, two social service counselors, a production director and a sales director. We are organized like any other business.

Many of the people who come to us are eligible for many types of federal handouts—aid to the disabled, welfare, and so on. But they don't want to sit at home and do nothing but collect checks. They want to become independent. They want their own self-respect, and so they come here looking for a job. Now, if the people who come here are seeking independence, we as an organization should do the same thing. That's why we don't ask for government support, and that's why we're not a member of United Way. There are many governmental and charitable programs we could apply for and are eligible for, but we won't do it.

Through our employment counselors, we try to place as many people as possible in competitive industry. We place between 6,000 and 10,000 of our people in private industry every year.

The thing we find about people who come to Goodwill is that they are victims of prejudice. Would-be employers say, Hey, you're in a wheelchair. You can't go through the doorway. We have no bathroom facilities. We have to worry about insurance. We don't have a job for you.

Many times a person might go to a counselor who is well meaning but says, "You can't become a lawyer because you're blind." Well, there are many students today who are going to college and becoming lawyers even though they are blind. Franklin Delano Roosevelt was handicapped with infantile paralysis, but he became president of the United States. A handicapped person can do virtually anything. Many people assume that because a person has a handicap he won't be able to learn, to function, to perform. Well, that's simply not true. Walk through any Goodwill branch and you'll see it's not true. You can't put a perimeter or a box around a person just because he's handicapped. That's part of the problem, people putting boxes around them, while you and I, the so-called nonhandicapped people, can soar to any heights we want. But in a sense we're all handicapped. I'm not a good speaker; you may not be a good swimmer. Everyone has some type of handicap.

Economic discrimination against the handicapped comes in many guises. For example, street corners aren't shaved down so people who are in wheelchairs can manipulate them easily. That just adds to the burden of the handicapped who are trying to find a job or trying to get to a job. Federal offices and post offices are notorious for the fact that the handicapped can't get into them with ease.

Another big problem for those with disabilities is that their families tend to protect them when they are growing up, making a lot of them unemployable. They don't allow their handicapped children to mature and gain self-confidence. They can't go outside to play because they are different. They get driven to school, if they go to school at all. When they reach seventeen or eighteen, they are so accustomed to having the family do everything for them that they don't have the confidence to go out and get on the bus or drive their own car in order to find a job. So they sit at home. These are people who need Goodwill.

Goodwill is a starting point, a place where the handicapped individual has the opportunity to get experience and learn good work habits. And with his work record, he can find a job on the outside that's productive for his employer and himself.

Our wage scale, approved by the California Department of Labor and the federal government, starts at $1.61 an hour. Most individuals start at that and progress from there. There is no top. We had a fellow here who was a dwarf and on crutches. He worked his way up to assistant bookkeeper; then he became our office manager, and he wound up earning close to $10,000 a year. He did an excellent job for us, and now he's working in the mayor's office at a much higher salary.

Often Goodwill is the employer of last resort. A lot of people who come here have never held a job, and so they have nowhere to turn except to us. If the person has determination—and just coming to Goodwill shows he has determination—we can help him climb up the ladder and get into competitive industry.

But there's another aspect to it. There are some people working at Goodwill who, because of the nature of their handicap, may never be placed competitively, because they have one arm or severe multiple sclerosis. They may not be fast enough or quick enough to work outside in private industry. Still, if they stay at Goodwill the rest of their lives, it's not only rehabilitation, it's a tremendous accomplishment for them. They could be sitting at home in a wheelchair, but they're not. For these people, working at Goodwill is just as good as working for U.S. Steel or the Bank of America.

I think a good question to ask is: What do we, the alleged nonhandicapped, owe those who have disabilities? Well, we have an obligation not to discriminate against them. Even when they go to church, many of our people are shunned. They're not considered part of the group because they're different, and when someone is different we all have a tendency to shy away from him. If you believe in helping people who want to help themselves, then possibly you have an obligation to share your discards to create a job for a disabled person. And if you feel an obligation to become more deeply involved, maybe you'd like to become an unpaid volunteer for Goodwill.

What never ceases to amaze me is the fierce determination of the people who work at Goodwill. One black man I'm thinking of was a basket case when he first came here several years ago. He had so many handicaps. I don't know the name of his disease, but for one thing he still has to have someone close his eyes at night or put coins on his eyes when he goes to sleep. He only weighs seventy or seventy-five pounds. He can't walk; he can't even crawl. His life is lived in a wheelchair. But he came here out of his own determination. We found that his mother had sheltered and overprotected him. As a matter of fact, his mother was a hindrance. We put him to work in the print shop, and nobody thought he'd be successful. At that time, we started him at twenty-five cents an hour. He became so adept at print work that he was able to go outside and get a job for $4 an hour. The president of the company where he works told me, "This man is our most valuable employee."

We had a girl with MS who had been bedridden for three years. But she had quite a will, and she was finally able to walk on crutches. Then she was able to walk with two canes. When she came to Goodwill she could hardly speak, and she couldn't write. She was put to work in the collections office. That's the division where they are on the telephones to the homeowners who call in and say they want a truck to come and pick things up. She had to learn to talk, and she had to learn to write. She learned to do both. She works as our receptionist now, and she has no trouble talking to anyone.

We have one man who is our candidate for Goodwill Worker of the Year. This is a competition that each Goodwill branch has every year. He's a victim of Hodgkin's disease, which is considered fatal; a patient is not supposed to live more than three or four years. This man, who is Spanish, didn't learn English until he was nine or ten years old, so he had a late start. After he graduated from high school, he of course had a difficult time getting a job because of his illness and because he was in a wheelchair.

He was thirty years old when he finally came to Goodwill. We asked him if he could do electrical work and he said yes, though he didn't know a thing about electrical work. But he observed and applied himself. And he was quite successful in learning that work. He mastered that job totally. Then he turned to transportation because he thought that would be interesting. He became a dispatcher for all our trucks. Then he got quite interested in other people. They would come to him with their problems. He talked to them and helped them. Now he's decided to become a counselor. He uses quite a bit of ingenuity in the way he manages his life. There was a time when he didn't have transportation, so he traveled seven miles a day on the streets in his electric wheelchair.

We had another fellow who worked with us who was also in an electric wheelchair. He had broken his spine in a fall. He came to Goodwill after graduating from college, and we employed him as a counselor also. After being with us for two years, he applied for and got a position with the state, and he's earning $20,000 a year.

You must remember that handicapped people are like anybody else. Cut them and they bleed. Make a joke and they laugh. Give them a job and they work.

Yesterday, Today and Tomorrow

Where in hell will it end?

—David L. DeWeese

HOWARD J. RUFF

"The best way to become a false prophet is to set a date for the end of the world and get it wrong," Ruff says. "But I think I can pinpoint some signs that indicate the certitude of a coming worldwide famine."

Ruff, forty-seven years old, has seven children and four foster children. Several of the youngsters scamper in and out of the living room of his large, comfortable house in Danville, an upper-middle-class suburb in northern California, about twenty miles east of Oakland. The sight of his well-fed, healthy children makes talk of famine and death from hunger seem particularly incongruous.

A former stockbroker, Ruff has gained his agricultural expertise from a close study of the subject since 1968. "It's an obsession of mine; it's all I do." He writes and lectures widely about the apocalypse of famine, earning between $25,000 and $30,000 a year.

Money is just a store of wealth, a medium of exchange, the transfer of wealth from one person to another for an exchange of services. But money, of course, doesn't have to be paper. For the Arabs, oil is money. For South Africa, gold represents money. As the largest exporter of commodities in the world, food represents money to the United States. But the production of food is so tenuous that I foresee a worldwide famine in which half a billion people will die.

First, you have to define famine. Famine is not just the inability to grow enough food for your population. More broadly and accurately defined, famine is the unavailability of goods for a variety of reasons.

The food the housewife buys in the supermarket is lubricated to move efficiently from one part of the country to another. We have become very interdependent. Food sometimes has to move from halfway around the world or halfway across the country to reach consumers. It used to be that the American farmer would eat what he grew and sell the surplus. Now he buys food from the market, like everyone else. There are a lot of kids growing up on farms who think milk comes out of cartons.

In order to have enough food, we are totally dependent on a sound economic system, which means a sound currency and free flow of credit worldwide. All the links in the food distribution chain become vulnerable when we don't have sound currency systems. England, Australia, Canada and Mexico have recently devalued their currencies, indicating that parts of the world's monetary system are in deep trouble. It seems to get worse each year. Anything that endangers the monetary system of the world endangers the world's farm economy. The flow of commodities from one part of a country to another or one part of the world to another is affected.

If the banks should fail in the U.S. and elsewhere in the world, which I think is a distinct possibility, currency would become worthless. There would be no useful medium of exchange with which you could reward the farmer for his goods, the trucker for his services, the supermarkets for their food and other merchandise. The distribution of commodities would become impossible.

Also, we are facing a real crisis in terms of the world's ability to grow food. This nation has always produced large surpluses. But now we are producing smaller surpluses per acre. The only way we've been able to maintain our surplus position and remain an exporting nation has been to vastly increase the number of acres of food planted. But we are producing less food per acre. It's simple mathematics.

As you expand food production, pretty soon you are going to find yourself on marginal land. Theoretically, you could farm the top of Mt. Whitney if you are willing to pay the price, but it is uneconomic, and of course no one will do it. Not only is the best land under cultivation, but a lot of our most fertile areas are being absorbed by the expansion of cities; those acres are under concrete. Another problem is that we have found ways of farming land so intensively that its productivity is dropping. You can't triple-yield a piece of land without eventually depleting the soil.

Changing climate and bad weather are also threatening our

ability to grow food in the entire northern hemisphere. In 1975 we came within two days of losing 75 percent of Iowa's corn crop because of drought. South Dakota Congressman Larry Pressler says that many counties in the eastern part of his state have been designated a drought emergency area for the past three years. Disaster conditions peaked in that portion of the country in 1976, with rainfall during the growing season running as much as thirteen inches below normal. As a result, South Dakota's grain production has decreased from 25 percent to 60 percent, with several counties now showing a 95 percent loss! Forty-one states, from Georgia to California, are currently suffering severe drought conditions.

I think the world's weather is changing permanently. The northern hemisphere is cooling slightly, which causes a shorter growing season, with cold, wet springs that make it difficult to get crops in. Droughts during the summer, followed by early frosts, have made farmers dependent on strains of grain which are vulnerable. These are grains developed for yield, not hardiness, and they have created all sorts of problems. Many of them are susceptible to various kinds of disease which, if they reached epidemic proportions, could wipe out major areas of our crops virtually overnight.

The best we can hope for is that our food production remains normal, but I don't think it is going to remain normal here or anywhere else. The Russians apparently lose as much as a third of their crop each year because of bad weather conditions.

We can't continue to give the world our food dollars. Our capacity is limited. We will find surely within a decade and possibly within five years that we are faced with worldwide starvation on a level that dwarfs any other catastrophe that has ever hit the human race.

I see famine occurring for sure within ten years because of decreasing food production, erratic distribution of food, and increasing population. The famine will start in the subcontinent of Asia, then spread to Africa, then to South America. You are also going to see an awful lot of deaths from starvation in this country. There is going to be mass hunger here. A certain percentage of our population is going to die. You will see terrible suffering. You will see social disruption. There will be a vast increase in the amount of crime. Still and all, we will be better off than the rest of the world. We'll still have food for most of our people.

We may be the only nation with food, the only people eating in a sea of starving nations. It will be a very dangerous position to be in, because many of these starving nations are now developing nuclear capability. We face the threat of war, and certainly commodity blackmail. Other nations will gang up on us and say, You provide us with what we need, even at the expense of rationing or allocation in your own country, or we won't provide you with oil or aluminum or zinc or any of the other vital materials your industrial economy needs for survival.

I believe that our standard of living has already peaked, and that we will never again have the standard of living we've had in the past. We are simply going to have to divide our resources with the rest of mankind or face a hostile world. I don't believe there's any alternative.

I'm not the only one predicting that half a billion people will die of hunger in the next ten years. Lester Brown, the president of the World Overseas Council, was quoted in the *National Observer* as forecasting precisely the same thing.

If half a billion people die, that's an enormous tragedy, but that's a half billion fewer mouths to feed. That really sounds more coldblooded than I feel about it. I don't mean it to sound that way. But what I'm saying is that, with its resources diminishing, the earth cannot continue to indefinitely expand its population.

Meanwhile, there are so many pressure points. We have a whole series of dangerous economic hurdles facing us in the immediate future. It's like a runner in a race, where each hurdle is getting higher and higher and the runner is getting more and more tired.

The first hurdle might be the bankruptcy of major cities. The Brookings Institution said in a report in December 1976 that eight cities are in financial trouble because of poor management, inadequate long-range revenue prospects and depressed economies.* The second hurdle might be the bankruptcy of New

*New York, Buffalo, Detroit, Newark, St. Louis, Boston, Cleveland and Philadelphia. "Their economies are going nowhere and their people are going elsewhere," the report said.

York State, then Massachusetts, and so on. The third hurdle would be a chain of bank failures as a result of the banks' large holdings in municipal bonds becoming worthless. Then the next hurdle could be the collapse of the great fortunes in the country which are heavily invested in municipal bonds and notes.

From there, it doesn't take much foresight to see that we could have food riots, people killing each other for a loaf of bread. It would be neighbor against neighbor in the streets. We had an indication of this in 1975 when New York City, on the verge of default, decided to stop cashing welfare checks. There were people standing in long lines at six banks to cash their checks, and riots nearly broke out. The police controlled the situation only when the order not to cash the welfare checks was counter-manded by the city, and the people got their money.

I think everyone has to make himself as independent of the system as possible. Everyone has to say, I will do whatever I can to provide commodities and security for my family against the time when food will be difficult to obtain. Then I won't be part of the panic when it occurs, nor will I be competing for scarce supplies. One thing I've done is to store food. I've stored an eighteen-month supply for my family and for some of my relatives who don't believe me and who think my ideas are a little strange.

In the near future, we are going to see a food allocation system similar to the allocation plans we had for gasoline during the relative shortage of oil in 1973. Then, eventually, we'll have food rationing. The Department of Agriculture already has a standby food rationing plan available.

But it's going to go beyond food rationing. For one thing, there won't be any more restaurants. If our currency collapses and there's social chaos and food is in short supply, what is a restaurant going to take in trade for a meal?

I'm sorry if I sound grim, but I don't see any solution. You can't have radical solutions, like sterilizing half of mankind. It's impractical; it can't be done. It's hard to say whether birth control is the answer. If you want an expert on birth control, don't talk to me, because I am not an expert on that subject, judging by the size of my family.

You have to deal with reality. You can't tear up the cities and put all that land into production. If you just tore up the highway and freeway systems in the United States, you could add some-thing like 8 percent to our food production in this country. But could we accept that?

I think we've already passed the point of no return. I'm not predicting the end of civilization. Mankind has faced these prob-lems before. The Roman Empire went under because it became bankrupt. The Romans were unable to fight their wars and pay their troops.

Whenever one political and economic system is destroyed, another comes to the fore. For a time, we may have a military dictatorship in this country. But I see an eventual return to democracy. Our democratic institutions and traditions are too strong for America to remain under a dictatorship for long.

But between the coming collapse and our renaissance there will be a horrible shaking-out period caused by our food short-age. Some 15 million Americans already go to bed hungry. What happens when the middle class and the rich don't have enough money to buy food because there simply is no food available?

DAVID NOVICK

The Rand Corporation—one of the nation's most prestigious think tanks—sits in orange and beige anonymity amid giant birds-of-paradise and palm trees in Santa Monica, California, one block from the Pacific Ocean.

Inside the four-story structure, Novick, who is seventy-one years old, is one of the presiding seers, an intellectually elegant expert on energy and economics. A ruggedly charming man with a booming, authoritative voice, he's been thinking his way into the future for more than three decades.

He's been adviser-consultant-economist to scores of private corporations and has served in a number of important government posts. In 1940 he designed the War Production Board's Production Requirements Plan and was a principal drafter of the economic sections of the National Security Act of 1947. He is also one of the nation's leading authorities on the world's supply of natural resources.

The U.S. energy shortage didn't begin in 1973, when the Arabs raised the price of oil. There was a 1967 Department of

Interior report that pointed out the increasing reliance of the United States on imports of petroleum. It was apparent then that U.S. production was declining, and that the U.S., which was once the biggest exporter of petroleum, had become the world's largest importer of petroleum.

What changed the situation around was the gigantic increase in U.S. consumption. This is true of energy in general. You look at any of the curves of consumption of electricity, gasoline and natural gas, and you will find that they have all gone up enormously, starting in the early mid-1960s.

Energy was cheap in that period, and consumption was encouraged. Husbands were blatantly advised to buy all kinds of electrical labor-saving devices for their wives. You were told that you shouldn't read by small bulbs. You were urged to have a 150-watt or 300-watt bulb; if you didn't have the correct protective lighting you'd go blind. The power companies said, If you buy a lot of electricity, we will make it cheaper per unit for you. So if you increase your consumption tenfold, you will only increase your cost threefold. Have a good time.

While we were having a good time, the shortage crept up on us. The energy crisis of 1973 would have overtaken us whether or not there had been an Arab-Israeli war, which to some extent resulted, for the first time, in a public display of oil politics and economic blackmail.

The important thing to remember, however, is that the shortage was not artificially created. As far back as 1970, an OPEC newsletter, which is issued quarterly, said the world market was changing from a buyer's market to a seller's market.

About that time the first move was made by the Arabs in the direction of raising prices. From 1970 to 1973 the price of petroleum almost doubled. Then, in 1973, it quadrupled on top of that. It went from roughly $1.50 a barrel to $2.75 a barrel in the 1970-to-1973 period, and then it went to $11 a barrel in 1973. It is now $13 a barrel.

The full impact of the higher price for petroleum is still to be felt in the United States. Cheap energy has always fueled the economy of this country. Our extraordinary growth from roughly 1875 onward would not have been possible without it. If energy had been as expensive then as it is now, we would probably be living in a quite different world. You wouldn't have all this highway and freeway concrete around, you wouldn't have all these automobiles riding on it, and you wouldn't have as many household appliances. You would have much higher labor input and much smaller machine input. You can only drive machines effectively and efficiently with low-cost energy.

You must remember, too, that energy isn't the only resource that is scarce now. Virtually all natural resources become scarce when you have a high level of prosperity. Energy is just the tip of the iceberg. When you have a prosperous society, people have the money to buy goods and they want them. The price of aluminum, of copper, of zinc, of all these things went up in 1974 following the increase in the price of oil.

The only thing that has stopped the Arabs from raising the price of oil much, much higher has been the depression in the West since 1974. The price of oil can go to, say, $15 a barrel only if there are enough nations who can afford to buy it. There is little point in raising the price of oil to what it eventually might be—$40 a barrel—if there are no or few buyers. But the price will increase starkly as the nations of the West return to relative prosperity.

In a year or two a gallon of gas at the pump will cost $1. Soon thereafter, it will be $1.25, $1.35, $1.50, because we are consuming more gasoline and apparently will continue to consume more gasoline than ever before in the history of this country. When you read those nice automobile sales statistics, remember that the only thing that drives an automobile is gasoline.

There are other factors compounding the situation of high prices and low supply of oil. We have built no new refineries since 1965. As a result, even if we had the oil in this country, we couldn't make it into gasoline. The big oil companies have chosen to build their refineries outside the United States, just as they have chosen to do their exploration for oil outside the United States. They get a better return on their investment that way.

Remember that you get everything you can think of out of a barrel of oil. Not only gasoline, but heating oil, kerosene, petrochemicals, textiles, fertilizer. As demand for all these products increases, the price will go up. Whenever there is high demand, there is a higher price. Less demand, if we as a nation could accommodate ourselves to that, would mean a lower price per barrel of petroleum.

If we keep on doing nothing, if we haven't the guts to initiate an effective energy policy, we will find ourselves more and more at the mercy of the Arabs. In October 1973 only 25 percent of our oil imports came from the Arabs. Today it is almost 50 percent.

We've been spoiled because we had a rare phenomenon in this country. From 1960 to 1965 we had no increase in prices for goods and services. In fact, we really didn't get inflation going hot until late in the sixties. It was induced in large measure by the Vietnam War, which was financed by borrowed money instead of taxes. In that period money was generally available, and money chases goods. When that happens, the price of goods goes up.

The question then becomes: Can you maintain prosperity without very much inflation? Inflation is a relative thing. I would say that almost all economists regard a 2 to 3 percent per annum price increase as very acceptable.

Probably more important than the prosperity here was the prosperity throughout the world. Look at Japan, which had a 16 percent per annum growth rate all through the sixties and into the seventies. Unheard of. Practically the same thing is true of West Germany.

The whole world is better off today than it ever has been in history in terms of the amount of goods we have. We may be killing ourselves in other ways, on the highways and through pollution, but in terms of goods, we've never had it better.

Whether or not we can hold inflation below 7 or 8 percent in the U.S. is largely a matter of government fiscal policy, the Federal Reserve Board's money policy toward business, and the attitude of labor unions. But our labor unions have been very, very modest in their demands for wage and benefit increases, despite all the headlines we read.

To make our economy viable, to lessen inflation and increase employment, the first thing we have to do is resolve the energy problem. And the first thing you have to do to resolve the energy problem is to introduce conservation. That means enforcing the 55-mile-per-hour speed limit. It means decreeing that new houses be well insulated. It requires a government subsidy program to insulate old houses, particularly in the northeastern and midwestern sections of the country, where the winters are long and harsh.

It means spending hundreds of billions of dollars on research. For example, when energy is transmitted from the powerhouse to the consumer, roughly 35 percent is lost. Maybe that can't be avoided, but I don't think we've done the research to find out. Copper prices would be as high as oil if we hadn't learned how to send long-distance telephone calls by microwave. We don't need the cables any longer. In the near future, you won't see any telephone wires between towns. In fact, you're seeing fewer and fewer of them now.

We have got to learn how to transmit energy from one place to another at minimum cost. We've got all this work going on in laser technology. A laser is simply a way of projecting energy. At the present time it is a very wasteful way, but who knows what a few hundred million more invested in laser research might accomplish?

Several hundred million or several hundred billion dollars isn't that much for what we need in terms of energy. After all, when the country's future is at stake, money becomes secondary. If you were to do the Manhattan Project today, it would cost around $1 trillion. And that is about what you have got to put into energy over the next century.

If we made that financial commitment, we would become self-sufficient in energy. However, in the meantime we would be forced to reduce our standard of living in order to provide the investment of that $1 trillion. We would have to stop making automobiles in such large quantities, and we would have to increase taxes and ration energy.

The question then becomes: Would the country stand still for such a program of severity and sacrifice? Well, we did it from 1940 to 1945. It's true that we had a commitment then to the war, that it was patriotic to deny ourselves goods; but now you must ask: What about a commitment to yourself, to your children, to the future?

Unless we do what I suggest, we are likely to become a mere appendage of the United Arab Emirates. If you are importing 50 percent of your oil from the Arabs, they have you by the

throat. Canada has practically cut us off. Venezuela has practically cut us off. We are getting a fair amount from Indonesia, but
that's small potatoes. Saudi Arabia is where the oil is, and with
that whole Arab gang.

Unless something drastic is done in terms of energy policy, I'm
not optimistic as to where we'll be by the year 2000. Nixon came
out with Project Independence, which was, of course, an overop-
timistic plan for self-sufficiency in energy by 1980. That was
ridiculous. Ford did little to improve the situation, and I've yet to
hear President Carter talk in terms of investing $1 trillion. Car-
ter has created a Department of Energy with 20,000 employees.
And he wants a higher tax on gasoline and gas guzzlers. But
that's not going to solve the problem. Unless we take drastic
measures the United States could be shaken by an energy crisis
in the 1980s worse than the Great Depression of the 1930s.

There should be a policy of building plants, refineries, coal-
processing facilities, that sort of thing. Even if this is done, it
doesn't mean that the energy crisis will be resolved immediately.
If the plan started tomorrow, we still wouldn't be in the clear for
fifteen or twenty years. In the meantime, we are going to have to
remain dependent on the Arabs.

You don't get anything for nothing. If we want to be free of
dependency on the Arabs, if we want to have a Western world
and a reasonably strong position in oil as well as other natural
resources, we really must be prepared to spend, if necessary, $2
to $3 trillion over the next ten to fifteen years.

Can we afford to? I ask you, can we afford not to? In my
opinion, what you have to do first is get back to basics. And the
most basic of basics is survival.

DAVID L. DeWEESE

*DeWeese describes himself as an economic conservative and longtime
student of government spending. Born in Atchison, Kansas in 1934, he's
vice-president of California's Union Bank (whose views do not
necessarily coincide with his own).*

*Blue-eyed, of medium height, he has on his polished desk a sheaf
of notes to which he occasionally refers during the interview.*

We have to ask ourselves whether government, Big Brother, is the servant or the master of taxpayers.

Congress and various governmental departments throughout our sprawling bureaucracy have made some very questionable if not strange expenditures of money in recent years.

Seventy thousand dollars was allocated to study Australian aborigines, and $20,000 to determine whether Polish pigs were superior to American pigs. For not planting cotton on her Mississippi plantation, we sent Queen Elizabeth II a check for $68,000.

The Federal Board of Tea Tasters, whatever that is, received $117,000; $59,000 has been expended to store 1,500 tons of feathers as "critical material" in the event of a national emergency. It took $70,000 to classify Indo-Australian ants. The taxpayers of the United States spent $298,000 for a study of summer camp safety which was later branded worthless in Congress. And there was no less than $19,300 spent to find out why kids fall off tricycles. And you thought it was because they lost their balance.

We were charged $121,000 for a study to find out why people say "ain't." Two hundred and four thousand dollars was wasted trying to find out why drivers get lost on freeways, Michigan State University was awarded $342,000 for a study in which students were asked where, when and with whom they had had premarital sex. And a $350,000 study determined that 48 percent of the American people believe in the devil. I always thought sex and the devil were matters best left to individual preferences, not government snooping.

A Florida congressman recently informed us that $81,000 was expended to study the social behavior of bears; $84,000 to find out why people fall in love; $37,000 to finance a potato chip machine for Morocco; and $17,000 for a dry cleaning plant for Bedouin tribesmen.

Congress in 1975 authorized $575,000 to establish a new National Commission on Supplies and Shortages. That sounds like a worthwhile idea, and perhaps it was, but couldn't the objective of this Commission have been accomplished by the existing Council of Economic Advisors, or the Council on International Economic Policy, or the Office of Management and Budget, or the Agricultural Economics Administration, or the Bureau of Labor Statistics, or the Federal Energy Administration, or any of the dozens of other government agencies?

It took 180 years for the federal budget to grow from near nothing to $100 billion. Only the subsequent ten years were needed to reach $200 billion. Incredibly, it took only the last five years to gallop to $375 billion.

In the United States today more than 13 million people are on federal, state or local government payrolls. The federal bureaucracy alone has increased 500 percent during a period in which population has increased only 63 percent.

What's happened to these federal employees during the recent inflationary spiral? Well, individually and collectively, they're faring much better than you and me. For every 3 percent rise in the consumer price index, they automatically receive a 4 percent pay increase. Perhaps you are also not aware that federal employees may retire after thirty years' service at the age of fifty-five with 75 percent of base pay, compared to your retirement and mine at age sixty-five at a below poverty level income from Social Security. These are the same people who insist on collective bargaining rights, including the right to strike!

In spite of the outrageously high taxes collected by our governmental agencies, the revenues they receive are never enough to satisfy their propensity for spending. Between 1964 and 1974 the federal government spent over $100 billion more than it collected, driving us deeper into debt, creating tremendous strains on our money markets, and assuring taxpayers that they will have more interest to pay each year on this growing debt. As unbelievable as it seems, the federal budget deficit is now running at an annual rate of $75 billion!

How much is $75 billion? I can only answer that by relating it to a basic statistic with similar magnitude. The entire gross national product of the United States in one year—i.e., the value of all goods and services produced—is less than $1.5 trillion!

Specifically, what does this $75 billion debt represent? In two words, Social Security. According to an editorial in the *Wall Street Journal,* future participants in the Social Security program, including those yet unborn, will be required to contribute in the aggregate that much from their income, plus interest, and it won't go to future beneficiaries of Social Security, but to those who are already participants in the program.

In 1950, the maximum contribution by both worker and employer was $45. Today it's approaching $900. By 1990, if we're lucky, the combined contribution will be $4,700 a year.

The unanswered question is: Will the next generation of Americans willingly be burdened with this monolithic monster of such incomprehensible proportions, or will they decide that such a burden was selfishly and unjustifiably thrust upon them and blast it into obscurity at the ballot box?

There have been several responsible studies of our existing Social Security system, all of which reach the conclusion that it's headed for bankruptcy. Then why can't we simply change course and put the program on a sound footing?

The primary reason is that economists for big labor, in tandem with the Social Security Administration itself, continue to extol the virtues of the existing program. But the Social Security Administration's own actuaries admit that there is a huge deficit in the program. Labor's position is that when Social Security runs out of money, it can be made up from the government's general revenues. Apparently labor has never been informed about or chooses to ignore our government's chronic budget deficits, which have occurred in fifteen of the last sixteen years and are the result of financing other social programs from general revenues.

Many people are under the mistaken impression that all the money contributed to Social Security since 1937 exists somewhere in an account waiting for us to retire. This is not the case. By 1981, the existing fund will be depleted. Sometime during the next few years Congress undoubtedly will devise a plan to increase receipts, which will amount to another mortgage on the pocketbooks of future taxpayers.

Then there's welfare. Never in the history of mankind has the opportunity for extortion and corruption been more readily available and more openly utilized than within our own welfare system. Gargantuan giveaways in the billions annually pass through our federal health, education and welfare agencies. The former Welfare Inspector General of New York State, George Berlinger, said that his estimate of $10 billion annually in rip-offs from welfare and various other governmental assistance programs is conservative.

There are hundreds of thousands of illegal aliens on our welfare rolls. They receive not only welfare payments but food stamps, Medicare, subsidized housing and other social services.

I suppose you read or heard about the woman who was arraigned on thirty-one counts of using eighty different names, thirty-one addresses, twenty-seven children, twenty-five telephone numbers, eight deceased husbands and three Social Security numbers to bilk social agencies of millions of dollars.

Police found that one member of the SLA, the outfit that kidnapped Patty Hearst, had a Medi-Cal ID card, a food stamp program card, a county welfare card, and a registration form from the U.S. Department of Agriculture's food and nutrition service. Only in the U.S. could a revolutionary be so well accommodated by a government he sought to destroy.

In 1964, there were 367,000 people participating in our food stamp program at a cost of $26 million. In 1977, 20 million recipients, equal to the combined populations of Arizona, Colorado, Nevada, New Mexico, Oklahoma, Missouri, Wyoming and Montana, inflated the cost to $5 billion. These recipients included striking workers, part-time students, runaways, and hippies in the underground culture.

The 20 million recipients are only half of the 39 million deemed eligible by our federal government to participate in the food stamp program. At the present time, the House Ways and Means Committee of Congress is also considering a proposal to spend $600 a year for a clothing assistance allowance for these same 39 million. That will cost taxpayers an estimated $6 billion a year, plus the additional cost of a new giant bureaucracy to be established under the name of the Clothing Allowance Assistance Administration.

There are other ways our ubiquitous government spends our tax revenues. Several years ago, the Indiana State Chamber of Commerce created a novel Federal Spending Clock. Every second a dial flashes to indicate that the federal government has just spent another $10,000—an average family's entire annual income. Every two minutes an ominous beep sounds to indicate that $1.2 million of tax revenue has met its inevitable destiny.

During the brief time I have been speaking to you, more than $10 million has been spent.

There are 868 federal assistance programs administered by forty-nine different government agencies. Exactly 183 different programs are administered by HEW alone.

Besides Social Security, Polish pigs, and welfare programs, where do some of our other tax dollars go? Since 1945, we have furnished more than $200 billion to more than 140 nations, two-thirds of which was in the form of outright gifts. How much of the remaining one-third we'll ever collect, of course, is subject to conjecture.

We have given India $9.5 billion in economic and military aid, helping that nation to avoid complete famine while concurrently doing nothing to earn our respect and friendship. Latin American countries have divided up $20.3 billion. Far Eastern nations are the greatest recipients of our munificence, consuming more than $60 billion, half of which was to help stem communism in Korea and Vietnam. This is in addition to the $150 billion we casually wrote off by involving ourselves directly in Vietnam. It would be nice, indeed, if we could reduce our national debt by one-third, which is the amount we have sent to our "friends" around the world during the past three decades.

We have also spent hundreds of millions of dollars to support revolutionaries, anarchists, fascists and Communists, all self-admitted enemies of capitalism, in something flagrantly called the United Nations.

You are probably not aware of one other very generous use of our tax dollars. The Export-Import Bank, underwritten totally by our federal government, loans billions under the guise of credit and loans, at interest rates popular fifteen years ago on terms approaching perpetuity.

Our government's national debt is approaching $600 billion. Were we to begin a conscious effort to reduce it, which we never will, at the rate of $1 million per day, it would take more than 1,600 years to repay.

Ronald Reagan recently said, "A government program once launched is the nearest thing to eternal life we shall ever see on earth."

Where in hell will it all end?

How much longer can we continue our excesses by transferring the costs to future generations?

How much longer can we continue the squandering of our resources as though they were limitless?

British historian Arnold Toynbee once wrote that of twenty-one notable civilizations in history, nineteen died, not from external conquest, but from internal decay, corruption and financial mismanagement.

It's a fair question, and I ask it again: Where in hell will it end?

NORMAN FLEISHMAN

"The economic implications of unrestricted growth of population are enormous," says Fleishman. "It's the most serious problem the world faces. It could result in financial catastrophe."

Forty-six years old, with dark hair and brown eyes that burn with the zeal of a crusader, he is the $22,000-a-year West Coast Director of The Population Institute, a nonprofit educational organization whose work is supported by grants from foundations.

"We have four children. We were going to have a dozen. We saw the light when I joined Planned Parenthood a dozen years ago."

The world's present population of 4 billion may reach 7 billion by the year 2000, and it may go as high as 12 billion. It is doubling every twenty-seven years. At the current pace the United States will double its population in about seventy-five to eighty years. At 1 percent rate of growth, we are increasing a little slower than the 2 to 3 percent growth rate in the rest of the world.

The world adds 200,000 more people to its population every day beyond those who die. That's 200,000 more economic units or consumers of the earth's wealth. It's breathtaking and frightening to think about. Whatever happened to the zero population growth movement? It never really got started. It's a mirage.

As population increases, it's very clear what's happening in the world—there is a widening gap between rich and poor countries.

The poor are getting vastly poorer and the rich are getting much, much richer.

The food you eat at your local Kentucky Fried Chicken outlet or a fish and chips place has been grown with the addition of cheap protein from the developing world. Fish meal from Peru, for example, comes up here to feed Colonel Sanders's chickens. But there are at least half a billion people in the world who do not have enough protein to sustain normal body growth. Mostly they are children and pregnant women. The fact that they are not getting enough protein means they are becoming more retarded every day. We are growing retarded people in two-thirds of the world. You tell me what is going to be the price in dollars for that condition.

It's the poor world that's growing at the rate of 2 to 3 percent. The rich world is increasing at about 1 percent. Mexico is supposed to double from 58 million to 116 million in the next twenty-two years. Mexico is already a disaster area. The peasants are expropriating land. In the north, they don't have enough water. The country can't feed itself. Since the peso was devalued in 1976, they are having terrible financial problems. In some parts of Mexico there literally isn't any money. People are using the barter system.

In other words, we are all in danger. India is adding 1 million people a month. Sometimes when I speak about out-of-control population growth, people say, Well, won't they just die? Poor people do die sooner than rich people, but they also reproduce faster. No, death isn't going to solve the problem. The demographics are in favor of life, with more people being born every day than die. The unassailable fact is that we're adding a fifth of a million to our world population daily.

If you cut a pie into four pieces, everybody gets a huge piece, right? But if you cut it into eight pieces, everybody gets a smaller wedge. Every day we are cutting the pie thinner. The world's resources are finite. We have a minimum amount of oil and coal, and we know how much there is, and there won't be any more in a couple of decades. What happens then? How thin can you slice the pie?

As population grows, each of us is worth less; our buying

power is less. What each of us owns of the earth is less. The simple equation is that by the time our population doubles, everyone on earth will own one-half as much as he does now.

It's said that we used to live in a cowboy economy: use it and throw it away. Now we are living in a spaceship economy where we must conserve and save. But we are not conserving and saving.

There's an excellent chance for a worldwide depression. All we have is the earth, but we are using it up, we are polluting it, we are beginning to have lower rather than higher economic expectations.

In the early sixties Premier Fidel Castro of Cuba used to say that by 1980 every Cuban family would own a house, an automobile or motorcycle, and a large refrigerator full of the most varied country-grown foodstuffs. The farmers would till the land in tractors equipped with air-conditioned cabins, working only a few hours a day. Such promises are no longer made in Cuba, where a marked slowdown in development has occurred. From 1975 to 1980 the government projects an annual growth rate of 6 percent, much lower than the 10 percent rate it claimed for 1970–75.

Brazil, after years of heady growth at 9 percent annually, is lowering its economic sights as the economy struggles with the high cost of energy and a swollen external debt. The economy of South Korea, which has grown at a yearly average of 10 percent over the past decade, is expected by the Bank of Korea to expand at only 4 percent annually for the next five years. In India, real income per person has declined from $45 per year to $41, a decline of 10 percent.

In Bangladesh the downward spiral is further advanced. Despite a bumper rice harvest in recent years, the average Bangladeshi is consuming less rice than he was fifteen years ago. The number of new mouths to be fed has simply exceeded the capacity of the country's farmers to expand their output. One foreign expert has described it: "Bangladesh is a look at the future."

The battle between population growth and efforts to raise or maintain living standards isn't confined to the poor countries.

Economic expansion has slowed visibly in almost all the industrialized countries, including the United States, Japan, Germany, the Soviet Union, France and Britain.

More Americans are living below the official poverty level now than five years ago. More people are currently unemployed in the industrial countries than at any time in the last forty years.

At the same time that the economies of the world are contracting, the demand for goods and services expands constantly because of population growth. Prices of petroleum, cereals, soybeans, and fish have soared since the sixties, and they have affected the entire world.

Increases in firewood prices, while less visible internationally, have been enormous. Firewood was a cheap, abundant source of energy when villages were small. As village populations grow, forests recede. Now wood prices are a primary topic of conversation among the poor from the Himalayas to the Andes. Price increases of two- or threefold over the past few years are commonplace. Today the average manual laborer's family in some West African cities spends nearly one-fourth of its income on firewood.

Escalating prices lead to demands for higher wages, which in turn lead to still higher prices. The result is continual inflation. Those who suffer most under the burden of scarcity-induced inflation are the poor, whether in the *barriadas* of Lima or the slums of Naples or New York. Worsening inflation means that those living at subsistence levels find themselves increasingly unable to make ends meet. When the price of grain triples, families that already spend 60 percent of their income on food can only eat less.

With 4 billion consumers already on the scene and 200,000 being added each day, scarcity-induced inflationary pressures may grow chronic. Inflation poses one of the most difficult challenges that political leaders will face in the years ahead. What they must now realize is that, without a marked slowdown in population growth, inflation simply may not be manageable.

People don't look at that one factor of the doubling of the population in a short span of years and see the economic relevance in it that affects us all. Businessmen don't seem to understand what their stake is in population growth. They still have the naïve philosophy that more is better. The Vatican has come out again and condemned voluntary sterilization and vasectomy. It's madness.

Another future powder keg, perhaps the most dangerous spot on earth, is Japan. Japan was lightly populated for millions of years, just a scattering of islands with not much land or water and not much in the way of natural resources. Now they have 116 million people on a few islands. They are so totally dependent on outside resources that when the oil boycott started in 1973 they were helpless in a matter of a few days. What if there was a boycott that lasted for a year?

Even though the population growth rate is slower in America than in most other places in the world, we are far from being out of the woods. By the year 2000 we're undoubtedly going to have massive metropolitan areas in this country. One belt will be San-San, from San Francisco to San Diego; Boswash, from Boston to Washington; and Chipits, from Chicago to Pittsburgh.

What happens when you have that many people living tightly together and there's a strike of truckers, a breakdown of power, or a total traffic jam?

The more congested we get, the more vulnerable we become. And I see us as a very vulnerable society by 2000. We might have a couple of billion people jammed just into our metropolitan areas by then. That's the way it's developing. More and more people are coming into the cities, and it's difficult to persuade people to live in rural areas.

Then there is another kind of problem on the horizon. You now have half a billion people starving. In 2000 you might have 2 billion who are starving. There's no telling what will happen. When you think of 2 billion starving people ready to do anything with nothing to lose, it boggles the mind.

Even now we're living in a brittle society just at the edge of a precipice. Virtually any economic problem could shove us over the brink.

The great question is whether there's any hope. The media have a tremendous potential for waking people up. But we've got to begin to think and talk differently. The word condom can't be mentioned on television. Yet 1 million teen-age girls get pregnant every year in America alone. Research has shown that almost none of the 1 million girls want their babies. They didn't want the pregnancy. But teen-agers don't have enough knowledge about contraception or abortion.

I am not saying that teen-agers should necessarily not have their babies, but they should be given a choice. They should be aware of contraception. However, I must say that, generally speaking, it's unwise for a teen-ager to have a baby. It almost never works out. You get child abuse. You get desertion. You get a woman on welfare.

Our standard of living can only be maintained if we start doing something about the population explosion now. In an overpopulated world, we should become pioneers of birth control. There's no other alternative to our survival. We can't make it without the rest of the world. America can't be an armed camp guarding itself against the rest of the world.

The main things that are needed now are awareness and education. I spent an evening recently with a man from Thailand who is trying to popularize condoms in his country. He hands them out everywhere. The Thai government allows condoms to be used as bus fares.

The condom is a very valuable piece of property; it accomplishes a lot in the world. It could accomplish much more. We tend not to talk about the condom in America. But by popularizing its use we could stop a lot of our VD epidemics and all those unwanted pregnancies among teen-agers.

Ideally, this planet should have half the population it has now, 2 billion instead of 4 billion people. But we are moving inexorably the other way.

How are we going to lose 2 billion people by the year 2000? Only with responsible parenthood. We have the methods available; we have contraception and, if necessary, abortion. But there is a parallel problem. People all over the world have to be better off financially. When people's incomes go up, the family size goes down. When they are desperate and starving, they just have babies as a matter of course. Increasing the standard of living throughout the world would mean a decrease in population growth.

There are a thousand causes of death and just one of birth. We can work with the methods we have, which aren't perfect, but they are pretty good. The technology exists in every drugstore in America. But we keep it in the back of the store. And we charge too much for the condom. Nobody is going to stop teen-agers from having sex, so the least we can do is to have cheap contraceptives and medical advice and sex education available. There should be vending machines with condoms wherever teen-agers gather—in coed college dorms, at drive-in restaurants, at movies.

Educating the country will be costly. But what we have is more costly. If two teen-agers have a baby and the boy leaves the girl and she goes on welfare, do you know what that will cost? It could mean twenty years of public support. The child could be born with a medical problem and cost $10,000 to $20,000 a year. And who wanted him in the first place? All the parents wanted was some fun, and they end up costing the taxpayer $300,000 for their child. Multiply that by thousands and you have a bill that's immense. All that money could be saved if contraception were available. I'm not advocating promiscuity; I'm advocating a recognition of penalties and cost in dollars.

It is perhaps an oversimplification to say that the condom can be the economic salvation of the world. But we don't know when we are going to come up with something to put in the water or some magic pill.

One child raised in America costs from $150,000 to $500,000 to support through college, depending on the family's income. People will spend several months looking at a house for $50,000 or $60,000. But a house isn't the largest investment you make in a lifetime; a child is. A child is an immense economic obligation, the greatest financial commitment you can make on earth. But few people think that way.

But we had better begin thinking that way. Otherwise we're headed for a world nobody will want to live in.

When I was a junior in high school, I used to worry when I heard that the sun was going to flame out in 4 billion years. But when you are talking about 7 to 12 billion people by the year 2000, you don't worry about what's going to happen to the sun in 4 billion years.